THE
HEARTLESS
STONE

THE

HEARTLESS

STONE

A Journey Through

the World of Diamonds,

Deceit, and Desire

TOM ZOELLNER

ST. MART

NEW YORI

www.stmartins.com

Library of Congress Cataloging-in-Publication Data

Zoellner, Tom.
    The heartless stone : a journey through the world of diamonds, deceit, and desire / Tom Zoellner. — 1st ed.
        p. cm.
    ISBN-13: 978-0-312-33969-2
    ISBN-10: 0-312-33969-0
1. Diamonds.   I. Title.
TS753.Z64   2006
553.8'2—dc22   2005033037

First Edition: June 2006

10   9   8   7   6   5   4   3   2   1

CONTENTS

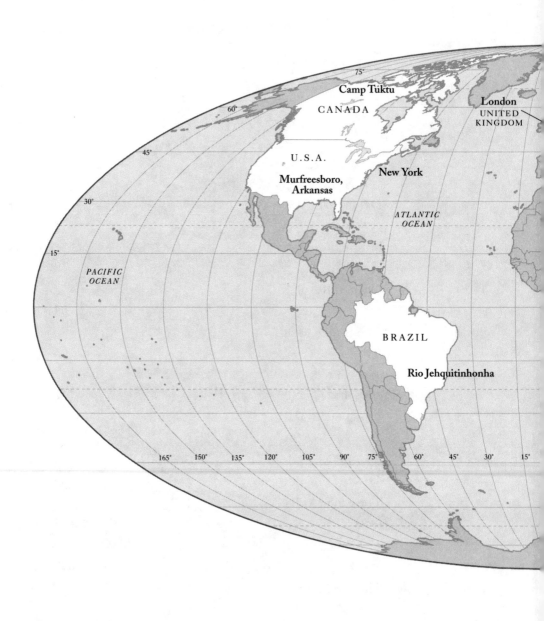

Camp Tuktu

CANADA

London
UNITED
KINGDOM

U.S.A.

Murfreesboro,
Arkansas

New York

ATLANTIC
OCEAN

PACIFIC
OCEAN

BRAZIL

Rio Jehquitinhonha

75°

60°

45°

30°

15°

165° 150° 135° 120° 105° 90° 75° 60° 45° 30° 15°

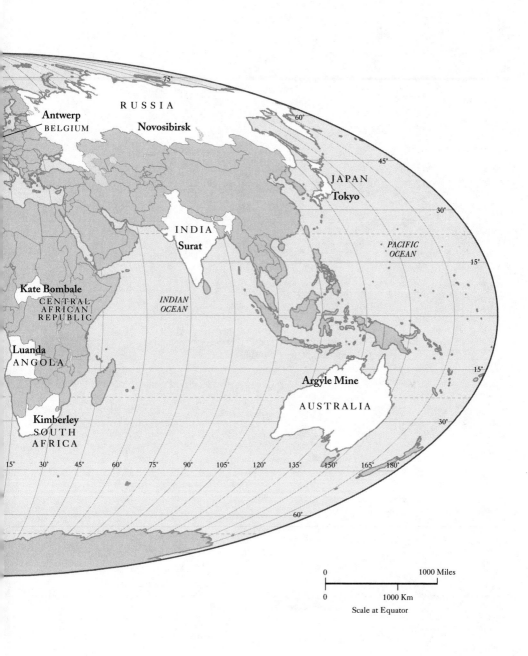

RUSSIA

Antwerp
BELGIUM

Novosibirsk

JAPAN
Tokyo

INDIA
Surat

PACIFIC
OCEAN

Kate Bombale
CENTRAL
AFRICAN
REPUBLIC

INDIAN
OCEAN

Luanda
ANGOLA

Argyle Mine

AUSTRALIA

Kimberley
SOUTH
AFRICA

75°   60°   45°   30°   15°   15°

0   1000 Miles

0   1000 Km

Scale at Equator

One

DYING STARS

Central African Republic

They had come across the river that morning, he said, as he took the stones from his pocket.

He set them in a line on the patio table. They looked melted and yellowish, as if someone had put them to a blowtorch. The smuggler and his three friends studied me as I held one up to the sunlight and tried to peer into it.

We're going to have to make this quick, said the man who owned the house. The police could come in, and then we'd all be in jail. He smiled vaguely at this thought. Across the alley, birds roosted in the broken-out window frames of a government building.

The smuggler watched me handle the rock. He said something in French to his friends. One of them tapped out a quick rhythm in his hand with the butt of his cell phone. Another glanced at the door to the alley and fingered the edge of the jacket he wore, even though it was a warm day.

You brought these from the Congo? I asked.

Today, he said. In a wooden canoe rowed over to Bangui. The mine itself was several hundred kilometers away, down a road into the jungle. I looked again at the dull yellow octahedron, wondering about its history, pretending I knew what I was looking at.

He is wondering who you really are, said the man who owned the house.

The smuggler placed the stones in the middle of a bank note, carefully folded it into a square, and made it disappear into his pants pocket. All four of them stared at me with flat eyes.

There are more where these came from? I asked.

Oh yes, I was told. Hundreds more. Thousands more.

Now: did I want to buy?

No. I have bought only one in my life. It was three years ago in California, over an ammonia-washed glass countertop. I was planning to ask my girl-friend, Anne, to marry me and was full of ever-deepening love. Jacqueline, the Asian woman behind the counter, showed me a series of stones, which she poured out of individual manila envelopes and set in a line. I peered at them all under a jeweler's loupe, as if I knew what I was looking at, and listened as Jacqueline explained the relative merits of each. She showed me the tiny angular hearts that clustered around the bases, like the petals of a flower.

There was one stone a bit clearer than the rest, slightly over a carat, and we haggled over the price a bit before I decided to buy it. Jacqueline fitted it into a Tiffany setting and I picked it up a week later. The stone was held aloft over the band in gold supports, like a preacher in his pulpit. I admired its sparkle. Jacqueline called it "the firing." I was then two weeks away from giving the ring to Anne on a precipice of land that over-looked the Golden Gate Bridge through a tunnel of cypress. This was to be a moment I had dreamed of since I was old enough to understand there was something special about girls.

Where did it come from? I asked her, just to say something. I was privately marveling at writing the biggest check of my life.

I don't know, she said.

Is there any way to tell? I asked.

Not really, she said. Probably Africa. That's where they all come from.

The place to go if you really want to see how some make their way to America is a nation called the Central African Republic. It is a landlocked crescent of ochre-colored earth about the size of Texas at the geographic heart of Africa. To fly over it at night is to fly over a carpet of complete darkness except for the occasional small cooking fire flickering up through the trees. There are no traffic signals, not a single mile of railroad track, and almost no electric lights outside of the capital city of Bangui. The nation is so poor that the government cannot pay its own employees any wages, and uniformed soldiers routinely beg money from passersby. Butterflies alight on the dirt roads and broad jungle leaves, and some locals try to make money by ripping the colorful wings off the butterflies and gluing them to paper to make artwork.

Children drunk on glue wander the filthy core of Bangui in broken flip-flops, begging for francs. Their T-shirts from Western aid agencies are often dotted with gummy clots; this is where they have smeared the glue to huff through the cloth. Shoe polish is another favorite intoxicant—it is spread on bread like jelly and eaten for a high. Still others take a stolen audiotape and soak it in a jar of water for a week. The resulting home brew brings strange hallucinations. Some of the street children will grab their crotches when they approach new faces for coins. Trading sex for money is common here, despite a national rate of AIDS infection estimated at one in every seven persons. "It's not always for money," a French schoolteacher told me. "Children need affection, to be touched is instinctual, and this is the only way a lot of them can get it."

The borders have been sealed to foreigners ever since the latest in a long series of coups toppled the government in March 2003, so there is really only one legitimate way in or out. That's the once-weekly Air France flight from Paris, which is inevitably crowded with a slice of the nation's tiny ruling class—the only ones who can afford the fare. The Sunday morning arrival of Air France is a free-for-all in the northern part of the city of Bangui. Hundreds of taxi hustlers and freelance luggage porters cram close to the perimeter fence as they watch the passengers step from one world into another, out of the air-conditioned cabin with its *fois gras* and Bordeaux and copies of *Paris Match* and into the fecund obscurity.

In a waiting room nearby, with thick wire mesh and tattered curtains covering the windows, are the departing passengers. They are protected like dignitaries from the masses outside. I learned later that some of them were almost certainly carrying a highly portable fortune in the folds of their business suits and warm-up jackets. They were able to carry wealth that equaled the annual wages of more than two thousand people. And without showing a bulge.

This is because the Central African Republic—corrupt, destitute, and nearly forgotten by the rest of the world—has been one of the best places on the continent to erase the history of a dirty diamond and smuggle it into the legitimate market.

I came because I wanted to see how it was done.

History has never been happy here. There have been people living in primitive agricultural settlements in this part of Africa at least five centuries before Christ, but today, the region is one of the most depopulated on the continent, a consequence of heavy slave-raiding activity in the seventeenth century. Arab bands from the north captured entire tribes and sold them to slave traders on the coast, and later on elevated blocks in Cairo. If any coherent records existed, it is likely that many American blacks could trace their ancestral lines to villages that disappeared centuries ago.

The French seized the region from an Egyptian sultan in the 1880s, named it Oubangui-Chari, and made it a department of a vast bloc of colonial real estate called French Equatorial Africa. They also built a plantation-style economy and set up the ramshackle capital of Bangui on a river port, positioned to move ivory and cotton out to the Atlantic. Export companies became the effective rulers of the colony. When André Gide visited the region in 1925, he called it "a country in ruins for the profit of a few." The adults were forced to harvest wild rubber while their children were taught to speak French and encouraged to forget their native language of Sango. The French also introduced their cooking, and in some of the farthest villages, it is possible to spend a few francs for a baguette, still gritty with black ash from the open fire it has been baked over.

When the independence movement swept Africa in the late 1950s, the region was among the first to break away from its colonial masters. The first president, Barthélémy Boganda, consolidated power in 1958 and tried to build a democracy out of the green web of clans and villages that shared little but language and hunger. The name, Central African Republic, was as empty as the results. The first of a long series of military coups took place eight years after independence, when General Jean-Bédel Bokassa and a band of soliders took control of the Presidential Palace.* Bokassa began an aggressive program of building up the nation's infrastructure, and his own wealth, in the process. About half of the 375 kilome-

---

*One of the rules of the Central African Republic is whoever can occupy this building by force becomes the de facto ruler of the nation.

ters of asphalt road in the country—mostly potholed streets in Bangui—can be credited to Bokassa's initiative at teasing development money in exchange for uranium that helped France build its nuclear program.

Bokassa's ego was titanic, even by the supersized standards of twentieth-century African strongmen. He built a new television station to broadcast his speeches, even though there were an estimated forty sets in the entire country at the time. He married seventeen wives, converted back and forth from Islam to Christianity, and had an extra-long military jacket tailored to accommodate all the various medals he awarded himself. But it was not enough. To the astonishment of even his most dedicated sycophants, he decided to declare himself "Emperor Bokassa I," and changed the name of his landlocked nation to the Central African Empire to suit his new title.

He had himself crowned emperor on December 4, 1977, in a spectacle that cost about a third of the nation's gross national product. Hundreds of mango trees that had lined Bangui's wide avenues were cut down to better accommodate the imperial procession, and a good portion of the capital's population was compelled to march behind a train of white horses imported from Belgium, pulling an antique coach decorated with golden eagles. Inside was the new Emperor Bokassa, almost lost within a 32-pound coronation robe with 2 million tiny pearls and crystal beads sewn into the fabric. Atop his head was a crown that cost $2 million, with a doorknob-sized 138-carat diamond as centerpiece.

It was an appropriate symbol, for diamonds had helped keep him in power. Bokassa had given several of his country's big-carat discoveries to his close ally and game-hunting partner, French president Valéry Giscard d'Estaing. The disclosure of the gifts embarrassed the French president, but not nearly as much as what happened in the winter of 1979. Bokassa decreed that all the nation's schoolchildren should wear uniforms—and the only uniform producer in Bangui happened to be one of his wives. Poor children (there is almost no other variety of child in Bangui) couldn't begin to afford the expense and a group of them threw rocks at the emperor's limousine one day in protest. An enraged Bokassa rounded up approximately one hundred children, innocent and guilty alike, and had them murdered. Bokassa killed many himself, and kept their remains in a refrigerator in his palace.

In the same larder he kept the corpses of some of the political enemies he had liquidated, and Bokassa was said to have snacked on their brains and hearts. The French were mortified enough to engineer a coup that relieved the emperor of power, especially after Bokassa claimed that he had surreptitiously fed human flesh to an unwitting President Giscard d'Estaing during several of their banquets together. The testimony of the palace chef at a 1986 trial was damning. Bokassa was sentenced to lifetime house arrest in a small house in Bangui, where he was treated something like an aged lion in a zoo. He died in 1996.

The latest coup—the ninth since independence—toppled the government of President Félix Patasse in March 2003. He had made the mistake of leaving the Presidential Palace for a brief trip to Cameroon. But he had also forgotten the other key rule of staying in power in Africa: Always keep your people paid. Soldiers tired of working for free refused to put up much of a fight against the rebels, so the revolution was relatively bloodless. The portraits on the walls of the Presidential Palace changed, but little else did. When I was there, civil servants were going into their fourth month without wages and the finance minister announced that no disbursements would be coming anytime soon. The treasury was bankrupt. The French ominously announced the deployment of a peacekeeping detachment. Soldiers with machine guns and rocket launchers cruised around Bangui in jeeps. At New Year's Eve 2004, the Central African Republic was again teetering on the edge of chaos.

"Listen. Here is something you must understand. Diamonds are an illusion, diamonds are a dream," said Joseph N'gozo, leaning back in his chair. He used to be an economic official with the U.S. Embassy, back when there was a U.S. Embassy. Now he was trying to make money in diamonds and not having a lot of luck.

We were having dinner at Le Relais des Chasses, a restaurant near the center of Bangui popular with French expatriates. Its name means "The Hunting Club." N'gozo wore a colorful African shirt and pinstriped banker's pants.

"They have no role in the tradition of our society," he said in accented English. "We mine for them only because it could make us some money. We want to work hard, the American dream. And diamonds are the price of admission to what we think we want."

Joseph owned a small mine in a sandy patch of river bottom, about eighty kilometers north of Bangui. He paid his ten crewmen the equivalent of $3 a day—top wages by rural African standards—to shovel the dirt out of the pit into sifts. The slurry is then washed in river water as the crewmen keep their eyes out for the glint of magic rock.

"They are not geologists," said Joseph, "but they know where to go. They can read a riverbank."

His miners hunt for what are called alluvial diamonds—those stones washed out of dead volcano cores by the rainstorms that pound Central Africa every summer. These are the easiest possible diamonds to discover and sell. They lie five meters below the surface at the most, and some can be found simply by brushing a few inches of sand away from the topsoil. There is no telling how many lie deeper—undiscovered and probably destined to remain that way—because heavy equipment, geological expertise, and working capital are all almost nonexistent here.

Even so, the nation's eighty thousand miners still managed to find the retail equivalent of $2.5 billion in gemstones in the sand every year. With shovels and sifts and sweat, they made the Central African Republic the tenth biggest diamond-producing country in the world. And for all of it, their pay was miserly, their days long and hot, and their country so poor that two-thirds of the population lived on an income of less than a dollar a day. According to the government, about 90 percent of the nation's diamonds were found by "artisans"—a euphemism for hired labor crews from rural villages. The work is dirty and miserable. The mines usually go no deeper than five meters underground, but the soil is unstable and walls often collapse, killing miners. There are no statistics to show how many are killed in mine accidents each year, but nearly everybody in the fields has heard stories of people dying this way. For almost everyone who lives in this part of Africa, however, this is the only kind of work that results in anything other than sustenance wages. It is the only real dream in sight.

"Diamonds can boost this country into boom times," Joseph said. His buoyancy seemed unshakable. The band onstage began to play a version of "She'll Be Coming 'Round the Mountain When She Comes," with the words in Sango. I ordered another beer and Joseph had another Fanta. Earlier in the evening, he had showed me the logbook that each mine operator is legally required to keep, called a *bordure d'achat*, or book of sale. It was in a small composition book with a grainy black-and-white cover, the same kind that schoolchildren use to copy lessons. Joseph showed me how a mine operator was supposed to fill it out by hand. Each diamond was to be listed on the right-hand side, and there were columns for the name of the miner who found it, the place it was found, its size in carats, and the name of the buying agency where it was sold. This was all you needed in the Central African Republic to verify that another diamond was heading to market.

Let's say a miner gets a diamond from someplace else? I asked. Like from a smuggler.

Joseph spoke slowly. "This system works in theory," he said. "In practice, this is very difficult to enforce."

The Central African Republic became a smuggler's paradise when two things happened in the late 1990s. The first was the outbreak of a vicious civil war right across the river. The second was the growing awareness that diamonds—the elemental symbol of love—were responsible for mass murder.

Bangui is the next major city north of the former Belgian colony that used to be called Zaire, the place that Joseph Conrad described in *Heart of Darkness* as "so hopeless and so dark, so impenetrable to human thought, so pitiless to human weakness." It was renamed the Democratic Republic of the Congo in 1997 after the longtime dictator Mobutu Sese Seko fled the country. Rebel armies seeking to topple the regime of the new president, Laurent Kabila, were able to purchase rifles and grenades by simply invading the diamond fields in the north and selling the plunder. Kabila fought the rebels with his own sale of the country's vast diamond reserves, creating, in effect, the same kind of kleptocracy that propped up Mobutu for three decades.

Soldiers—often no more than twelve years old—frequently went to work themselves in the mines, and the shovel became as important as the Kalashnikov as a tool of war. Diamond fields became important military targets, and those who tried to defend them would occasionally be crucified to trees. Some of the stones were taken out of the country via midnight transfers at remote airstrips. But many were sold blatantly in the open to buying offices in the capital of the Congo, which in turn forwarded them via air cargo to various European cities. Many of them wound up passing through the second floor of a dull concrete building near the financial district of London.

This was the selling office of the De Beers Consolidated Mines, Ltd., one of the most lasting monopolies on Earth. It had been founded by strongmen in the heyday of colonial Africa and carries with it a nimbus of invincibility and near-royal confidence in its mission to keep the price of diamonds high by limiting their availability and inflaming demand with heavy-barreled advertising campaigns. Billions of dollars worth of rough diamonds used to be stored in its basement vaults, and its wholesalers are the most powerful elite of the jewelry world. De Beers is not quite the evil empire that its critics make it out to be, and I would come to learn that its majestic facade concealed a surprising level of incompetence, but it still maintains a level of control over the industry today unparalleled in any other commodity trade. And critics charge that it turned a blind eye for several years to the true source of all the gems being dug up by warrior children, which eventually found their way onto the fingers of American brides.

Diamond sales raised more than $1 billion to pay for the violent quagmire in the Congo which involved seven nations and killed more than 2 million people through starvation, disease, and slaughter between 1998 and 2002. Though despicable, nothing about the diamond-based financing was technically illegal. And it was good business, too. The cargo of African wars made up as much as 14 percent of the world's entire diamond trade. There was no way to sort the bloody stones from the clean ones, and the diamond industry had no interest in separating the two. Once they were shipped to Antwerp or London, they were dumped into bulk sales pouches like wheat seeds poured anonymously into the bins of a Kansas grain elevator. Jacqueline was right: there was simply no way to tell where my fiancée's ring had come from.

Good intentions sealed the Central African Republic's fate. A British organization named Global Witness published a groundbreaking report in 1998 called *A Rough Trade*. It exposed the runaway use of diamonds to fuel African civil wars, especially on the part of a rebel army in the former Portuguese colony of Angola. Stories also began to leak out about the diamond-vending Revolutionary United Front of Sierra Leone, whose doped-up soldiers used machetes to hack off the hands and arms of thousands of villagers in an attempt to keep them from voting. The phrase "blood diamonds" entered the Western vocabulary and De Beers was shamed into closing its buying offices in Angola. Retailers proclaimed themselves shocked their diamonds might have been used to buy guns or machetes. "The thought that a Tiffany product, no matter how indirectly, could be linked to the horrific events of Sierra Leone absolutely and figuratively makes us lose sleep," Tiffany & Co. CEO Michael Kowalski told *The Washington Post*.

Feeling the pressure, South Africa and forty-four other diamond-producing countries developed a cursory method to stem the flow of blood diamonds known as the Kimberley Process. Now the daily loads of gems being flown to Europe had to come with a certificate declaring they were not mined in a nation in a technical state of war. The diamond industry hailed it as a giant step in the right direction. But human rights groups criticized it as superficial and full of loopholes. And one of the many problems was this: The capital of the Central African Republic—with six buying agencies and a direct pipeline to Antwerp—is a ten-minute canoe ride from the edge of the Congo.

"Officially, the government wants to make it all legal and regulated," Joseph told me as we sat next to the Oubangui River. "But unofficially, there's smuggling. I can take a stone and put it into my mouth. Under my tongue. Bam, it's gone."

How brazen is the smuggling? The statistics of production and sale are almost laughable when you line them up next to each other. I'm saying "almost" because there is much death and suffering in the gap where some arms merchants make a tidy profit. The mines of the Central African Republic are capable of producing about 500,000 carats a year, at most. But the diamonds that showed up in Antwerp with the Central African Republic listed as the official country of origin amounted to nearly twice that in 2000. This gap persists today, and it isn't hard to guess where the extras are coming from.

"This is the subject nobody wants to acknowledge," said Reinhard Moser, the project chief for Radio Ndeke Luka, the nation's only private radio station. "It is laughably easy to smuggle diamonds here. Nobody knows the true volume."

Only tiny drops from this underground crystal stream can be clearly glimpsed, and then only for a moment. When I told the men from the Congo that I couldn't buy any of their diamonds that morning on the patio, they left angry. I saw them later that day outside the high metal walls of a diamond-buying agency whose office was on the road to the airport.

Three more pebbles, tossed into an ocean of dreams.

I've had my share of truly awful moments—the kind that you wish you could blot out of your memory for good because they hurt so much—and one of them was the Tuesday night in February that Anne took the engagement ring off her finger and handed it back to me.

We were sitting on my couch, in the midst of what would be the last of an agonizing series of discussions over whether we should go through with the wedding. The last three months of the engagement had been bad, full of doubts and silences, and in retrospect, we made the right decision; but I will still never forget the look on her face as she removed the diamond and handed it to me. I stared at it in my palm. It was still a little warm from her hand.

After she walked out the door, I put the ring back into the blue box it came in, the one that closed with a snap. I tucked the box in the corner of my top desk drawer, put some old phone bills over it, and promptly got drunk. For the next week, I opened the box each night just to see it, and it made me cry each time.

After that first week, I didn't look at it again for a long time.

There are bullet holes in the garage walls at the buying agency, souvenirs of last year's revolution. The finance director pointed them out to me with something like pride. This was one of the first places looted. "What, you think the guys before you didn't get everything?" he had asked the twelfth band of thugs who shot their way inside. This company was lucky. One of the six other licensed agencies saw its offices burned out.

This agency was one of the most heavily fortified buildings in Bangui, outside of the Presidential Palace. It looked like a colonial estate. The walls fronted a dirt street littered with trash and crawling with beggar children, but inside the compound was a tended garden, a television satellite dish, and a Range Rover. There used to be a large illustration of a diamond on the front gate, but that had been painted over to conceal the true business of the place and the wealth inside. Not that it was a big secret in Bangui. This was the mouth of the pipeline to Antwerp, where virtually all of the Central African Republic's diamonds would enter the Western market.

"Look, let me be honest with you," the director said, about half an hour into our conversation. He was a Belgian, about thirty years old, with gray patches salted through his hair. "I didn't come here to help this country. I didn't come here to build hospitals. I could say that I did, but I'm not that kind of liar. I came here to do business, nothing more. But I really think the government should stop paying these thieves and put the money into schools or a hospital. When you see all this misery and the people all around not getting paid wages, it breaks your heart. All over the world, people believe diamond buyers are making huge profits. But those days are over. We're fighting here like crazy, man. We have to take a lot of discomfort for our profit."

This was after the point at which he felt comfortable enough with me to produce, as casually as if he were brushing away a fly, a Beretta pistol from his waistband, to show how he'd welcome looters when the next coup arrived. Almost as thoughtlessly, he dug out a piece of rough that had been sold to him not long ago. It was 27 carats, about the size of a big ripe blueberry. How much had he paid for it? About $52,000. I played with it idly in my hands while I asked him about the illegal flow of diamonds in and out of the country. He was quick to explain that he and his company were not involved, but readily admitted that it was common practice by others.

"I don't buy diamonds from people I don't know," he said. "In any profession, you have good and bad. But we are taking a lot of risks to establish these offices in unstable places. Smuggling is smuggling."

This, of course, has been a feature of the diamond trade for centuries. There is simply no better way to move around a large sum of money in a small place—almost no mineral is worth more per gram. This is the signature fact of a diamond, and its curse. It is why violence and deception trail it like mist. There are lots of places on the body to tuck one away. Jean-Baptiste Tavernier, one of the first European diamond merchant kings, visited India in 1665 and reported of the miners: "And their wages are so small they do not manifest any scruple, when searching in the sand, about concealing a stone for themselves when they can, and being naked, save for a small cloth which covers their private parts, they adroitly conceive to swallow it."

How does the smuggling happen in the Central African Republic today? I wanted to know.

The finance director took the berry-sized diamond from my hand, held it upward, and fixed me with a stare that I was unable to read.

"Take this and put it in your ass," he said. "You can walk out of this country with a half-million dollars in your ass. Six stones, that's about the size of a small piece of shit. Sell it to a gangster. Watch TV, man. That's what's happening in reality. . . . You will always find people willing to do something for you the moment you offer the right price."

Seeing a legitimate diamond is a lot harder than seeing a dirty one in the Central African Republic. I went down to the Ministry of Mines, which was in a motel-shaped building wrapped around a dusty courtyard. I asked one of the senior deputies, a genial English-speaking man named Cyriaque Gonda, if I could take a look at a diamond-producing region that week.

Certainly that could be arranged, he told me. There are two large mining districts, both along broad river valleys and both about a day's drive from Bangui. But there was a small problem. It was illegal for foreigners to enter these areas. I would need a permit and a letter of permission from the minister and those things would cost me $200, payable in U.S. dollars.

"But I don't want to buy any diamonds," I said. "I don't want to dig for any diamonds. I just want to see where they come from."

"Yes, certainly," said Cyriaque. But $200 American is what it would cost. In cash.

"I don't think I'm going to pay," I said, wondering if this was a legitimate fee.

"Sorry," said Cyriaque. "That is the rule."

What was the big secret? I wondered. This was a mineral that underwrote a huge part of the economy. Diamonds were responsible for up to 60 percent of the nation's export income, and slightly more than half of them were clean. Wouldn't they want to show them off? I had already spent $130 of my dwindling cash at the Ministry of Communications for a press permit, signed by the minister, Parfait M'baye. He was supposed to have been one of the actors in the March 2003 coup that brought the new government to power. M'baye now occupied a dingy two-story office with a stone wall out front and an empty flagpole tipping to the side. Each ministry here is its own province, and every request from the outside is an opportunity to create more paperwork and collect more fees. The French have left their legacy in Central Africa and part of it is the worship of government process, no matter how shaky the government or pointless the process.

I left the ministry, annoyed, and started walking along Avenue Boganda, past roadside ditches filled with trash and old grayish water, thick enough to be like gelatin. Street vendors sold cell phone covers, plastic dolls, and cooked goat meat from plywood shelves balanced on tires. The air was hazy with *harmitaan,* the mixture of veld smoke and desert sand blown down from the Sahara that particulates the sky every winter. There was a wooden arch at the entrance to the main traffic roundabout, a remnant of the Bokassa era. I walked under it and up the gentle hill to the high gates of the 1960s-era Presidential Palace, where a right turn would take me back to the hotel where I was staying.

I had gone several paces down a broad asphalt avenue—by far the smoothest in Bangui—before I realized the voice screaming in angry French behind me was screaming at me.

I turned around. A man wearing a white suit rushed over and flashed a handwritten document covered in ink stamps and encased in plastic. After two minutes, I understood the word *gendarme* and he understood that I spoke extremely poor French. "Your passport," he said in English, and I handed it to him. "Come with me," he said, taking me by the arm and leading me inside the gates of the presidential compound. "What is the problem?" I asked, trying to keep my voice casual. He didn't answer. He had an almost perfectly circular patch of white hair on the back of his head.

We walked up a grassy mall, up a flight of steps, and into a formal waiting room with marble columns, a chandelier, and a large oil painting of President Bozize on the far wall. This was apparently the antechamber to the president's office. There was something wrong with the electric lights in the room; they kept flickering on and off, and the room flashed from light to dim. I sat in a leather chair and watched as the policeman in the suit gestured angrily to another policeman and pointed over at me. Then they both disappeared.

I had a five-minute wait before I was taken outside the gates to a police station and made to stand against a plaster wall. Beside me was a rectangular hole where a light switch had been ripped out. "What did you think you were doing?" a man in a uniform asked me in broken English. "I don't know," I said. He shrugged, and turned away.

What *had* I done? I had just refused to pay a fee to the Ministry of Mines. Was that the problem? Or could they have somehow known that I had been sitting on a patio in the suburbs when a smuggler and his friends tried to unload three diamonds from the Congo? That would be a year in jail for me.

The man with the patch of white hair came out of a room with a padded door. He took my hand in a limp mortician's handshake and said in careful English: "My work here is done. Good-bye." And then he smiled for the first time, showing me his teeth. Another policeman took my arm. He and two soldiers in camouflage led me out of the station, through the streets of Bangui, where the roadside market was in full clatter. A few of the vendors stared at me.

"Can you tell me where we're going?" I asked, again in the friendliest voice I could summon. I got silence for an answer.

We walked south toward the port of Bangui, the one the French had built in the 1880s to ship cotton and diamonds down the river to the Atlantic. It looked like it had not been used in decades. There was a blue-barred gate in front and soldiers standing sentry at the edges.

"Why are we going into the port?" I asked my escorts. They only waved me forward impatiently, across the concrete tarmac and around the back of a two-story warehouse. There was a door wide enough for large cargo that led into a dim chamber. Dead electric bulbs hung from wires in the ceiling.

The two soldiers behind me unslung their rifles. They were held casually, but the muzzles were pointed at the approximate region of my ankles.

"You want me to go in there?" I asked. For the first time since being arrested, I began to get frightened. I could feel my hands start to tremble. Visions of an impromptu execution and a river burial began playing in my mental cineplex. They must have somehow found out I had met with diamond smugglers.

The policeman urged me forward, and we walked into the cargo hold together, down a dark hallway, and through a series of rooms. They were filled with trash, and loose wires hung from the ceiling.

Though it was ridiculous—I had done nothing wrong—I felt twitchy all over, my back especially. If they were going to shoot me, would it be here, without warning? Or would I be talked to first, made to understand, spun around to face the rifles?

The soldiers led me to a cement staircase and I was motioned to climb. On the second floor, I was led into the dim office where a sign on the door proclaimed SECRETARIAT OF POLICE. The man behind the desk had rheumy eyes, the sunken face of an AIDS victim, and hesitant English that was still far superior to my French. He wanted to know where I was staying, who I was working for, what my mother's name was, why I had walked in front of the Presidential Palace.

"The palace?" I asked.

"That road is forbidden for passage," he said. "There was a sign there."

"I am very sorry," I said. "I didn't see it."

Before I had left for Africa, a friend supplied me with an emergency tool: a letter written on some stationery from *Time* magazine with a nonexistent editor's scrawl at the bottom, identifying the bearer as a freelancer on assignment. I had used it the day before with a low-level official at the Ministry of Communications to convince him I hadn't come to Bangui to smuggle out diamonds, even though appearances probably indicated otherwise. In a nation without tourists or a U.S. Embassy, there were few other reasons for me to be there. What the letter was really intending to say, of course, was: "This person has friends concerned for his whereabouts. Please do not kill him." I was certain *Time* would forgive me this case of petty misrepresentation in a tight spot. It was a magazine I had always enjoyed, that much was true.

I pulled the letter out and showed it to the secretariat. He studied it for several minutes, eyes flicking up at me frequently, as if he were trying to reconcile the inflated person referenced in the letter with the one before him.

"It is very lucky for you that you were not taking photographs," he said finally.

I was handed off to another police official, this time by guards with Kalashnikovs safely behind their shoulders. He sat me down in front of his desk and began writing out a lengthy document in French. This was to be my "statement," he explained. I could see my name, my birthday, my hotel room number, and my parents' names in the jumble of words I couldn't read. Behind the policeman, through a dirty louvered window, was a view of the Oubangui River. It looked as far away as Miami. Fishermen in canoes paddled close to the Congo shore. I wondered what they were carrying. I thought of Anne, my lost fiancée, and the ring I had given her. Had her diamond come across this same river, in the shadow of a dark warehouse that was really a police station?

This, of course, was the Central African Republic personified: The government was too preoccupied with remaining in power and fighting off counterinsurgents to do much about the smuggling. This was a world where a lone person walking outside the walls of the Presidential Palace was of much greater concern than illicit diamonds coming over from the Congo. The French had left the nation with almost nothing, except for their language, their bread, a few rotting military bases, and their rigid legal system, which strained out gnats while entire camels were swallowed. It was like the diamond registry book that Joseph had showed me: so easy to sleepwalk through the motions, so oblivious to what was really happening. Around this carefully inefficient house of law, a vast green anarchy groaned.

After an hour had passed, the policeman finally put the finished document in front of me, lettered carefully in French. It was three pages long. He handed me a pen.

"I can't understand this," I told him, through a boy in a T-shirt who knew a little English. "*Je ne parle pas français*. I can't read it."

"He says you must put a mark on it," the boy told me.

I looked at the policeman and shook my head, unafraid of being shot anymore. If it was going to happen, it would have happened already, and the passage of time had probably calmed things down. Either jail or the demand for a hefty bribe was coming down on me, but either was going to be far better than signing a confession to an unknown deed.

"He says you must mark it," the boy repeated.

I shrugged apologetically and shook my head and did nothing. The policeman looked at me with unfiltered contempt, tossed me my passport across the desk, and told me, in words that I did not understand, but did, to get the hell out of there. And I obeyed.

A month after Anne broke up with me, I moved back to my hometown in Arizona and took a job as a reporter at the local newspaper. Anne and I maintained a careful friendship over the phone for a few weeks. Then she stopped taking my calls.

I made halfhearted inquiries about the best way to sell her diamond. Then I stopped. For reasons I couldn't explain, I still wanted to keep the ring. But at the same time, I couldn't bear to have it near me. I put it into a silver martini shaker and took it to my grandmother's house. "Can I keep this here?" I asked her casually, setting the shaker amid other knickknacks on her fireplace mantel. "Sure," she said. I didn't feel like talking about what was inside.

Half of a year went by. Our planned wedding date, June 16, came and went. I spent that day at the bottom of the Grand Canyon, sitting in the shade of a cliff at the time when the ceremony was supposed to have begun. *Then I thy sovereign praises loud will sing, That all the woods shall answer and their echo ring.* I dreamed about her almost every night that summer, and saw her in the faces of strangers.

One night in September, as the dreams were beginning to fade, I went over to my grandmother's house for our regular Monday night dinner. I usually did not look at the mantelpiece to see the martini shaker during these get-togethers—I usually tried to ignore it—but for some reason, on this night, I gave it a glance.

But it wasn't there. It was gone.

"What happened to the martini shaker I put there?" I asked.

"Oh, that was yours?" she said. "I was wondering about that. I moved it to the living room."

I went to fetch the silver shaker from its new place, which happened to be on top of a rock-walled indoor planter that held much fascination for me as a child. I opened the shaker. It was empty.

"Did you find a blue box in there?" I called to my grandmother. All the spit in my mouth had thickened to paste.

"That was a gift from Nonie," she said, referring to an old family friend who had recently died. "She started giving all her fake jewelry away. I didn't want to upset her by telling her no."

"What happened to the box?" I asked. "There was a ring inside."

"I gave it away," said my grandmother. "It went to St. Vincent de Paul the other day."

At this moment, my uncle Fred interjected, "No, the guy isn't supposed to come by until tomorrow. Tuesday." He retreated to the other room and brought out a small blue box. "Is this what you were looking for?"

Anne's ring was inside, the stone balanced on its prongs. It was really the first time I had looked at it since the week she had left me. I felt as though I might vomit.

I confessed to my grandmother what the fuss was about—that the ring wasn't Nonie's; that it had belonged to my lost fiancée, the one I had never wanted to talk about; that I had been keeping the ring at her house because it made me incredibly sad to have it near me; that I didn't blame her for almost losing it and that it was my fault for being so closed-mouthed about the whole thing; but that I was too upset to eat anything and had to leave right then. And then I drove away.

"You'll want to watch the guys who go off by themselves to take a shit," said the man in the purple basketball jersey. He was selling adapter cords for cellular phones, but not the phones themselves, from a small wooden platform next to the side of the road.

"They're the ones who are trying to steal," he said. "They'll swallow a diamond and then shit it out a day later. They'll paw through their waste to find it." He showed me how this was done, raking his fingers carefully across his palm.

His name was Beinvena Yelbana, twenty-eight years old, and he used to be a *nagbata*, or diamond laborer from the city of Carnot, and he had certainly never shit a diamond into his palm. If he had, he might not be here on Avenue Boganda, selling adapters next to a drainage ditch. He told me how he had made and lost an overnight fortune in his father's small diamond dig.

"It is hard work and you have to concentrate," he said. "You have to control yourself. It has big money, but there are big risks. I had so much money, I didn't know what to do with it. I spent it all on wives"—by this he meant girlfriends—"and alcohol. And other things. But I can't remember where it all went."

Beinvena's fortune came to him in just one magnificent day, when he saw the dull wink of a diamond in the sift he was washing in the river. He had hauled the dirt to the river himself from the mine, more than two kilometers away. Beinvena's arms were on fire from the journey. But that didn't matter anymore. There was a huge party that night and he got drunk. The stone was given to the collector who had fronted the equipment money. Nobody ever told Beinvena what price his stone commanded—a frequent complaint among village miners in Africa—but Beinvena still got paid a handsome finder's fee, and proceeded to waste it all.

This, of course, made him exactly typical of any young man caught in the riotous flush of a mineral dig. There's a reason why prostitutes and saloons followed mining camps; why pickup truck dealerships offer such easy credit near the smelter. "Mining the miners" has always been a better bet than mining itself, and not just in Africa. Something about the combination of youth and shovels does not lend itself to good money management anywhere. Beinvena's wealth had come and gone like a summer daydream under the baobab trees. His diamond, it might be said, was not forever.

"When I look back on my life," Beinvena told me, "I know I haven't gotten any good things. You have to work by faith, or else it's just an illusion."

An illusion, a phantom, a dream. Those were the words that the Central Africans kept choosing to describe the diamonds that lay under their earth. They were hidden in the sands, in the ghost riverbeds, millions of them, an otherwise useless pebble that had no place in the cultural history or spiritual tradition of the region, but one that the white men valued supremely and were willing to pay rewards that far surpassed any other. The world outside had decided that pure value could not be concentrated any more effectively than inside these little bits of carbon, which became, with polishing and cutting and marketing and advertising and cooing, the gems that fired under light, the signal mark of possession, the very zeniths of love and victory. And so Central Africa bent itself daily to feed that hunger. It sent a million carats a year to Belgium, and half of them were even legal. But what was there to show for it when the digging was done and the diamonds flown out?

"I'd like to see a mine," I told my translator, Alexie. "Can we?"

"It is very difficult," he said. "The problem is that transportation is very expensive. There are bandits on the roads. And permission is needed to enter into the mining areas."

"Let's not worry about that," I told him.

Alexie had been a graduate student at the University of Bangui until his adviser quit and no other faculty member would agree to read his thesis. He had three children he was raising on his own, and he told me his wife had left him for the witch doctor in his home village the previous year. He resembled a smaller version of Martin Luther King Jr., with calm almond eyes and a sobriety of purpose. Alexie's slippery answers sometimes drove me crazy (every other sentence seemed to begin with "The problem is . . .") but I grew to appreciate his wits in the backcountry.

It took time and bargaining and several glasses of beer drunk on the porches of Alexie's many friends, but after three days, we had a Toyota Land Cruiser at a price of $130 a day, not including fuel, but including a surprise: a driver, a backup driver, and one of Alexie's jobless relatives tagging along as an "apprentice." A friend from the United States had come along with me to shoot some pictures of wildlife. We looked at each other and shrugged. A bigger posse would make us look more important, and possibly less attractive to bandits, anyhow.

We obtained some official-looking paperwork created on a borrowed computer, announcing an *Ordre de Mission* which displayed the name of Parfait M'baye in boldface, and composed a vague paragraph in French that explained our group was "collecting information about economic development."

"This must be stamped," I was told. "But the police will take care of that."

They did. We left the center of Bangui in the predawn chill and promptly hit the first of what would be almost two dozen checkpoints. They were ostensibly to prevent the movement of armaments around the countryside, but it soon became clear that their actual purpose was to provide a source of income for the penniless soldiers assigned to guard them. The checkpoints were often nothing more than a bamboo pole over two buckets. I learned that "coffee" is the Central African code word for "tribute to police." Alexie was usually able to get us waved through the checkpoints after brief parleys and a minimal amount of coffee money. Before long, our dubious *Ordre de Mission* was dripping in official ink. "Stamps are very important in this country," said Alexie. The French process lives on, generations removed from the heavy colonial hand.

About twelve kilometers out of Bangui, we ran into trouble. A policeman at a checkpoint wanted more than coffee from Alexie. He was clothed in the usual government camouflage jumpsuit that makes police and military indistinguishable, but he was also wearing an imperial glower that seemed to have the entire village cowed. We weren't the only ones having a hard time. I watched as he ordered a decrepit van behind us torn apart. Fieldworkers watched silently as the contents of their bags were dumped on the pavement.

After half an hour of bargaining, Alexie was still unable to get him down from the outrageous figure he was wanting. I went over to talk to him.

"We have authorization from the minister of communications," I said.

"Minister! Who is the minister?" demanded the checkpoint captain. "He is in his air-conditioned office while we are out here suffering." But he would not look me in the eye. Off to the side, I watched as one of the workers from the junked van—an elderly man in the long robes of a Muslim—was ordered to his feet at the point of a gun. The soldiers went through his pockets.

I pulled out a notebook.

"What is your name, sir?" I asked the soldier, through a supremely uncomfortable Alexie.

This received no answer, and so I asked again, uncapping a ballpoint.

"What is your name, sir? We will be talking to Parfait M'baye when we return to Bangui."

Five minutes later, we were rolling again. The pavement soon gave way to rutted ochre. We eased over a creek on a bridge made of wooden market pallets lashed together. Naked children waved and screamed to us from the water. At first I thought they were calling *bonjour*. It was only later I learned that few people in the villages speak French with any degree of fluency, and what the children were really screaming was the Sango word *mahjoo*—which means "white man," a rarity in the bush.

We were heading into the substrata of the country, the true ancient régime of the Central African Republic, the pole-and-mud villages that had somehow outlasted the slavers and the Arab raiders and the missionaries and the distant tussles in the capital, scratching out a life in quiet obscurity for thirteen hundred years among the baobab and poho trees. The morning fog began to burn away, the cinder-block huts gave way to dirt, and the jungle closed in.

Diamonds are strangers to the surface of the earth. Their true home is the iron silicate and magnesium soup at the mid-regions of the earth's interior known as the mantle. Pressures are enormous here. At temperatures approaching 2,000 degrees Fahrenheit, small grains of carbon that found their way here are pressed into something new. The heat and the weight of the mantle press sheet after sheet of new carbon onto the grain. And eventually it becomes almost unbreakable. The carbon atoms of a diamond share an extra electron with each of the four carbon atoms that surround it, and their bond with each other forms a tight cube. This is the strongest linkage of atoms known to chemistry. It could not survive the lighter regions of the earth's crust, where carbon is expressed as a much flakier substance called graphite. The hellish foundry of the earth's innards, at depths approaching 120 miles, is the only birthing place for a diamond, which takes its name from the Greek *adamas*—which means "indomitable."

Diamonds found their way into the world of man by being blown out of the cones of ancient volcanoes millions of years ago. The streams of lava and slurry punched up through hard-rock fissures near the crust and exploded up into the air. If the magma was traveling fast enough—the necessary speed has been estimated at 100 miles an hour—the diamonds it bore along had a tiny chance of surviving the rapid expansion of gases near the surface. The concept is like that of a NASA space capsule requiring the precisely correct angle and velocity to reenter the earth's atmosphere without being incinerated. If the magma moved too slowly, the diamonds fizzled away in a sigh of gas. What we wear on our fingers and around our necks are the lucky survivors, the sperm who won the race.

When the ancient volcanoes died and eroded away, the vertical dykes that carried the lava hardened into carrot-shaped fossils. These daggers into the earth are packed with a grayish-green rock called kimberlite. Pipes of kimberlite are sought-after prizes for geologists, but only those that moved their lava fast enough are worth anything. Of the six thousand known kimberlite pipes on the planet, barely a dozen are known to contain enough diamonds to be "economically feasible"—that is, to justify a large mine. This means almost nothing to the diamond miners of Africa, because if you lack the trucks, drills, rolls, chutes, and the hundreds of millions of dollars it takes to properly exploit the kimberlite pipes, your only alternative is to look into the rivers that may have carried rough jewels away from their hidden volcanic portals. You simply dig a hole in the riverbed, sift through the sand, and hope to get very, very lucky.

There is an enduring mystery concerning the birth of a diamond. How did the inner kernels of diamonds—those seedlings of foreign carbon—find their way into the mantle in the first place? There are three theories. One is that the carbon occurs naturally in the mantle, in a way that scientists do not precisely understand. A second holds that the floors of some of the earth's oceans dumped a load of silt and organic material through diagonal cracks in the basalt crust. A small number of these carbon bits survived the journey into the mantle and had the ultra-strong layers of crystallization wrapped around them over time, as an oyster spins pearl thread around a piece of sand.

This would mean that the heart of a diamond was once a living thing—a bit of seaweed, perhaps, or the speck of a trilobite. The negative numbers of isotopes seen in eclogite diamonds are strongly reminiscent of life-based carbon, lending strength to the idea that humans and diamonds share a common ancestry.

This theory was thrown into doubt in 1981, after a meteor found in the Allen Hills of Antarctica chewed up a saw blade that researchers at the Smithsonian Institution were trying to run through it. What could ruin steel quite like that? It turned out the meteor was seeded liberally with diamonds. Scientists theorized that those tiny diamond chips buried in the mantle may have been planted there by ancient meteor strikes. The hypothesis gained strength six years later, after astronomers at the University of Chicago found diamonds no bigger than 20 angstroms across while using a spectroscope to view a supernova. "It seems necessary to invoke an extra-solar origin for the diamond," the Chicago researchers concluded in a paper published in 1987. The tiny gems were suspended in deep space, the discharge of a dying sun. Quite literally, stardust.

How do you find a piece of star in a place like the Central African Republic? The customary way is to have a dream about it.

We came to the town of Boda, which was a kind of supply center for the mines. Muslims owned most of the markets, where oil lanterns and giant sacks of milled flour were sold. Loud music came from a bar where men were getting drunk in the middle of the day. There were a few buying agencies ringed with high walls. There was a wide main street, crisscrossed with rain rivulets and sloping down to an anemic creek. Boda reminded me of a rawer version of Placerville and Ouray and Park City and the other nineteenth-century boomtowns of the Sierras and the Rockies.

I sat on top of the spare fuel drum lashed to the back of the Land Cruiser while Alexie bought bananas and bread from a store and Hassa, our driver, drank coffee from a jelly glass at a nearby stand. A man in a beige shirt came up and spoke French to me. I quickly understood he was a police officer and reached for some coffee money. But he didn't want it. He had just taken a job as the police chief in a town fifty miles away. Could we give him a ride? The chief climbed in with a single suitcase, spread a foam mattress out in the back of the Land Cruiser, and coasted along with us, as if in a raft, looking up at the darkening sky.

We came to the edge of the Lombaye River in the middle of the night. It is too wide to be bridged with wood. There was an iron ferryboat on the other side—the only way across. Two children who lived nearby volunteered to paddle across in their pirogues and unhitch it from its cable. A man from a village on the other side had a habit of locking it up for himself, they said, even though it was government property. It was the only way we could pass. I gave the children some francs, crouched by the water's edge, and waited. The only sounds were the receding hush of paddles in the water and the croaking of frogs. The river spread away like a lake under moonlight. Presently, I heard the sounds of clanging iron from across the river in the darkness, as the children worked to unlock the ferryboat.

Another vehicle soon joined ours at the water's edge. It was a battered station-wagon ambulance carrying more than ten people. I walked over to talk to one of the passengers, a fortyish man in torn pants and a filthy tank top. He introduced himself as N'Djiewa Sylvin, a *nagbata*, and said he was hitching a ride back into the mining regions. He was broke. The biggest diamond he had found in his life was only 4 carats big—a stone that would easily be worth $50,000 in American retail prices, the income of three well-fed lifetimes in Central Africa, but it had left him without even a good pair of shoes.

I asked him how he knew where the diamonds were, and he said that he looked for maps in his sleep. These dreams were sent from the ancestors and they would point the way.

"Dreams always bring good answers," said N'Djiewa. "I am often told in my dreams to share my food with children. If I do this good deed, I may find a diamond the next day. If I don't find it, one of my neighbors will find it because of my dream. If you get a dream that you have a new flashlight, that means you're supposed to get that flashlight."

Could the prophetic dreams ever fail? I asked.

N'Djiewa said no.

"I'm going to keep mining until I die," he said, just before the iron boat came drifting across the river toward us in the broth of darkness.

We slept that night on the floor of a shack in a village whose name I never learned, where a kind woman fed us bowls of curried goat when we arrived. My sleep was patchy and broken. I was beginning to have dreams of my own. Before I left for Africa, I started taking an antimalarial drug called mefloquine, whose label warned ominously of "psychiatric side effects" and "vivid dreams." Friends of mine who had traveled in the tropics had warned me about this. One who spent months in India said he had strange thoughts about murdering his traveling companions. He concluded that if he had known how unpleasant the chemical blowback was, he never would have taken the trip. Other reactions I had heard about were milder, but the common experience was dreams that seemed uncannily real.

I awoke from a polychromatic sludge that night, not knowing where I was, and heard somebody speaking in harsh and scratchy French. I twisted around for a look, but could make out nothing in the shack except for moonlight coming in through the slats. Then: a small red dot about ten feet away. I became aware that it was the police chief, listening to Voice of America on his shortwave radio.

I heard more about the diamond dreams the next day from a younger miner walking the road with a shovel over his shoulder near the village of Katopka. His name was Narcise Blede, twenty-three years old, and he said the divinations that came to him in the night weren't always from his ancestors. He had dreamed of having passionate sex with a rich white woman the night before a big-carat discovery the year before.

"She came driving up to my house with a new car," he said. His friends next to him laughed, but he didn't appear to be joking as he told me the story through Alexie.

"It was a very good dream," he said. "I was screwing the spirit."

I asked what he had found recently and he gestured to a friend. The friend pulled out a small cardboard matchbox bearing the words *Le Boxeur.* Inside was a sickly yellow chip, a sad discolored little half-carat.

"Diamonds are full of spirits," he said. "Very powerful. If the diamond is too big, people can go crazy and die."

Dreams and spirits. What was happening in the Central African Republic was the emergence of an entirely new folk religion. French corporations have dug diamonds out of the sand here since the 1880s, but the large-scale recruitment of the countryside into mining didn't gear up until the Bokassa era, when lust for imperial glitter became a presidential obsession. The president had died, but the mania hadn't. In just thirty years, diamonds had transformed the economy of the backcountry. But they had changed even more than the dreams of young men—they were changing the culture itself. The yellow rocks from the mantle had been almost unknown before, with no place in the ceremonial or religious heritage of the M'Baka, the Niam-Niam, the Baminga, the Mondjombo, or any of the tribes, and now a whole set of mythologies was laid onto their slippery surfaces.

Most of them revolved around the spirits of the dead.

Near a small village called Kate Bombale is an outcropping of black rock. It is atop a hill, just north of the thin ochre track that leads to a nearby mine. "That's where the spirits of the diamonds are living," I was told, as we bounced along the road. "We pray to it whenever we go past."

There were eight men from Kate Bombale with me, packed into the back of the Land Cruiser. They were taking us deep off the road into the jungle to show us where they hoped to find their salvation. Purple blossoms and twigs fell into our hair as the vehicle thwacked through the dense brush. The men ducked their heads. Pythons are sometimes known to fall from the trees this way.

We came to a series of shallow excavations next to the Loame River. They reminded me of gravel pits dug next to highways. The men from the village said the first diggings had been done with a bulldozer commissioned by a diamond buyer from Boda. The rest of the work they did themselves, with nothing more than shovels and sifts. It was like panning for gold in the California Gold Rush, except the Americans of a century and a half ago had better equipment.

The chief of the mine, Yango Michel, was a very old man by Central African standards at fifty-seven. He stood at the bottom of a pit and told me: "This is the exact spot where my son found a six-carat. I was proud. But I would have been prouder if it had been a better color. This is how you know if you have a good gem: If it looks like a candle, good. If it is colored like a bottle, it is bad."

I asked Yango about the dreams and he told me that his were mostly about chickens.

"The spirit comes and asks you to make a sacrifice," he said. "I often hear it asking me to buy a white chicken to share with the children. Diamonds follow good deeds. The spirit then says, 'I have heard you, I am your grandfather,' and then it tells me where to go and dig."

They took me down to the river and one man showed me how he sifted the ore in a wood-framed screen, looking for the magic octahedron. There is a song to the dead—a low guttural chant—that is sung as they work the sifting boards:

> My ancestors
> If you really exist
> From the work I do now
> Give me five carats
> Ten carats
> Twenty carats

I stood at the edge of the river and looked up the cutbank at the line of men from Kate Bombale. This was the bottom of a vast supply chain—

the place where the death of a star met the world of commerce. Between them and the end user stood a colossus, with value-adding stops in Boda, Bangui, Antwerp, Bombay, London, New York and other American cities. These men would be paid perhaps $200 for a gem that would easily retail for $40,000 in a mall in Albuquerque.

They were hungry and discouraged. The merchant from Boda who bought their diamonds never told them what kind of profit he made from their labor. They suspected—correctly—that they were being swindled, but they were powerless to do anything about it but keep digging and hope for a large discovery. They had tried to talk to their member of the national Parliament, but had heard nothing.

I asked them if they knew how their diamonds would eventually be used when they left Africa. They answered no, they had no idea.

"In America," I said, "it is traditional for a man to give a woman a diamond when he asks her to marry him," and this set off a round of laughter. They had never heard of such a thing. It was ridiculous to think of. I was asked through Alexie if I was joking, and I assured them I wasn't.

The only Muslim convert in the village, a twenty-two-year-old father of two named Bayo Arnaud, beamed down at me from his spot on the cutbank. He said: "In our world, diamonds bring riches to a village. If in the United States, you use a diamond to buy a wife, that shows how much richer you are than us."

There was not a trace of irony or superciliousness in his tone. He meant to express sincere—if puzzled—admiration for the special kind of dowry that the West had created from the stones their dead grandparents showed to them in their dreams.

Before I left the Central African Republic, I bought a few paper cards decorated with the wings of butterflies. They had been arranged to make familiar shapes: a man, a hut, two birds, a tree. It seemed to be a reflection of the country as a whole, wings torn off a living thing to make an image of something alien. It has a kind of beauty, but it is beauty at the expense of terrible pain.

And what gives diamonds their hard and remorseless beauty, really? Whether they emerge from the death of a star or the life of plankton makes no difference, for these chips from the earth are nothing more than an empty cage for our dreams—blank surfaces upon which the shifting desires of the heart could be written. A diamond is a philosopher's stone of the existential variety, for it is like the world itself: spoken into existence only through whatever meaning we choose to assign to it. For men like Joseph N'gozo, it is an elusive ticket to middle-class respectability; for the killers in the Congo, it is a down payment for more guns; for madmen like Bokassa, it was visions of immortality; for the miners of Kate Bombale, it is their ancestors come to life again; for Beinvena Yelbana, it is only a way to eat something more than manioc for another day. And for me, it is love curdled to quiet sorrow, a stone attached to my heart like a tumor, representing all my hidden longings and failures. We look into the stone and see only ourselves firing.

Anne would come to wear it once again. Time passed and we reconciled. I apologized to her for not loving her as I should have and she forgave me. And we sat together at a long banquet table. There were guests on either side of us. I was holding her hand and she mine and we chatted as though nothing had ever come between us. I could not remember being so completely at peace. Her engagement ring sparkled on her finger.

But as we ate an appetizer, I said to her, "Anne, something is bothering me. I can't remember exactly when it was that we got back together."

"Neither can I," she said.

"I can't remember how that happened," I said.

But I decided it didn't matter—we were together again, that was all that was important—and I kept eating the hot peppers on my plate, letting the warmth of forgiveness flow over me. But the feeling did not stay.

"Anne," I said after another pause. "I'm starting to wonder if you're real or not."

"Please don't think about that," she said, looking at me with the green eyes I had loved so much.

"You're not real, are you?"

"No," she confessed. "I'm not."

I knew then that I had only a few seconds left and I moved to hold her in my arms, to cradle what was already tattering away into mefloquine wisps.

It was a sleep so deep and a malaria dream so vivid that it took me at least a full minute to come completely awake and realize where I was: alone, under the spreading veil of a crinoline mosquito net, next to the Sangha River, in Africa.

Two

MIDNIGHT SUN

Canada

At the beginning of every summer, a small committee holds a meeting in the tin-sided municipal building in the town of Cambridge Bay. The meeting is never advertised and is not open to the public. Its purpose is to calculate how many people in town are old and sick, and to estimate the number who will die in the coming year.

The estimation is necessary because Cambridge Bay is in the part of Canada that crumbles apart into islands as the globe tilts toward the North Pole. It is 280 miles above the Arctic Circle and built upon a bed of permafrost. Only during a two-month window in the summertime is the ground soft enough to be opened. And so after the town officials secretly arrive at a number, the Public Works Department is sent out to the graveyard north of town to dig that many graves, and even then, the earth becomes hard as marble at a depth of only four feet. The shallow graves are filled in throughout the winter as people die, and at each funeral, everybody eyes the remaining holes.

"The elders don't like it that we do this," said Mark Calliou, the hamlet's senior administrative officer. "But it's a necessity. If we miscalculate, we have to store the corpses in the maintenance shed all winter." This would be disrespectful, but not a health hazard. There is no fear of corpse decomposition in the Canadian Arctic, where average winter temperatures are around 20 degrees below zero.

There is another problem with dying in Cambridge Bay. Bodies do not always stay buried here. After being exposed to the air, permafrost tends to heave upward, and corpses are known to rise to the surface after burial, pushing limestone rocks and the sterile polar dirt out of the way as the ground beneath them puffs like dough; it is not unheard of for a family to visit the cemetery only to see the corner of a relative's coffin poking out of the rocks, and the wooden cross knocked over. The Public Works Department must then re-dig the grave and pile more rocks on top to keep the coffin down.

Cambridge Bay has very few buildings with foundations and those that do—the new dome-shaped high school, for example—must be equipped with an aerating mechanism to artificially chill the soil underneath. Otherwise the heat of the building would thaw the permafrost into dirty gelatin and the entire structure would slide off its footing and tip into the ground. Fickle earth: the dead rise, but buildings sink.

Laying an aerated foundation, like nearly everything else in Cambridge Bay, is extremely expensive. The windswept settlement of twelve hundred is on the southern tip of Victoria Island in the Arctic Ocean, across the Coronation Gulf from the north coast of the North American continent, more than a thousand air miles from the nearest asphalt road and two time zones away from the territorial capital at Iqaluit. Everything in the town's two supermarkets must be moved in by airplane. A handful of wilted asparagus costs $12; a quart of orange juice $9. Whiskey is not sold openly—it's against the law—but the going rate for a bootlegged fifth is $300.

I flew into Cambridge Bay's lone dirt airstrip one day in August and was met on the ground by a man named Wilf MacDonald. He is a short, balding man who speaks with a hollow Canadian brogue that sounds almost Scottish. We climbed in his pickup truck and headed toward town, a jumble of wooden clapboard houses and tin sheds on the edge of the tundra. There was a dirt dock, a small generating station, some cylindrical tanks that held a year's supply of heating oil, a giant red military antenna that no longer broadcasts anything. A few dead seals rotted on the beach next to the fishing boats. Wilf took me inside his house, which is a converted Canadian federal post office that sits on pilings, and poured vodka into cans of ginger ale. It was the time of year when daylight lasts twenty hours a day and we drank until the long gray sunset, which was at 1 A.M. Wilf told me he used to be a plumber in Montreal, where he had a side business in "midnight moves," that is, helping people skip out on their back rent by moving them in the dark. He could clean out a house in two hours. Those who would stiff a landlord would also stiff a mover, of course, so Wilf had to be prudent. The best insurance, he told me, was to load a television or stereo in the front seat of the plumber's truck. If he failed to get his cash, he just drove off with the appliance. Wilf moved to Cambridge Bay to be a plumber and wound up as the town coroner.

"Propane-sniffing used to be a big thing among the boys in town, eh?" he told me. "This one time, five of them were in a shed down by the docks sniffing off a bottle, and one of them lit a cigarette. Two of them got blown apart and there wasn't much left to bury. I went to collect evidence and found a gloved hand about two hundred yards away, eh? It was still holding the lighter. Pink Bic lighter."

Wilf is now in the business of supplying food and other provisions to camps in the interior of the island, and business is booming. The next morning, he hustled me out to the airstrip and put me on board a De Havilland Twin Otter plane bound for the middle of the island. I shared the cabin with a load of frozen steaks, Gatorade, breakfast cereal, and potatoes. The window was a pane full of gray. It was too early for snow cover, and the stony barrens below stretched to a horizon muddled with fog. Down there were a rash of shallow lakes, and patches of sickly green that were fields of moss and dwarf shrubs. They are virtually the only plant life that can survive in the alkaline till. Victoria Island is what biologists call a polar desert. Despite its nearness to the North Pole, the annual rainfall of about sixteen inches a year resembles that of more arid drylands, and islands farther north in the Arctic archipelago receive less precipitation than the Sahara Desert. The island is about the size of Nebraska, but not a single tree or any wild plant taller than a baseball grows here.

The dominant animals are called musk ox—enormous hoofed beasts that look like buffalo from another planet. Their ancestry dates to the last ice age, and Victoria Island is one of their last free-roaming pastures. The Inuit on the coast—the people who used to be called Eskimos—used to hunt them to supplement their seafood diet. But few of the Inuit ever ventured far off the coast to find them. The inner regions of the island were hostile terra incognita to them, and to the rest of the world. Detailed maps of the interior did not even exist until the 1950s. But the previously unknown regions of Victoria Island are now being mapped with awesome care, its innards vivisected like a cancer patient.

Willy the pilot started to descend and I saw human leavings for the first time—a pile of crates and some blue oil drums. We banked around in a sharp half-circle and came down with a bump and a clatter on a bare patch of dirt. There were fat tundra-tires on the Twin Otter—Willy never needed an airstrip.

I stepped out into the chill and took several sharp breaths. The air felt almost metallic in my lungs. This was beyond the outposts of the settled world; the nearest house was a nine-day walk to the south, with nothing but sand and polar lakes in between. What would happen, I thought, if I were left here on my own? Would I last even a day? Willy spread a black net on the ground and we started loading the crates of food on top of it in neat piles.

We were almost finished when the mutter of a helicopter sounded to the north and grew louder. The helicopter eased down near Willy's plane in a squall of rotor wash and dust and I was still wiping my eyes as a short redheaded woman full of smiles dashed over to me with her hand extended.

"I'm Vicki Yehl, project geologist," she shouted. "Welcome to diamond camp."

It used to be said that North America was a great place to sell diamonds but a lousy place to find them. Not anymore. Diamonds were first discovered in a remote part of Canada's Northwest Territories fifteen years ago, setting off a rush that pushes farther and farther north into the Arctic every year. Canada has quickly become the third largest producer in the world, second only to Namibia and Botswana. Two major diamond mines, each with campuses as big as steel mills, are pulling an estimated $1.7 billion worth of rough diamonds out of the tundra every year. The rocks are of gem quality, vodka-clear and icy, and have the added benefit of coming from a stable nation with some of the toughest environmental laws in the world.

Canada began producing its diamonds just as human rights groups were beginning to denounce the chaotic diamond economies in Africa that were being used to finance bloody civil wars. Africa's misery was a priceless public relations gift, but one that the retailers chose to emphasize with drawing-room delicacy. "Born under the northern lights more than a billion years ago, Canadian diamonds are pure in every sense of the word," oozed one glossy advertisement, adding: "There are other diamonds. Let the others wear them." To further secure the high ground, the retailers began putting tiny inscriptions of Canadian iconography onto the girdles of their stones—maple leaves, polar bears, igloos, Inuit inukshuks, "everything but a hockey stick," in the words of one industry observer. The inscriptions carry a specious air of authority to them to reassure the consumer, a mark of indemnity against the generally unsavory business of how the stones reach the marketplace. The vast sums of money at stake are pushing the hunt for diamonds farther and farther toward the North Pole, to places like Victoria Island, where the idea of hunting anything but caribou would have been laughable twenty years ago.

The story of how diamonds were first discovered in an Arctic lake is the story of an old geological puzzle eventually unlocked by technology. That, and pure ornery stubbornness.

North America didn't seem to be blessed with much kimberlite, that peculiar type of clay tube that brought pressurized carbon to the surface 100 million years ago. Stray pipes of it had been accidentally discovered in Pennsylvania and parts of upstate New York, but they were bereft of diamonds. There was only one known rich pipe anywhere in America, under a cow pasture in Murfreesboro, Arkansas, but its promoters had never been able to develop it into a full-scale enterprise. There didn't seem to be any other good kimberlite anywhere on the continent—but there was a frustrating mystery. When the Midwest was being settled and plowed in the nineteenth century, loose diamonds kept turning up in strange places: a well on a Wisconsin farm, a gravel pit in Michigan, creeks in Indiana.

In 1893, a geology professor at the University of Wisconsin named William Henry Hobbs read a newspaper story about a boy who had found a 3.83-carat stone while playing in a cornfield. Hobbs began collecting stories about diamond finds in the Great Lakes region and charted them on a map. They formed a loose arc across the region. That shape spoke a loud message to Hobbs. In 1899, he published an article in the *Journal of Geology* speculating that the diamonds showing up in roadside gravel pits and farmers' fields were not products of the local soil, but had been carried south by glaciers, which had receded from the upper Midwest at the end of the last ice age, some ten thousand years earlier. The true diamond fields, then, should lie somewhere to the north.

But where? No substantiated kimberlite pipes had ever been found in Canada. And even if those stones turning up on Midwestern farms had been refugees from the Arctic, how could a prospector hope to uncover the true source in one of the harshest places on the globe? The upper fourth of the North American continent is a sheet of granite and gneiss called the Great Slave Craton. It is the core of the continental plate—a layer of granite 100 miles deep that is, in geologic terms, flat as a sidewalk and just as hard. Farming anything on the craton is nearly impossible above the 60th parallel, which is on the same latitude as the southern tip of Greenland. A carpet of spruce and jack pine coats the unsettled land. The trees vanish entirely just above the Great Slave Lake into a moonscape of granite and icy clear lakes. The only greenery out here is lichen and tough little shrubs that bloom like Irish heather during the two-month Arctic summer. Snow flurries are common in August. Winter temperatures here routinely plunge to 40 degrees below zero, cold enough to crack steel. The Dene Indians to the south ventured here only during seasonal caribou hunts; to them, this was a land of starvation and death. They called it *dechinule*, or "land of little sticks." To the early French fur traders, this was *les Terres Steriles*, "the Barren Lands." Today's residents like to call it "Tomorrowland," because their section of the Canadian map is always covered up by the word "tomorrow" during television weather forecasts. The stations thought nobody cared about the weather up there.

In the summer of 1985, a geologist from British Columbia named Chuck Fipke began hiring some of the float planes out of Yellowknife Bay to fly him to the barrens. The rate was $700 a day and Fipke always paid cash. He would wait until the plane was aloft before giving exact directions, and then mutter something about looking for gold if he was questioned. Fipke ordered the pilots to land on the lakes, splashed to each shoreline in hip waders, shoveled dirt and sand into burlap bags, labeled them carefully, and sent them back to his lab in Kelowna for analysis. The pilots thought he was slightly crazy and nicknamed him "the Sandman." Fipke *was* more than a little erratic, but he had a secret that would unlock the puzzle of Canadian diamonds.

The same heat and pressure in the mantle that forged diamonds also created a shower of red garnets. If you found blood-colored specks in your siftings, you were on the right track—every sandhog from Brazil to Botswana knew that rule. But in the mid-1970s, a postgraduate fellow at the Smithsonian Institution named John Gurney discovered something astounding about the garnets. He took ore samples from South African mines and put them under a microprobe, which is an expensive piece of equipment that analyzes the chemical contents of stones. Gurney noticed a key similarity between the South African garnets and tiny garnets embedded within diamonds taken from other mines. Both sets were deep purple, and proved high in chrome and low in calcium—an unusual and distinct combination. Interesting enough from an academic perspective, but Gurney's insight had the potential to make somebody extremely wealthy. The G10 garnets were the only certain chaperones of a diamond. They were the key for separating a bad pipe from a good one. If you found lots of garnets in your samples but none with the G10 formulation, you didn't need to waste any more time on that site because you didn't have a diamond pipe.

Gurney resisted an attempt from the De Beers cartel to buy his research. He instead passed a copy to a Toronto mining firm called Falconbridge, which entered a joint venture with Fipke's tiny outfit to look for diamonds in Canada's Northwest Territories. But in 1982, citing cost concerns, Falconbridge pulled the plug. An irritated Fipke and a geologist named Stewart Blusson decided to form their own exploration company called Dia Met, which prompted the mysterious sampling missions out of Yellowknife Bay in the summer of 1985.

One of Fipke's burlap bags of dirt had been collected north of a large lake called *Lac de Gras*, or "Fat Lake," which had acquired its name from the Inuit. They thought the bands of quartz on the shore looked like caribou fat. When Fipke put the soil from Lac de Gras under the microprobe, he couldn't believe what stared back at him: nearly a thousand purple G10 garnets. This was the surely the tip of a huge pipe. To throw off potential spies, Fipke started staking out areas around Lac de Gras under the name of a shell corporation: Norm's Manufacturing ("Norm" being the name of the elderly janitor who cleaned his lab in British Columbia).

Fipke hired a crew of friends to take further samples from the area, and in April 1990, they found a huge green chrome diopside—another surefire indicator—on the shore of a small lake near a spot called Misery Point. The kimberlite pipe, Fipke realized, was not hiding under the surface granite. It was instead under the lake, where a glacier had ripped away the head of the pipe more than seventeen thousand years ago. A pool of snowmelt was concealing the scar.

It was an epiphany that will probably go down in diamond lore as something akin to John Marshall spying a lump of gold in a twinkling California river. The accumulated evidence was persuasive enough for the Australian mining giant Broken Hill Proprietary to buy a large share of

Chuck Fipke's struggling company. They slung a drill rig out onto the ice at Misery Point and started digging.

That was the beginning.

Vicki Yehl is the kind of geologist who falls in love quickly, and she was starting to fall in love with this pipe.

The target was officially called BI-04-01, but the geologists had nicknamed it "Snow Bunting." The magnetic maps showed it as an intense blue stalagmite some ninety feet below the surface. That was strongly suggestive of one thing: kimberlite.

"It looks good," said Vicki, staring down at the map. "This is one of the highest-rated bodies on the whole property. But we don't know how deep it goes. We don't know the shape of it."

I was sitting with her in front of the oil stove in the "office tent" at Camp Tuktu—a cluster of twelve canvas shacks huddled together on a gentle slope near the geographic center of Victoria Island. From a distance, it looked like a little frontier town in a movie western. There was a kitchen tent, a shower tent, a tent where the drill samples were stored, several bunk tents facing each other like storefronts, and a single lonely outhouse standing like a gunfighter at the northern end of the avenue.

This was the third summer of the camp's existence. It was originally bankrolled by a Vancouver junior mining company called Diamonds North Resources, Ltd., which had restaked some of the properties originally claimed by the De Beers cartel in the wake of Fipke's discovery. The De Beers geologists had found some diamondiferous kimberlite on Victoria Island in 1997, but eventually decided it wasn't worth the trouble. Starting up a mine is phenomenally expensive, and Cambridge Bay—let alone the middle of the island—was just too remote and hostile a place to bring in the necessary equipment and make it profitable. Diamonds North thought it might be worth a second look. The company formed a partnership with the wealthy mining conglomerate Teck Cominco to see what might be made of pipe formations like BI-04-01. They called up Wilf MacDonald in Cambridge Bay, hired a cook and a helicopter, and sent Vicki and a team of seventeen other people up to the Tuktu region to find some diamonds, or at least some good indicator minerals that could give their stock price a bump.

The chances of success were slim; Vicki knew that. Most diamond geologists go through their entire careers without finding a single profitable formation. If you were extremely lucky, you got to find one. Nobody ever found two. It was a job rooted in failure, she liked to say. Even now, the only diamonds Vicki ever saw were in the jewelry store. But she was still in love with this pipe.

All the right signs were there. Snow Bunting appeared to be part of a dike formation, which meant it was once an underground sheetlike channel for lava. Volcanic dikes are thin and many of them have spikes of kimberlite erupting upward like frozen geysers. There was only one way to find out what was inside. Vicki had ordered the helicopter to pick up the drill with a long cable and fly it to a spot directly on top of the formation. Drilling would start tomorrow.

She had been looking for diamonds for four years. Her specialty was zinc, but when her company found out she had spent a summer on a diamond dig in Guyana, they put her in charge of the Arctic operation. She had been excruciatingly shy as a child and hated meeting new people. The world made sense to her only through puzzles—crosswords, rebuses, jigsaws. Classmates considered her a nerd and left her alone. It wasn't until her junior year at the University of Toronto, at twenty-one years old, that she began to lose her shell and discover boys. She met her future husband while renting a movie. It was her first night in Vancouver, and she had just been hired as a beginning geologist with Teck Cominco. Feeling a bit lonely, she went into the corner video store for a movie and a two-liter bottle of Coca-Cola. She thought there was a flirtatious edge to her conversation with the clerk, and became a regular at the store. One day she marshaled nerve and asked him, "So would you think it was corny if I asked you to a movie?" He didn't think it was corny at all.

The clerk—Herb was his name—turned out not to share her love of geology. He was a logger's son whose father was never home. Herb summed up his personal feelings about the Canadian wilderness with the saying: "Log it, mine it, pave it, and then I'll put a computer on it." On their honeymoon in 1999, she took him to some volcanoes in Hawaii and showed him the remnants of magma bursts. He carried the camera around his neck as she led him to calderas and tubes and dead pahoehoe channels. The entire island chain was a big pile of hardened magma, she told him. Most of it lay underwater. They bought a place in Vancouver at about the same time that Vicki's company decided there might be something profitable that De Beers had missed in the Arctic. Herb was promoted from store manager to IT technician for the video chain. He tried to get used to Vicki's summer absences. But she was starting to remind him of his father—always gone. Ultimately, they divorced and she went up to Camp Tuktu, ate a lot of Doritos, and put on weight. The extra pounds were now mostly gone; at thirty-four, she was anxious to be over the marriage and move on with her life's work, which was discovering things.

Now: this pipe. The drillers would work around the clock, in twelve-hour shifts, until they hit the kimberlite. She had no expectations of seeing a diamond in the core sample—that would have been the equivalent of being dealt a cold royal flush in poker. Petroleum drillers get showered with sour crude and gold miners usually see gold, but a diamond geologist never sees the thing hunted, only the traces. Even the richest mines have to crush an average of a ton of kimberlite ore to find a single carat. But a good core sample might, back in the lab, show the kind of G10 garnets and nearly invisible microdiamonds that made mining executives happy and stock prices rise. That was the whole point of their being out here.

"You know, I think about this sometimes," she told me at the oil stove. "It's really frustrating on one level that we're out here doing this instead of trying to cure cancer or something." She gestured at the map. "Do I care about diamonds? Not in the slightest. It's the looking for them that excites me. The intellectual pursuit. Hunting for things. That's my love."

Vicki went to talk to the drillers in the kitchen tent and I bundled up to take a walk. It was about nine o'clock in the evening, but the sun would not be going down until after midnight. I put my hands in my pockets and headed in a direction I thought was north. I trudged and trudged until I could look back and see the camp only as a tiny set of white specks clinging to a rise in the tundra. All around me was a panorama of emptiness.

I went over the top of a swale to a point where I could see perhaps forty miles off to the west—an immense gulf of Arctic grass and gentle hills going off to the edge of the world. It reminded me of eastern Montana without the barbed wire and the highways. There was a time when the Great Plains might have looked this way to the first settlers, equal parts magnificent and terrifying, a blank page on which they might try to etch a new life, if they could.

I felt my heart turn over slightly in a way I hadn't felt for quite a long time. It was the feeling I used to get on long road trips as a child, going to my grandmother's house in rural Kansas, looking out the car window at the vast spread of the world and the great romantic mystery that, to my eyes, it must have held and that it would surely yield. Years later, I came across a sentence in the autobiography of C. S. Lewis, the British theologian who wrote the *Chronicles of Narnia* and a man with a deep respect for myths. He described the moment, at age ten, where he read a poem by Longfellow and felt a sense of inexorable, boundless "North." "Instantly I was uplifted into huge regions of northern sky," wrote Lewis. "I desired with almost sickening intensity something never to be described (except that it is cold, spacious, severe, pale, and remote) and then . . . found myself at the very same moment already falling out of that desire and wishing I were back in it."

I knew immediately what he meant by that word "North," even though I could not begin to describe what it means or why it exists.

I scrambled down a steep bank and looked at the lethargic Tuktu River, one of several rivers to bisect the heart of Victoria Island. It looked like a sheet of black marble. The channel was flat and sandy, and dotted with rocks in the midst of the water. There were cloven tracks in the sand where caribou had come for a drink.

Nothing was moving, not even the water. It was completely quiet. I stood still for a long time as it grew darker and listened to the most immense silence I'd ever heard.

Victoria Island was discovered because of a faraway obsession.

At the beginning of the mercantile age in the sixteenth century, the European powers began trying to find a shortcut to the Pacific Ocean and to the spice markets of Asia. The overland routes through Persia were too long and hazardous to support a large-scale shipping enterprise. Mapmakers figured there had to be another way over the top of the world. The expeditions of John Cabot and Christopher Columbus seemed to prove the existence of a long landmass standing in front of the Orient, but little was known about the region or its size. When navigators tried to imagine the places beyond the northwestern ocean, they saw landscapes of wild surmise. There were stories of gold mines worked by a race of dwarves, whirlpools that dragged entire flotillas to their doom, magnetic currents so strong they spun compass needles in circles and pulled the nails out of the timbers of approaching ships. The cartographers decided there had to be a great saltwater river that connected the two oceans. Whoever could control it would automatically dominate the world's economy. The idea soon gained royal sponsorship and the quest to find the "Northwest Passage" to China and India became a foreign policy obsession.

One of the first serious attempts to go around North America was made by Jacques Cartier in 1535. He sailed up the St. Lawrence Seaway and mingled with a band of Huron Indians, who told him they came from a nearby village—a *cannatta* in their language. Cartier translated the word as "Canada" and used it to describe the entire region. The expedition spent the winter near the present-day city of Quebec, where a quarter of his men died of scurvy. Six years later, Cartier returned to the St. Lawrence and sailed up the Cap Rouge River, where he became fatally distracted. There was a pile of shiny stones on the riverbank. The crew judged them to be diamonds—the legendary gems of India, lately procured by the Portuguese for the crowns of monarchs. "When the Sunne shineth on them, they glister as it were of fire," wrote an excited Cartier in his journal. He had two barrelsful shipped back to the king of France. Their arrival created a stir in Paris until the king's jewelers came back with a verdict: Cartier had been fooled by an unusually luminescent variety of quartz, which was then thought to be the host rock for diamonds. The incident made Cartier the subject of ridicule. It also became the root of some French slang still used today. *"Un diamant de Canada,"* or "Canadian diamond" is a fraud meant to fool the gullible, the equivalent of selling the Brooklyn Bridge.

The map of North America took further shape after an ex-pirate named Martin Frobisher accidentally sailed into Hudson Bay in 1578. He had been hired by a group of London traders who called themselves the Company of Cathay and were willing to front large sums of cash to qualified mariners who thought they could discover the secret route to the Orient. Frobisher made it clear that he wasn't taking the job to make anybody rich. Finding the passage was, for him, a route to personal glory. "It is the only thing left undone whereby a notable mind might be made famous and remarkable," he said. On his second voyage to the interior of Canada, he made a mistake similar to Cartier's—he got distracted by minerals. On an island in the middle of a strait, one of the ship's officers discovered a deposit of black rock with flecks of gold. After returning to England with a sample of the rock, Frobisher turned his attention from the passage and went back to Canada to dig. He shipped 200 tons of the mysterious black ore back to England for assay. The shiny metal turned out to be pyrite—fool's gold—and Frobisher's reputation collapsed, just as Cartier's had over the "diamonds."

The Northwest Passage remained elusive for the next three centuries, even as the French lost their grip on the New World, and the American colonies pushed deeper into the western wilderness. The hope of finally locating the channel was at the heart of the 1803–06 expedition of Meriwether Lewis and William Clark. "The object of your mission," wrote President Thomas Jefferson in a letter to Lewis, "is to explore the Missouri river, & such principal stream of it, as, by its course & communication with the waters of the Pacific Ocean, whether the Columbia, Oregan, Colorado or and other river may offer the most direct & practicable water communication across this continent, for the purposes of commerce."

They found no such watercourse, but hope remained alive. In 1820, the British government sent a dull-witted but ambitious naval lieutenant named John Franklin on an overland expedition across the northwestern part of Canada. He and an entourage of twenty-seven started out from the settlement of Fort Providence in August carrying just two casks of flour, two hundred dried caribou tongues, and some moose meat. Franklin was confident there was plenty of summer left to travel, and that the Indian hunters in their group could keep them well fed with wild game. He was wrong on both counts. The snow came early and the expedition was forced to make winter camp barely two weeks later. It was the first of many miscalculations. The following summer, the expedition arrived at the mouth of the Coppermine River at the Arctic Ocean, but perilously low on food. The men were forced to eat moss and boil their own shoes for sustenance. Franklin split his expedition into three groups for the trek back across the empty tundra, leaving some of the starved and diseased behind to die in the polar desert. Surviving members of one party included the surgeon Dr. John Richardson, his beloved friend Robert Hood, and a French-speaking Iroquois named Michel Teroahaute. One night, Teroahaute brought into camp some meat he claimed was from a wolf that had been speared by a deer's horns. But as Richardson chewed, he became convinced the food was really from the bodies of some of the men who had been left behind to die. Ten days later, Richardson came back into camp from a moss-hunting trip to find his friend Hood dead, a bullet hole in the center of his forehead. Teroahaute insisted that Hood had been toying with his gun and shot himself accidentally. Richardson remained silent, but as soon as he got the chance, he ambushed Teroa-haute on a bend in the trail and shot him in the back of the head. Only nine men staggered back into Fort Providence alive, but the incompetent John Franklin became a popular hero in Britain. The newspapers called him "the man who ate his boots," and he was rewarded with the command of a second expedition to find the passage six years later, with Richardson again signing on as a surgeon.

It was on this trek that Victoria Island was first spotted off the northern coast of North America. Lieutenant E. N. Kendall climbed on a hill and spotted a thin gray stripe of land across the water. In his diary entry of August 4, 1826, Dr. Richardson wrote: "As soon as supper was over, I also set out to enjoy the gratifying prospect, and from the extremity of the cape on which we were encamped, and which was named in honour of the Right Honourable Lord Bexley, I beheld the northern land running north-north-west till it was lost on the horizon on a north 73 east bearing . . . On the strait, separating the two shores, I bestowed the names of our excellent little boats, the *Dolphin* and *Union*."

Richardson did not know it, but he was looking at the Northwest Passage that evening. The fabled waterway to Asian riches and the centuries-old grail of kings and cartographers turned out to be a twisting path between a maze of Arctic islands, frozen solid for most of the year and completely useless as a travel route. But this would not become clear for several more years, and only as the result of a disaster.

Sir John Franklin—he was a "sir" by then—was given command of a third expedition to find the Northwest Passage in 1845, and his departure from London became a celebrated event. Balls and receptions were held in his honor, and his two ships, the *Erebus* and the *Terror*, were among the most lavishly equipped of the Royal Navy. Among the comforts on board were 916 jugs of rum, 914 cases of chocolate, 4,573 pounds of pickles, 7,088 pounds of tobacco, 18,000 cans of biscuits, and a set of monogrammed silver spoons. A whaling ship spotted Franklin two months later as he headed into the entrance of Lancaster Sound, and the white unknown beyond. That was the last time anyone saw him. He was supposed to send word of his safe passage through the Arctic from Russian Siberia the following summer. When two years passed with no word from Franklin, the British Admiralty grew worried and offered £20,000 to any man for the safe rescue of the expedition, half that sum for any news of their fate.

Almost overnight, the craze to find the Northwest Passage turned into a new kind of obsession: finding Franklin. His attractive young wife, Lady Jane Franklin, became a media superstar. Engravings of her face filled the London papers. She was portrayed as the widow-to-be who never gave up hope that her husband might be found alive somewhere in an Inuit village or starving in the hull of one of his ruined ships. Songs and poems were written in the missing man's honor and his fate became the subject of intense parlor-room speculation. More than forty separate expeditions were dispatched to Franklin's rescue over the next thirteen years. They returned with little hard evidence of what happened to Franklin, but with a wealth of new information on the Arctic, both geographic and anthropological. Franklin's old friend Dr. Richardson set out on his own rescue mission and produced detailed reports of four separate bands of Inuit. The blank spots on the Arctic map gradually filled in, and the Northwest Passage was identified as the ice-choked disappointment that it was.

The first real clue to Franklin's fate emerged in 1854. A group of Inuit told the explorer John Rae that dozens of white men had starved to death south of King William Island. They showed him coins and spoons that could only have come from the *Erebus* and the *Terror*. Five years later, one of the last rescue parties came upon a discovery—two skeletons in a longboat beached on the ice. Nearby was a stone cairn with a handwritten message hidden in a biscuit tin in the center. "Whoever finds this paper is requested to forward it to the Secretary of the Admiralty in London," said the message, which went on to report that the ships had been entrapped in ice in the spring of 1847, but that the party was well. A second message written in a shaking hand in the margins, however, reported that two dozen men had since perished, including Franklin. "And start tomorrow, 26, for Back's Fish River," the note concluded, indicating the survivors were setting out overland on a nearly impossible 900-mile march to the southern frontier at Fort Providence. Their remains have been discovered over the years, scattered along that march line, many bearing saw marks at the edges of their bones. The last surviving men had turned to cannibalism in an effort to save themselves.

The fantasy persisted, however, that members of the lost Franklin expedition must have found succor among the Inuit bands that fished and hunted on the southern shore of Victoria Island. This theory helped create the notoriety of the Arctic explorer and self-promoter Vilhjalmur Stefansson, who spent the winter of 1909 on the island and reported finding a tribe of "blond Eskimos" who had surprisingly light hair and European facial features. Could they be the bastard offspring of the starving English sailors? Stefansson was widely ridiculed for this explanation, but it did not deter him. He had his own ideas about Victoria Island—great utopian images of a northern kingdom of commerce webbed with electric wires and air routes.

Stefansson was the son of Icelandic immigrants to Manitoba. After being kicked out of the University of North Dakota for "insubordination," he later graduated from Harvard with an anthropology degree and the idea that Franklin had failed, in part, because he did not adopt the traveling methods of the native Inuit. He convinced the American Museum of Natural History in New York to fund his wide-ranging expedition to the Arctic in 1908. Stefansson spent four continuous years living among the Inuit and learning their culture. Some of the thirteen groups he visited seemed not to be aware that Victoria Island even was an island. His diary entry for February 25, 1909, makes a deadpan observation: "Scarcity of women is noted. There are no single women, but several single men; no man has two wives but several women have two husbands. Exchanging wives is practiced and little or no sexual jealousy."

He returned with an idea almost as big as the Northwest Passage. The Arctic, he claimed, was not the harsh white netherworld of popular imagination. It was instead an ideal place for the extension of civilization, a great expanse of rich land destined to be conquered, fenced-off, and settled as the American Great Plains had been in the previous century. Stefansson published a 1913 book called *The Friendly Arctic* that laid out this theory. The famous Arctic cold was no worse than an average Dakota winter and could be easily weathered by a man of good constitution, he said. Stefansson concocted an elaborate historical diagram purporting to show how civilization was born in the equatorial heat of Mesopotamia and had marched steadily northward over the centuries, from Jerusalem to Rome to London, and would eventually reach the Arctic, a seat where man was destined to rule the world. Stefansson brooked no criticism of his pet cosmology. He invested in a disastrous venture to create a giant cattle ranch of reindeer and musk ox on Baffin Island. An energetic lecturer and an aggressive debater prone to shouting, he dismissed all his critics as "illiterates"—his favorite insult. But to his many detractors, Vilhjalmur Stefansson was a blowhard and a fool, known as "Windjammer" or "Will-

Yell-More," another huckster of Canadian diamonds. He died in 1962, having foreseen innovations like polar airline routes and ice-breaking submarines, but without witnessing the great commercial empire he envisioned in the Arctic.

The U.S. military had other ideas for the place. In 1952, a team of scientists issued a frightening report from the Massachusetts Institute of Technology: the nation was vulnerable to a sneak Soviet missile attack over the North Pole. A necklace of radar stations across the Arctic could provide a fifteen-minute head start on a retaliatory nuclear strike in case World War III should break out. The Bell System got the contract, agreements were signed with the Canadian government, and the "Distant Early Warning" system went online four years later. It was a chain of sixty-three stations across the polar desert, each with a team of U.S. Air Force servicemen assigned to an exceptionally boring task: waiting in the nowhere for missiles that never flew.

It was a different kind of obsession than the search for the Northwest Passage, but this, too, was an enterprise that changed Victoria Island forever. The radar stations, known as the DEW Line, became a magnet for jobs and liquor, and Inuit girls started to get pregnant by the servicemen and contractors. Cambridge Bay grew from a trading post into a permanent shanty settlement. Oil tanks were built at the dock to keep the new houses warm throughout the winters. The government in Ottawa decided the best way to manage the thirteen hundred or so nomadic hunters on the island was to introduce them to a wage-and-town life. You could get welfare benefits only if you had a fixed address and a last name—foreign concepts to most Inuit. Some of the first residents were issued metal dog tags to wear around their necks. A Catholic priest built a small church out of sandstone and tar paper in the 1950s, but it was abandoned shortly thereafter. Somebody got drunk and rammed a city water truck into it a few years ago. When I went by for a look, the floor was littered with garbage and FUCK was spray-painted on one of the walls.

The church is the closest thing the town has to a historic site, unless you count Mt. Pelly, a crenellated mesa a few miles out of town. Its Inuit name is *Uvajuq*. It is the highest point on that part of the island. Civilizations everywhere have a natural tendency to sanctify local mountains, and the Inuit are no exception. The story they told about Uvajuq was about the immortal giants who used to roam the earth before the time of the ancestors. They wandered looking for food, but found nothing that could satisfy them. The caribou were too small for them to eat. A rival group of giants, meanwhile, came across a small bird. It hardly seemed big enough to eat, but they split it among themselves equally and it was enough to satisfy them. The other tribe of giants was not so wise. A family of three— father, mother, and baby—were too proud to scavenge for anything but big food. They died of starvation, one after the other. The father, named Uvajuq, was the last to lie down on the tundra and his body became covered with a shroud of stones. The sharp ridges in the slopes are supposed to be his ribs.

A hard gray rain started coming down in the early morning hours on Tuesday, and the temperature dropped below freezing at Camp Tuktu. The helicopter pilot, a tall Austrian military veteran named Michael Podolak, announced that he didn't feel safe ferrying the drilling crew back and forth in the midst of a storm.

"The Chinese rule, my friend," he said to me. "No fly, no die."

Michael wore a turtleneck and wraparound Oakleys and stood as if a shower rod had been rammed into his spine. I found out later he had been piloting a Bell 206 that crashed in a northern Alberta swamp four years previously. The rotor had folded down and chopped through the flimsy walls of the cabin and into his feet. Nearly every bone in his right foot was shattered. He had to walk out of the swamp two miles on the ruined foot. He was lucky: a folded rotor usually amputates the pilot's legs.

Vicki had no choice but to call a weather day. The decision would cost Diamonds North and Teck Cominco about $20,000 in lost time, but there was no alternative. Most of the drillers disappeared into their sleeping bags. A few sat in the kitchen tent and played game after game of euchre, while the camp cook, Tara Furhe, cooked a huge pot of Thai chicken soup for lunch.

Tara is a magazine-model blonde with a boyfriend in Vancouver and a graphic arts degree she never uses.

She grew up among miners. Her father was a placer hunter and he made her spend every summer with him rooting around in the mountains of British Columbia for gold. When she turned eighteen, Tara told him what he could do with his summer job. She went off to college, accumulated a mountain of debt, and heard about a drilling crew who needed a kitchen supervisor. She faked her way in, even though she knew nothing about cooking. Mistaking a pork roast for beef, she set the oven too low and the roast bled a lake of pink juice all over the men's plates. They proclaimed it the best they'd ever had. She was now spending her twelfth summer in mining camp, and always swears never to come back.

"You think you've got it out of your system and then it creeps back in," Tara told me while we played cribbage. "I think it's like what women say about childbirth, you always forget the painful parts. Everything here is so pure and beautiful. You can look as far as the eye can see and it's all untouched. I think I crave the untouched."

Part of her personal mythology centers on the Arctic. In 1958, when her father was a young man, he signed on for a job bulldozing a temporary road over the ice from Yellowknife all the way up to the DEW Line. The company was ill-prepared and badly led. The lead Caterpillar bulldozer went through a soft place in the ice and sank; its driver barely escaped drowning in the freezing water. The weather turned and the spare fuel froze to jelly. The crew pulled the diesel drums into the bulldozer cabs to warm them up a little, and then siphoned in warm petroleum from the engines to pour over the jellied fuel. An open spark would have meant death. Any mistake at all, in fact, would have meant death. Tara's father came home from that trip with $10,000 and bought a house. She has made him tell that story over and over.

Danger is always stalking the edge of Arctic mining camps. It couldn't be any other way, far away as they are from rescue, and beholden to the fickle weather. Drill sites near the coast require one member of the crew to stand guard with a rifle watching for polar bears—by far the meanest and most deadly species of bear in the world. Most of the drillers have at least one story of being left out on the tundra in bad weather without food or shelter. The camp manager, Mike Merante, told me he once got dropped off with three other men to gather samples on Somerset Island. The helicopter failed to show up at the designated time. The mood among the crew evolved from annoyance to anger and then to near panic as night fell and snow began to come down. All they could do was build a small windbreak out of rocks and wait. At first, Mike tried to make a game out of throwing snowballs at an imaginary target on the tundra. But everybody lost interest as the temperature dropped. They huddled in the red plastic chopper flags and told all the jokes in their memory, especially the dirty ones. Mike had no food except a bag of trail mix he was reluctant to eat too quickly.

Dawn came, and still no helicopter. Everybody was out of jokes and too nonplussed to throw snowballs. There was nothing to do but count the minutes. At dusk, the helicopter finally clattered in to pick them up. It turned out the pilot had misread the GPS coordinates and realized his error only when somebody back in camp pointed it out to him.

"When you're out there in those kind of conditions," Mike told me, "one hour feels like a *day*."

The miserable weather dragged on at Tuktu. The rain let up around 3 P.M., but prospects did not look good. The weather station at Holman on the northwest edge of the island was reporting an eastward moving curtain of freezing rain and high winds.

"That's h.s. weather, my friend," said Michael the pilot. "Holy shit weather. No fly, no die." He cackled and went back to his laptop, where he was watching the zombie movie *28 Days Later* on DVD. Hard winds pounded the camp during the night, but the rain did not arrive.

The next day, it was calm enough for Michael to feel comfortable flying a crew to the drill site. But there was another problem. Diamonds North had a smaller camp 250 miles to the northwest, on a place called Banks Island. The geologist and his team had apparently decided to fly out on a Twin Otter and left their helicopter pilot behind. It wouldn't have been a big deal, except nobody had heard from the pilot in the last twenty-four hours. He should have appeared at Tuktu camp that morning. The radio was silent.

"It's a bit of a pooch screw," Vicki told her supervisor in Vancouver over the satellite phone. "I just hope he makes it here. We don't want anything icky to happen."

Vicki was a cool poker player, but I could see the indent in her forehead. The pilot, Steve Verdyne, was a classmate of hers from high school. His helicopter was not equipped with pop-outs, the inflatable devices on the skids that can keep a craft afloat if it goes down over water. If Steve's helicopter had crashed on land, he could conceivably use the survival kit and wait for a search party. But Banks Island was separated from Victoria by ten miles of open water. If he had gone down in that, he would stay alive perhaps ten minutes.

Michael called over the radio from the drill site. His voice was quiet, but his Austrian accent was sharp.

"Vicki, I want to see some affirmative action on Steve. He has five kids. And if he's in the water, it will be bad. So, ah, I would like to see some affirmative action on this now."

"Yes. We're working on it. I don't know what you want me to say," she said, and put down the receiver.

Nobody had to tell her what it meant to go down in a helicopter. Her company had been exploring some zinc formations on Baffin Island in the summer of 2001 when a crew failed to show up on time. A magnetometer walker noticed a plume of smoke coming over a rise in the tundra and ran over to see a pile of burning wreckage. The bodies inside were charred beyond any recognition. Two people had been killed at the scene. The third survived two more weeks in a burn unit. One of the dead had been Vicki's twenty-one-year-old assistant.

She made another call to Vancouver, trying to get in touch with Steve's helicopter company. "Yes, that's what I said." She gave the helicopter's call signal again. "Gulf X-ray Zulu Uniform."

Ten minutes later, the company called back. They had finally contacted their pilot and he told them he was safely over the strait. Vicki relaxed enough to drink a cup of tea and type in some notes.

Steve's helicopter touched down at Camp Tuktu near suppertime and Vicki walked out of her tent to meet him.

"WTF?" was the first thing she yelled over the rotors. *What the fuck?*

Once he was inside a tent, Steve told her the fuck what.

"The geologist borrowed my GPS yesterday and he erased all my waypoints without telling me," he said. "I had already copied them down by hand and I had to work off my notes. If they tell me to go out to Banks Island again, I'm telling them to stuff it. That place is a mudhole."

If Vicki finds her dream pipe, this is what might be coming to the middle of Victoria Island: a giant pit in which you could fit at least four major sports stadiums, a residential complex as big as a Chicago convention hotel, a water treatment plant big enough to service a city of fifty thousand, a landing strip where at least five chartered jets full of passengers land each day.

This is a description of the Ekati Diamond Mine, built in 1997 near the spot on the Arctic prairie where Chuck Fipke found his kimberlite pipe. It is the largest diamond mine in the western hemisphere, unearthing nearly 3.5 million carats every year, which is about 4 percent of the entire world's output of diamonds. From the air, it looks like a space colony plunked on the surface of an alien planet. Ekati sits in the midst of spectacular isolation. It lies 200 miles away from the nearest asphalt road, or even the nearest human settlement, and any piece of equipment that can't fit on a 747 must be hauled in by truck during a five-week window in the dead of winter when the contractors plow a makeshift road across the ice sheet. When a security consultant from South Africa was flown in for a look, he was appalled to find the mine unprotected by a fence. "Why would we need a fence?" an Ekati official asked him. "If you walk away from here in any direction, you will surely die."

The plane back and forth from Yellowknife is called "the bus," and I was invited to fly on it for a visit one Tuesday in August. The operations manager of the mine, a youngish bald man named Todd Harkies, took me to the edge of the giant excavation called the Fox Pit and we looked inside. It was a cone-shaped hole bored into the site of what had once been a tundra lake. There were terraces cut into the earth at twenty-foot intervals. Dark green stripes of kimberlite were marbled through the exposed earth. A string of giant ore loaders, their tires eleven feet tall, was at work down in the center of the pit, near a pile of rock rubble. "This isn't going to make us any money for the next four years," said Todd. The diamonds lay farther down below, he explained. The pit, one of eight on the property, would eventually get four times as deep before the kimberlite was mined out. Until then, it would be continuously worked every minute of every year, through the Arctic winter of all-day darkness and the cold that averaged 37 below zero, enough to chip the teeth off the claw-bucket blades. Exposed skin starts to freeze and die after sixty seconds in that kind of weather. But work never stopped in the pit.

Hardly anybody who works here ever sees diamonds. The final separation process is carefully controlled, to the point of obsession. One of the only corners of the processing plant not monitored by security cameras is the passageway leading out, where a small repository is fastened to the wall like a poorbox in a cathedral. It is called "The Last Chance" station. Here a thief may turn from evil without penalty. A sign next to the box warns: "Any product found on your person during an exit search will be regarded as 'intentional removal.'" Visitors are solemnly admonished not to touch or pick up any stray rock material on the premises, though diamonds are almost impossible to find with your bare hands even in the richest kimberlite. An average of 250 tons of rock must be crushed to find a single carat. A person could spend weeks sifting through it with a hammer and trowel before finding anything worth pocketing.

This doesn't deter the managers from shrouding the separation process with a mystery worthy of a Mormon temple ritual. Superbackgrounded "level four" security clearance is needed to access the fortified part of the Ekati plant where diamonds are cleaned, weighed, logged, and packed into containers for the flight to Yellowknife. I was not allowed to see this room, but was told the daily output of diamonds would fit in a small supermarket coffee can.

Given the casual way I had seen rough stones pass through many hands in African buying offices, the level of security here—loudly touted in Ekati's promotional materials and omnipresent everywhere on the Arctic campus—seemed paranoid to the point of foolishness. It was as if the security had a double function as a giant PR device; an apparatus designed not so much to protect the diamonds as to *advertise* them, to inflate their aura of holy mystique. I asked an Ekati security executive about this, and he said: "You have to understand what we're working with here. A handful of diamonds is worth a fortune." There are days, he said, when that coffee can–sized package flown to Yellowknife is worth $18 million. A plant manager put it another way. What the company is trying to stop is not so much petty, one-time pilfering but the establishment of an ongoing criminal enterprise. A dextrous sorter, for example, might be tempted to start switching valuable diamonds with cheaper gems and fence the originals in Montreal.

"It's to protect the community, really," the manager told me. "Diamonds are worse than drugs, they're so small and valuable."

Tools of corruption, but also tools of construction. They were, after all, the seeds that had made the whole improbable edifice spring up in the tundra, in the same region where the last of John Franklin's men had eaten the leg muscles of their companions on their march away from the wreck of the *Erebus* on the shoals of the Northwest Passage. Few people who worked at the mine, though, seemed to have much personal affinity for the gems. "Thank God for women," was all Todd Harkies would say. A production technician named Mike Axtell told me a story about a manager who called all the employees together when the plant first opened to announce that some diamonds would be on view in another room. "I don't really care what they're worth, I'm not going to go," Mike had said. This provoked an enraged rebuke from the manager. "If it wasn't for these diamonds, you wouldn't have a job!" he had yelled.

It was true. Diamonds built this space pod in the barrens. Diamonds lured powerful sums of capital to the ragged fringe of Canada and created high-wage industrial careers in a depressed economy. Diamonds brought prosperity to the six organized groups of Inuit and Dene natives who managed to lay a convincing ancestral claim to the place on the barrens where Fipke found his pipe. BHP had laid down native hiring quotas and made a series of outright cash payments—the exact amounts remain confidential—to tribal groups in exchange for the privilege of mining on the tundra.

Diamonds were also responsible for a truly awesome feat of earthmoving. It happened at the only other diamond mine in Canada, which is on the edge of a polar island barely ten miles from the Ekati site. Diamondiferous kimberlite was found there by a struggling company named Aber Resources, Inc., right after Fipke's discovery broke in the national press. A beginning geologist named Eira Thomas (a college classmate of Vicki Yehl, as it happened) ordered a drill slung out onto the ice of Lac de Gras near the end of April as the surface was turning into slush. Melted lakewater was seeping into the drill shack when Thomas pulled out her last cores and shut down for the summer. One of the cylindrical samples happened to hold G10 garnets, and the ultimate rarity tucked inside: a 2-carat diamond. It would prove to be the first fruit of one of the richest deposits ever discovered.

The problem was the lake. This pipe wasn't under a small pond, like Chuck Fipke's had been. It was beneath one of the largest lakes on the barrens, Lac de Gras, one big enough to actually have a name.

Diamonds weren't like crude oil. You couldn't just build a metal platform above the water, stick in the drill, and suck out the mineral. You had to peel away the land, layer by layer, with trucks and hammers and explosives—the classic inverted-cone method of open-pit mining. There was one way to get at the pipe: 13 billion liters of water would simply have to be moved aside.

Aber and its partner, the British mining conglomerate Rio Tinto, set about to create the largest private hydraulic project the Arctic had ever seen. They would encircle the diamonds with a dike and then pump out all the water, exposing the critical acres to air for the first time since the last ice age. But the engineers faced the same problem as the gravediggers in Cambridge Bay: how could you prevent the permafrost from melting, and then heaving upward? It couldn't keep a coffin down, it couldn't support the foundation of a house, and it certainly couldn't be expected to hold up the largest dam in the North American Arctic. Artificial cooling mechanisms would have to be built in those sections of the dam that straddled the island.

The problem was compounded by the shoreline. Permafrost is one of the most complete sealants in nature—it fills every crack and fissure and nothing can leak through it—but the lake bed wasn't frozen. It was made of glacial till, the wash of boulders, rocks, and sand swept there by a glacier ten thousand years ago. The till went fifteen meters deep. It was strong enough to support a dam, but too porous to prevent water from seeping through. Unless it could be sealed somehow, the diamond pit would be constantly filling with lakewater.

Rio Tinto's engineers decided to drive an impermeable wall through the till and down into the bedrock. It was made of "plastic concrete," more flexible than the conventional building variety, with a low cement content and a fine-ground clay called bentonite. This wall was sandwiched by 6 million tons of crushed granite. The trapped water was fished out, the pumps were turned on, and after two years of construction work—most of it in the cold and all-day darkness of the ten-month Arctic winters—the pipe was ready to give up its diamonds.

The dike would bear a strong resemblance to a Mississippi River levee if it weren't in the middle of the tundra. I went out on top of it with Scott Wytrychowski, the project's chief environmental manager, and the one in charge of keeping the water quality of Lac de Gras up to Canada's rigid cleanliness standards. He is a pleasant man, with a trim goatee on a round face. He peers up from little eyeglasses that look delicate but have side shields on them, as on a welder's mask. At one time not long ago, he was the fifth largest landholder in the Northwest Territories. This isn't because he is fantastically rich, but because he and some friends used to run a helicopter service during the days after Fipke found the diamond pipe near Misery Point. Every junior in Canada was in a hurry to stake all available land on the barrens—anything that didn't move—and Wytrychowski did it by simply tossing the line stakes out a specially designed window on the helicopter. The mining companies often wanted to keep their presence a secret, so it was Wytrychowski's name that went down on the claim forms.

The great fascination of his life is water. He views it in a mystical way, almost holy, in the same way that other men may think of the frescoes of Titian or a Beethoven sonata. Water is the most commonly used solvent on the planet, Wytrychowski told me. It actually becomes lighter as it gets colder. It reaches the point of maximum molecular density at 4 degrees Centigrade—take it anywhere south of that and the molecules actually start to push apart again. The globe is two-thirds water. So are people. Nations fight wars over it. Future civilizations won't be drilling for oil. They'll be drilling for clean water. When Wytrychowski went to Las Vegas on a vacation, it was Hoover Dam he wanted to see. He couldn't have cared less about the gambling or the musicals.

Nor does he care anything for diamonds, he told me.

"That's what the public wants," he said. "To me, it doesn't matter what's in the pit. My job is to mitigate the impacts. My goal is to leave the water in the lake as clean as it was when we came in. It's one of the largest resources we have, in both quality and quantity. You'll find more ions in bottled water at the supermarket."

Wytrychowski was proud of what had been done here, and of his role in the project. The point of the endeavor was immaterial to him; what mattered was the work done in its name. The dike had displaced more water than a Roman aqueduct. The year it was completed, 2002, it won a Certificate of Merit from the Canadian Council of Professional Engineers, the highest construction honor the nation has to offer. The project would provide a lesson and a pioneering example for future generations of builders who sought to mold the landscape of the Arctic.

Should it matter that the motivator for it all happened to be a stone that stood for vanity? The Egyptian pharaohs had commissioned the largest building project of the ancient world for similar reasons. They put hundreds of thousands of slaves to work for life, floating stone blocks up the Nile, polishing them, shaping them, and wrenching them into place, expending their life's muscle and sweat and brains so that one among them could go into the next world enveloped in magnificent rock. It was earthmoving—and social engineering—on a mammoth scale. The organizing power helped make Egypt the most advanced civilization of the world at the time, but all in the name of a ridiculous goal. It might as well have been building a ladder to the moon or making the Nile flow in a circle. It was brilliance chasing absurdity. At the heart of the pyramids was an appalling moral vacuum. But that folly had—almost by accident— forced a miserable kind of genius into the world.

Should humanity ever die out, archeologists from another planet might wonder what to make of this gigantic dam in the Arctic. The ruins may be difficult to find. In approximately 2024, when the complex has been fully mined out and no diamonds are left, Rio Tinto has promised to take down the processing plant and the maintenance sheds, cut a flow channel into the granite dike, and let 13 billion liters flood back in behind the walls, leaving the level of Lac de Gras an estimated one inch lower than before, with a giant terraced pit concealed underneath.

"Everything keeps fucking up, holy fuck," said the driller. He was a big Cree Indian named Rusty and his voice was calm and flat, like he was ordering a cheeseburger.

It had been a bad shift at Snow Bunting. They had worked through midnight, through the long Arctic summer sunset, and through the darkness, only to see one minor disaster after another. The casing rods had gotten frozen in the hole by some melted permafrost, and the core barrel had gotten stuck. They had to leave the whole expensive apparatus stuck where it was and start drilling another hole. Plus, it was starting to get uncomfortably cold during the four-hour nights, even in August. The men drank hot coffee and warmed themselves by the propane heater when they weren't attaching rods.

The drill house was a small wooden shack without a roof. It had been slung here on a helicopter cable, piece by piece, to this spot about a mile away from a river with crumbling banks. It was an unremarkable place, lonely and barren like every other place on the island, except that it was on top of the kimberlite pipe Vicki was in love with.

The science of drilling has not changed much since the early days of the Texas oil field derricks. You start with a drill bit sharp enough to cut through rock. You screw that tool to the end of a long heavy metal pipe. You attach that rod to a cable and hoist it up perpendicular to the ground with a derrick. Then you ram the rod into the earth and start corkscrewing your way through the bedrock until you go ten feet. Then you screw another rod on the end and keep drilling. All along the way, you keep bringing up smooth tubes of rock about the size and shape of cucumbers. These are the "core samples"—tiny geological peeks at what lies below.

Despite the broken rod and the lost hole, the night shift had made a little progress. The men kept the pipe coming—they got paid a dollar bonus for every foot drilled, and their salary wasn't at all dependent upon whether anything good came up. They'd put steel pipe all the way into the mantle if they were told. Around dawn, the new hole started to intersect the spot where they had lost the rod. The foreman, Jay Clarke, knew it when chewed-up pieces of the old pipe started floating up in the water near the drill hole. Down in the piss, he called it. Black metal down in the piss. He pressed on the drill switch and it whined like a table saw cutting board. The crew hauled up the rod and screwed on another, fifty pounds. One man rubbed his hands and winced. If you were a driller, tendonitis wasn't a possibility; it was a certainty. But he had a kid to take care of back in Alberta, the offspring of a high school marriage. Plus, the money was better than good.

"I work my ass off for two months so I can live like a king for a week," he said.

At around 7 A.M., the helicopter arrived on schedule and Vicki came over, donning her hard hat in the midst of the rotor wind.

"So, no kimberlite tonight," Jay told her.

Vicki looked at the row of rock tubes laid to one side of the shack. It was a crude linear picture of what lay beneath their feet. There was a line of black clay going crumbly. And then, from deeper, something marbled and smooth, the color of Irish Spring soap. She let a little spittle drop through her lips, rubbed it into the stone, and looked again, closely.

"Oh yes, there is," she said.

Who will be digging the diamonds out of the island if Vicki should get lucky? There was little doubt about that. Cambridge Bay doesn't have the labor pool, so all those miners would have to come from Yellowknife, the capital of the Northwest Territories and the home of almost everybody who works at the two existing diamond mines on the barrens. The Indian name for the town is *Somba'K*, which means "the money place." Few cities have earned the title more than Yellowknife.

Previously a sleepy frontier outpost, the city has exploded with cash in the time since Chuck Fipke found his diamonds under the lake. Starting salaries are among the highest in Canada, even for menial jobs. Real personal income has almost doubled in a decade. The logo of the city's bus system is a sketch of a glittering diamond. You can now call a stretch limousine to take you back and forth from the airport. A special detachment of the Royal Canadian Mounted Police has been assigned to watch out for signs of mafia infestation, and now even the rudest shack seems to have a new Ski-Doo snowmobile tucked out back. There is now a population of approximately eighteen thousand, a modern hospital, a Wal-Mart, four car dealerships, some coffee bars, a squat downtown of office buildings, and two small indoor shopping malls.

But Yellowknife still has a ragged edge under the diamond wealth. The town is literally at the end of the road. If you're going north of here—in fact, if you're heading any direction at all but south—you're taking an airplane. On clear nights, the aurora borealis bends away in the night sky like a glimmering bicycle tire. Men's-room fistfights and drunken brawls are still commonplace at the Gold Range Bar, notorious all over northwestern Canada as a hazardous place to start a conversation. My first few nights in town, I stayed in a hotel that consisted of two double-wide trailers welded together. It was down the road from a kennel of sled dogs who yipped all night. They sounded like a beachful of seals. This is also a town where a tin shed has a historic marker bolted to one side, and not as a joke. The shed had been put up by the Hudson Bay Trading Company in 1936 and was one of the oldest structures for 500 miles around.

The town was hastily erected around the lake in the early 1930s after bush pilots found traces of placer gold. A minor wave of hysteria swept through the Canadian media and the woods around Yellowknife came off sounding like the new Klondike. A magazine called *The Beaver* ended a typical story in the exultant tones of a newsreel: "Mining on countless occasions has been the forerunner of new colonization, and miners have led the pioneers to opening up distant lands for settlement and civilization, to new jobs, houses and fortunes for men and women. Who knows, today the Northwest Territories may be at the threshold of destiny!"

Hopeful young men, many of them freshly mustered out of service in World War II, listened to the hype and headed north to find their own veins. One of them was a native of North Dakota named Louis Garskie. He knocked about the woods of the Northwest Territories for more than a decade before finding a gold deposit on the shores of Sproule Lake. With some financial backing from a greengrocer, Garskie set to digging. He milled the ore himself on a large stone slab, using a heavy top rock to grind the diggings the way an Aztec wife would grind cornmeal. This yielded four beer bottles full of coarse gold that Garskie showed off around the bars when he came to town. His grinding stone is now planted in the gravel in front of the departure gates at Yellowknife International Airport as a historic exhibit. A marker says: "Garskie was self employed, self-reliant, living off the land and he had a totally independent lifestyle."

Not a single word of this is true. Garskie was about as independent as a salaryman in a downtown high-rise. Everything he did was driven by the notion of gold as a glittering object that society had decided to value, and his fortunes were entirely dependent on people's willingness to buy his otherwise useless product. The frenzy for gold that buzzed in the south was what drew Garskie to the woods—the same things that pulled all of his fellow émigrés and dreamers to a place where nothing edible could grow, the sun never appeared in the winter, and the cold could kill a person in thirty minutes.

Garskie and the prospectors like him had an important place in the history of the Canadian Arctic. They were the vanguard of a heavily capitalized obsession, one of the latest of a long series of waves. It always took a kind of madness to pull the outside world up here—a pattern that kept repeating: the lust for the Northwest Passage, the search for Franklin, the corralling of the Eskimo, the fear of nuclear war, a gold rush. And now diamonds.

When the weather got warm enough, I left my trailer hotel and walked three miles outside town, down to a rocky hill near an inlet of the Great Slave Lake. In a stand of jack pine, I rolled out my sleeping bag, put my wadded-up jeans under my head, and looked upward through spears of trees at the night sky. A high shield of clouds covered whatever there may have been of the northern lights. I had brought a bottle of wine from the liquor store to help me sleep, and I drank it down as I listened to the silence.

My thoughts drifted to Anne, as they often did during periods of solitude. It had been more than three years since she had taken the diamond ring from her finger and given it back to me. There had been other women in my life since, but none that had moved me enough to want to propose again. Perhaps I had wasted my only chance. Perhaps the love I had known with her was the kind that became harder to find with every year that I grew older and further away from the broad horizons of youth. In any case, I had only myself to blame. That was the hell of it. I drank the remainder of the wine and looked at the clouds. An unknown time later, I fell asleep.

Vicki had now seen the kimberlite pulled out of the Snow Bunting pipe, and she was beginning to have her doubts. For one thing, she should have been seeing a continuous line of thirty to forty feet of kimberlite, but the night's drilling had recovered only three feet before the line went to limestone again. It could be, of course, that the drill had only nicked an edge and that the heart of the pipe hadn't been intersected. But there were only so many more drill rods she could shoot at it—one or two at most—before she gave up.

"I don't understand the shape of this body at all," she murmured, looking at the magnetic map again.

More than almost any other science, geology requires a theatrical cast of mind. If you or I were walking through a river valley, we'd probably see trees and a pleasant stream. A good geologist would see tumbling cliffs and grinding plates and tremendous explosions of magma. The surface of the earth—what we see all around us—is a history of violent events. Peaceful moments disappear but catastrophes remain. The earth is continually remaking itself, building up and breaking down, but remembering its history in a cortex of stone. A mountain range that stood high as the Rockies 300 million years ago is today a thin band of red sandwiched in the ground underfoot. An ocean is a sprinkling of halite underneath a desert. A continental collision is a ridge of basalt. A vanished glacier is a hill of sand. Geology is autopsy.

Picturing the diamonds below Victoria Island requires you to look across the empty Arctic and imagine the pips and pops of small volcanoes erupting all around like pimples emerging on an adolescent face. The magma underneath the surface became charged with carbon dioxide and rose to a point some two miles below the surface, where it flowed in streamlike channels under the caprock. When a stream encountered a fissure in the ground, the lava suddenly burst upward into what geologists call a "blow," forcing the topmost rocks open like a curtain, and vomiting up a mixture of hot clays and olivine. This is kimberlite, the host rock of diamonds.

There has not been a documented burst of it in the last 50 million years. Volcanoes simmer around the world today in various geothermal hotspots, but kimberlite is an antique. Its emergence in the prehistoric world was both rare and quite weak by the titanic standards of vulcanism. Mount St. Helens exploded in Washington State in 1980 with the force of five hundred hydrogen bombs. An average kimberlite eruption, by comparison, would have been like a single load of TNT.

This helps explain why diamond deposits can be so hard to find. Ordinary volcanoes are literally mountain-sized, and many of their corpses exist today as giant peaks. The largest kimberlite pipes, by comparison, occupy a space no larger than a few football fields. It takes imagination to see these jeweled daggers in the upper part of the continental plate, but it takes a crew of four and a drill to get a close-up look.

Drilling for kimberlite is an inherently frustrating enterprise for a geologist. It provides a peephole into the ground just slightly thicker than the circumference of a broom handle. Trying to divine the shape of a kimberlite body through drilling might be compared to standing twenty feet away from a billboard and trying to read the message only by looking through a narrow paper tube. Move the tube around enough, and you'd eventually be able to understand the billboard, but every glance you took through that tube was going to cost your employers at least $50,000.

So far, that had not been a problem. The bosses back in Vancouver had every confidence in Vicki—enough that they were risking up to $2 million on this summer exploration. Despite her habit of falling in love with pipes too quickly, she was a talented geologist and a natural manager. Nobody doubted who was in charge of Camp Tuktu. She had been a recluse as a child, it was true, but somewhere along the way, she learned how to talk to men with the right mix of amiability and insouciance. In the towel-snapping atmosphere of mining camp, this went a long way. Her first year on the job, she asked a geology student to go dump some lye down the outhouse hole to keep the stench down. He misunderstood, and sprinkled it on the seat. The next man to use the outhouse was a big driller named Pearly and he spent the next week walking sideways. Vicki herself changed the bandages on Pearly's ass every night, bending him over samples in the core tent.

She was respected, but she still had costs to manage and this was hardly a sure thing. De Beers had explored this same formation for three years and decided it was a bust. Diamonds were here—there was little doubt of that, even though nobody in camp had actually seen one. But of the seven thousand known kimberlite pipes in the world, only 0.01 percent were diamondiferous enough to justify a mine. The odds would be even worse in an end-of-the-earth place like Victoria Island, where the nearest qualified labor pool was three hours away by jetliner.

The wind picked up again that night, though without any rain, and a group gathered in Mike Merante's tent for a "manager's meeting"—a term understood to mean that somebody was going to produce a bottle of smuggled whiskey. We poured it into cans of ginger ale and listened to the wood and canvas creak in the night breeze. The talk drifted from hockey to fishing and then into what the chances were of returning in the spring for more drilling.

"My gut says this is going to be a mine," said Mike. He was a bearded man with a ponytail and he was sitting in the kind of white plastic chair that sports bars have on their patios.

"I've got confidence we're going to find something," he went on. The oil stove made half of his face orange. "Those cores are too good. We're walking on top of a mine."

Later on, after the whiskey ran out and the gathering slowly broke apart, he shook his head and laughed. He had been in Canadian mining camps his entire career, and at age thirty-seven, he had never once been on a diamond exploration that had turned into an exploitable discovery.

"All for a fucking ring," he said.

By morning, Vicki had officially fallen out of love. The new drill hole was showing kimberlite down at 167 feet, which was not nearly shallow enough. She still had no clear picture of how the pipe contoured underground. All she knew for sure was that it wasn't very straight and it wasn't very wide. Her geologist's mind had pictured it as a shimmying carrot, a kind of frozen tornado that managed to dodge the lines sent down by the drillers. It didn't matter—all economic logic said that the top of Snow Bunting didn't appear large enough to justify any bulk sampling, or even any more drilling.

"You can't get too attached to these things," she told me. "If we got enamored with every hole, we'd wind up with a lot of broken hearts. If you're not getting it, you move on to the next." There was love, but there were also cold equations. In her mind, she was already rehearsing a presentation calling for ice drilling in the spring. There were several round lakes that she'd noticed from the helicopter that looked like kimberlite tops.

Vicki called Vancouver on the satellite phone to confer, and then ordered the rig slung over to another pipe. This one's name was Centaurus, and it lay about fourteen miles away from Snow Bunting. The magnetometer readings were encouraging—there was a bright circle of blue that promised a lot of dense kimberlite. It was a shape that had potential. A Diamonds North crew had drilled there last year, but lost 300 feet of rod and had to quit. It was worth another chance and she could get several good holes into it before the onset of blizzards in September.

Three

DESIRED RESULTS

Japan

The woman brushes back her hair. An engagement ring sparkles on her left hand. She has a calm smile and well-scrubbed features, and is in the flower of her early twenties. She wears a simple sundress, but the spear of a neckline points downward and there is the breath of rococo sexuality around her.

The words next to her say: *This very moment. Dreams for our future spread over the green fresh field of our promised life. A diamond is forever.*

This magazine advertisement was the first of a wave to hit the nation of Japan in the late 1960s. It was an attempt by the De Beers organization to create a new market for diamonds in a place they had never been sold.

It was a risky move, for diamonds have no place at all in traditional Japanese culture. This is partly the result of geology and partly the result of trade patterns. The geothermal currents under Japan created plenty of volcanoes over the eons, but not the special kind that produced the host rock of diamonds. Seafaring merchants might have introduced the stones from India, but the insular character of Japan prevented them from establishing a trade. The diamond craze that swept European royal courts in the seventeenth century therefore missed this corner of Asia entirely. Even after Japan was pried open to outsiders with the help of U.S. Navy gunboats in 1847, the Japanese government banned diamond imports until nearly fourteen years after the surrender on board USS *Missouri* that marked the end of World War II.

The Japanese had no need for diamonds mainly because the engagement ring did not have a place in their historical notion of romance. The nation had a long tradition of arranged marriages and—for the men—a stoic "samurai" detachment from the indecency of bride-hunting. "It used to be that if you were a good samurai with a good income, the people around you would find you a wife," one senior Japanese executive told me. "He doesn't have to chase the girls or win the heart of a beauty. Trying to attract the attention of a woman was regarded as nothing that a samurai should do." The Western notion of pursuit-based courtship (with the endpoint of an engagement ring) was foreign to a culture where arranged marriages were the norm. The Shinto marriage ceremony, called the *yuino*, involved a formal banquet where the two families exchanged gifts or money and the young couple drank rice wine together out of a wooden bowl. No rings were ever exchanged.

But in the mid-1960s, the De Beers cartel looked at Japan and saw potential. The J. Walter Thompson advertising agency was hired to flood the Japanese media with advertising touting the rings as a symbol of Western sexuality and prosperity. Ads from this period were aggressively American in their tone and style. The men were dressed in snappy suits and there were sports cars in the background. And the women, noted the journalist Edward Jay Epstein, "were involved in some kind of activity that defied Japanese traditions, such as bicycling, camping, yachting, ocean-swimming and mountain-climbing." It was never stated explicitly in the text, but the visual cues were powerful. Diamonds are new. Diamonds are cool. Diamonds are not of the hidebound Japan that suffered humiliating defeat in the Great Pacific War.

De Beers could not have picked a better time to hit this note. Japan was then two decades and a generation removed from the horrors of bombing and slaughter in World War II. The Tokyo Summer Olympics of 1964 had functioned as a kind of coming-out party for the rebuilt nation. Japan was growing in industrial strength and prosperity, and young people were earning more and more money. The long occupation by American G.I.s had also brought things like Hollywood movies and jazz and baseball. The people were developing a taste for what popular magazines of the 1950s called "the bright life" of electrical goods first imported from America like refrigerators, televisions, and fluorescent light bulbs. With the scars of the war finally healing over, there was more room for luxury spending.

The timing was right, and the message was perfectly *new* and perfectly *old* at the same time. De Beers cleverly tapped into an existing cultural receptor by linking the diamond with the ancient *yuino* ceremony. Jewelers were encouraged to sell the engagement ring as one more gift to add to the festivities. Young professional men were given an easy guideline for how much they should spend to make their brides happy. "Three months' salary" became a constant refrain in the advertisements, which also depicted a stream of "will-you-marry-me?" proposals of a type then slightly alien to the Japanese mind.

The campaign succeeded beyond anyone's most optimistic projections. In 1966, the year of the first advertising blitz, less than 1 percent of Japanese women received a diamond ring when they married. By 1981, that figure had rocketed to sixty percent. And after another decade of sustained advertising and hype, close to *ninety* percent of Japanese brides received diamond rings as a part of their marriages. What had been previously unremarkable had become essential.

The Japanese view of diamonds is now showing signs of change, but the story of how De Beers first sold the engagement ring to the Japanese still ranks as one of the greatest marketing coups of all time. It is also a powerful example of the ways in which advertisements can directly influence, and even reinvent, the culture at large. Japan had been turned into the second-largest consumer of diamonds in the world. The courtship ritual had been remade along with it. A custom older than the tea ceremony had been twisted into a new shape to accommodate a consumer product. And it had been done in just twenty years, through a campaign of excitement around an object that had been previously considered on the far margins of general acceptability, if not actually worthless.

Put simply, capitalism's ultimate trick had been pulled off. Somebody had finally learned how to sell rocks.

The winning formula was discovered in the United States, thirty years earlier.

In 1938, a letter arrived at the New York offices of the N. W. Ayer & Son advertising agency. It bore a South African postmark. The letter purported to be from a man named Raymond R. Byrne, who went on to explain that he had been asked to seek a partner in the United States to take on a very special advertising job. The organization Byrne represented was what the agency would later refer to as a "unique and challenging client"—De Beers Consolidated Mines, Ltd., which was then effectively barred from doing business in America because of its price-fixing policies. But at that point, America was the only nation that could save it from what seemed like ruin.

De Beers was in a crisis of oversupply. Prices had collapsed during the worldwide depression of the 1930s and the bankers of the South African cartel were concerned about its ability to make good on its obligations. With Nazi Germany on the brink of invading Poland and Europe sliding toward all-out war, the future for gem diamonds looked bleak.

De Beers had controlled the world's diamond trade since 1888, when it had bought up all the best mining claims in South Africa, but its monopolistic ways prevented it from doing any direct business in America thanks to antitrust laws. Diamonds could still legally make their way to the United States through a tangled chain of wholesalers. But the war threatened the artificial scarcity that made diamonds valuable, and now De Beers needed to hire a partner to sell their message to ordinary Americans.

Their choice of agency could not have been more apt. N. W. Ayer & Son, founded in Philadelphia in 1841, had built its reputation on heartland values. The firm's list of white-shoe clients grew in the advertising boom of the 1920s and the company came to represent some of the biggest names in corporate America. Ford Motor Co., R. J. Reynolds Tobacco Co., United Airlines, the Bell System all used Ayer to sell themselves to the world. De Beers now turned to Ayer to save it from disaster.

One of the counterintuitive truths of business is that it rarely makes sense to cut the advertising budget during a recession. In fact, the thing to do is step on the gas. Procter & Gamble took this route at the bottom of the Great Depression in 1933. The company used its dwindling earnings to buy a spree of radio time reminding cash-strapped families not to forget staples like Crisco cooking grease and Camay soap. It sponsored a series of cliffhanger serials such as "Vic and Sade," "Ma Perkins," and "Forever Young" that made liberal mention of Procter & Gamble products. This introduced the phrase "soap opera" into the popular language and boosted P&G sales to the point where it became a market leader in several categories. While other household-product makers failed, P&G ended the 1930s in robust health. This lesson in the power of advertising was not far in the past when De Beers made its first major assault into America.

Ayer's president at the time was a Winston Churchill look-alike named Gerold Lauck who had come over from Welch's Grape Juice. A brilliant but erratic adman prone to fits of depression, Lauck ordered his creative team to do nothing less than create a new place for diamonds in the American psyche. Crucial to the strategy—as it would be crucial in Japan thirty years later—was to move the gem away from its former role as a trinket for the rich and turn it into the indispensable symbol of romantic love. In this way, the ads could lay claim to some of the most vulnerable and urgent territory in the human heart.

There was some precedent for this. The notion of giving a woman a ring to mark a union was an ancient one in the Western world. It was first documented among soldiers of the Roman Empire who tagged their chosen women from a village with straps of leather tied around their fingers, which in turn probably descended from the custom of tying the legs of a capture-bride with bundles of grass so she could not run away. The practice lived on symbolically through metal bands and had been enshrined in the Christian wedding ceremony, but in the 1930s, it was not common to link a diamond with the arrangement. In the public's mind, diamond rings were still associated with aristocrats and stuffed shirts and gangsters. Interesting to look at, but hardly practical, and certainly nothing that a young working family would want to buy. De Beers, through its American agent N. W. Ayer, set out to fundamentally change this attitude. "For it is the public, particularly those millions in the middle-income group, who must be influenced in their thought, taste, habits and fashions, if the sale of diamonds is to be increased," concluded a confidential report presented to De Beers in 1939.

A mission this big required a bold stroke. Lauck commissioned a series of original paintings from some of the world's top artists, including Pablo Picasso, André Derain, Jean Hugo, and Salvador Dali, to grace the top of a series of four-color ads to be placed in the nation's top magazines. The paintings were not of diamonds but of pastoral scenes, foreign cities, churches, and rustic landscapes—art that would not look out of place hanging above a mahogany table in the Harvard Club. The images telegraphed the idea that diamonds themselves were classic works of art. Gems of various sizes were tastefully portrayed in a small box below, with a chart listing approximate prices, and the legend: "Your diamond, though it may be modest in cost, should be chosen with care, for nothing on earth can take its place." The price chart was key not only to hooking male readers who had no idea what a diamond ought to cost, but it also functioned as a dodge. The cartel was prohibited from selling diamonds in the United States—that was the job of the jewelers—so it could not quote exact retail prices. But it could lay down a semispecific range that would give young men a roadmap to what would likely be the most expensive purchase of their lives thus far.

The key assumption of the campaign was that a diamond was an absolute requirement for any young man preparing to marry. It was not just one of his many options, but *the* singular imperative—the *only* thing that would do. This was a brazen denial of three centuries of American cultural history, in which diamond rings were generally regarded as foppish extravagancies. Not once in the early Ayer ads is there a reference to "new"—ordinarily a favorite word of admen. There is not a hint of anything being cutting-edge or trendy or modern. There was instead an overt expectation that the reader was *of course* going to play the game just as his ancestors had (even though they probably hadn't). It was an audacious move, but one based on a principle that works with surprising ease in the marketplace, as well as in politics. The rule is this: Assume a desired thing to be true and proceed forward in that belief without apology. If you are charismatic enough and persistent enough in the delivery, the public will eventually accept your assumption—no matter how unbelievable—as objective reality. De Beers had thus created a "fact" in the American mind.

Besides the obvious appeals to love, there was a curious fixation on death and mortality in the early magazine ads. The words were set in unctuous type and read as if they were intended for carving into marble.

"A man approaches his harvest years realizing quite definitely that he has not labored for himself alone," read the copy of one 1939 placement. "Then comes his greatest satisfactions—the dignity and well-being that reward one who proudly has carried his family name and fortune. How in terms more precious and permanent than he has discovered shall he express to those he loves his life's work and affections? His clue lies in the delight of his wife at an ancestral necklace, his daughter's joy in the possession of a family ring, that in these timeless jewels lie the most expressive symbols of the fruits of the earth."

In addition to the grammar convolution typical of the early ads, this spot featured a bleak painting by Salvador Dali of a chest of drawers standing in the foreground of a desert plain. If the reader got lost in the

Yoda-speak, the Dali painting made it clear: wealth outlasts life. And De Beers was there to help.

Ayer produced another ad the next year, entitled "Shoal of Time," that forced the reader to contemplate his own death and the probability that nobody would remember him when he was gone. The only solution? Diamonds, of course.

"Few men can found a city, name a new star, shatter an atom," said the copy. "Few build for themselves a monument so tall that future generations may point to it from far off, saying, 'Look, that was our father. There is his name. That was his lifework.' Diamonds are the most imperishable record a man may leave of his personal life."

The ads harped not just upon the inevitability of death but also on the ravages of age. Customers were also told that their marriages would probably get dull and boring as the years went on, and that the best part of love always fades away. Those feelings, therefore, must be captured like a bird and housed in the cage of a diamond.

From a 1940 magazine ad: "Days go by in breathless beauty—nights in which each star marks a bright anticipation of the future. Endless they seem to young people caught up in love's first awareness and yet already they are fleeting. . . . Fortunate indeed are those who carry with them out of the flame of their dreams some tangible object to grace a lifetime's mature happiness with the memory of this first sweet halcyon."

And the bigger the better. Otherwise, the marriage will be second-rate, warned another ad, which cautioned couples against the "underestimation of their new estate's loveliest ritual. . . . Postponed in favor of more perishable chattels, it can never shine with the glory of their first love. Mature regrets are inevitable should it prove unworthy."

More than a bulwark against boredom, a large enough diamond could even be used as insurance against a cheating spouse. A 1944 ad aimed at couples about to be torn apart by the draft featured a drawing of a solitary woman toying with a long stringed instrument. The case was made *pianissimo* in the copy: "Through all their wartime parting, this shining symbol, their engagement diamond, so close to her, by him so well remembered, inspires an inward courage that disdains all doubt and fear." The next year featured another solitary woman and the legend: "See on her finger—the ring-set star that guides his thoughts in swift succession to her round the earth's great curve." Message to women: no French prostitutes for this G.I.

Another spot entitled "For the Times She Is Not There" even gently suggested to the male reader that his wife could be *replaced* with a diamond if she should ever die. "For no man knows how much he loves his wife, until one time, she isn't there. It is such quick inarticulate moments of realization that are eventually expressed in diamonds."

Many of the early ads were penned by a woman who wasn't married. Her name was Frances Gerety, and she had been one of N. W. Ayer's only female copywriters in the Philadelphia headquarters before being transferred to New York to work directly under Lauck.

Even a casual reader of the diamond ads in the 1940s can see a theme fighting its way to the surface, like notes of a melody gradually coalescing into the backbone of a symphony. In one ad, Gerety quotes the poet Robert Southey: "Like a diamond, its holy flame forever burns." In another, an original saying from an anonymous copywriter, probably Gerety: "In the engagement diamond on her finger, the memories will shine forever." In 1948, Lauck asked her to inscribe some words underneath illustrations of gemstones in the price chart. The background was a deep blue that suggested timelessness and oblivion, but the gems were colorless and could have been rubies or emeralds. Something quick and brief was needed to identify the stones as diamonds. Lauck was on his way to South Africa the next day and made it clear she needed to give him something to show the clients. An exhausted Gerety took the layouts home and worked until 4 A.M. With the sun about to rise, she still had no signature line. But she said later she had been "surfeited" by an idea throughout the De Beers campaign and it tumbled out naturally.

"I closed my eyes, asked for help from above, wrote something down and went to bed," she recalled.

She took her tagline into the office the next morning, where it received a relatively tepid reception. "Nobody jumped," she said. "It was just a way to sign the advertising." Lauck took the slogan with him to Johannesburg. The immediate reaction of the client was not recorded, but somebody at De Beers must have seen a winner. "The brilliance of the phrase is not just its simplicity, but also its depth and breadth of meaning," one executive remarked years later. "In these four words are concentrated all the emotional and physical properties of a diamond." Gerety's late-night scribble would eventually be deemed the most successful advertising slogan of all time by *Advertising Age* magazine. It would grace countless magazines and billboards around the world for the next six decades and become a part of the Western cultural vernacular. De Beers has it carved in glass at the entrance to its London headquarters. It may be the ultimate monument to the power of advertising to conjure deep and profound significance out of nothing at all.

A *diamond is forever.*

The "forever" idea was aimed primarily at men, who, according to Ayer's surveys, were the ones buying up to 90 percent of diamonds. Women had a strong influence on the decision, but men were the ones actually spending the money and controlling the terms of the purchase. Market research would later reveal a surprising intercouple dynamic. It was often the *men* who wanted to buy a bigger ring, while the women, who would actually be wearing it every day, lobbied for a smaller purchase in the interest of spending more money on the wedding and the first possessions of a new household.

"While men invest the DER ["diamond engagement ring" in agency jargon] with a great deal of meaning, women are less likely to recognize this importance and often exert *downward* pressure on price due to other marital priorities," said one of Ayer's internal strategy documents.

It went on to report a remarkable conclusion about the role of diamonds in the male psyche. A 1990 marketing survey seemed to suggest that men would choose to put key investments—such as a mortgage or a car payment—in jeopardy for the sake of the ring. A stunning 59 percent of men indicated they were willing to do this, while only 22 percent of women said they would want a diamond at the expense of other priorities.

The author of the strategy paper (whose name appeared nowhere on the document) suggested that forty years' worth of advertising had elevated the diamond to a place in American pop culture that went beyond a token of love. For the majority of males, it seemed, the diamond had come to represent their progress into manhood.

"For men, engagement was seen as a momentous occasion, signaling a major life change," said the report. "To them, the DER was viewed as the true mark of adulthood and all the responsibility that goes with it—family, home, a steady job, a lifestyle of permanence. Because men invested the DER with so much importance and meaning, it was also a source of pride that had to be sufficiently expressive of the occasion."

This trenchant insight into the male mind was the key to the raging success of the diamond ring campaign in the United States. The ads may have spouted pompous gobbledygook, but they tapped into an urge that may be even more central to the human condition than sexual love: the endless quest to make larger meaning out of those desires.

Love is love because it is a transcendent act, something bigger than ourselves—a selfless surrender to another. Buying a diamond ring was a way for an inarticulate man to approach all the messy and slightly embarrassing feelings running though his veins and marshal them into a clean receptacle. He could use a tiny stone to impose some order on the wildness in his nature. Wallace Stevens never wrote about diamonds, but his poem *Anecdote of the Jar*, written in 1923, captures the structural idea:

> I placed a jar in Tennessee,
> And round it was, upon a hill
> It made the slovenly wilderness
> Surround that hill
>
> The wilderness rose up to it
> And sprawled around, no longer wild
> The jar was round upon the ground
> And tall and of a port in air.
>
> It took dominion everywhere.
> The jar was gray and bare.
> It did not give of bird or bush,
> Like nothing else in Tennessee.

But before they could buy the ring to limn their passion, men first had to make an emotional commitment. The author of the strategy paper compared the magnitude of this decision to the only other surrender in a young man's life that claimed as much time and dedication—the decision to join the U.S. Army (which was, perhaps not coincidentally, another famous client of N. W. Ayer). Whether he was pledging his life to a woman or to a country, it seemed that a man had to be led down the road slowly and gently. Neither was a quick sale. Noted the strategist: "Like a decision to join the Army, the decision to purchase a quality Diamond Engagement Ring requires a major commitment which can only be made if positive attitudes are developed over time, and the final sale is carried out on a face-to-face basis (for De Beers through a local salesperson, for the Army through a recruiter)."

These "positive attitudes" were all about male commitment. For women, the subtext was judged to be something different: giving in to sexual desire. In a revealing 1982 article in *The Atlantic* magazine, Edward Jay Epstein used several of Ayer's internal documents to explore the psychology behind diamonds and their role in the courtship process. "The male-female roles seemed to resemble closely the sex relations in a Victorian novel," writes Epstein, and then quotes from a memo explaining the agency's somewhat lizard-brained view of the buyer's thoughts:

"Man plays the dominant, active role in the process. Woman's role is more subtle, more oblique, more enigmatic . . ." The woman seemed to believe there was something improper about receiving a diamond gift. . . . Yet the study found that "buried in the negative attitudes . . . lies what is probably the primary driving force for acquiring them. Diamonds are a traditional and conspicuous signal of achievement, status and success." It noted, for example, "A woman can easily feel that diamonds are 'vulgar' and still be highly enthusiastic about receiving diamond jewelry." The element of surprise, even if it is feigned, plays the same role in accommodating dissonance in accepting a diamond gift as it does in prime sexual seductions: It permits the woman to pretend that she has not actively participated in the decision. She thus retains both her innocence—and the diamond.

Like cigarette makers before them, the diamond sellers targeted the young and hoped to hook them early with these subtle messages. De Beers' ad agents sent wall charts and questionnaires to five hundred junior high school teachers in 1991 in hopes of creating diamond "educational kits" for preadolescents and teenagers. Newsletters were drafted to drop into the mailboxes of college students.

The drive to convince men to "trade up" and buy bigger diamonds was showing positive results, reported Ayer, and the agency pointed to the results of one survey as proof. A selection of grooms was asked to respond to the statement, "It wouldn't be a real engagement without a ring." The number of men who "agreed completely" or "very much agreed" with that assertion went up from 41 percent in 1988 to 54 percent two years later. It was significant, the agency went on to note, that men were being asked to buy not so much a product as an *idea*. And what a powerful idea it was—the man's sense of himself as a lover and as a provider, and the woman's sense of herself in deciding to have sex with him. This is what Ayer meant by the "true value" of the object it was hoping to introduce to young men and women: the web of personal myth that each individual would naturally spin around the stone.

De Beers understood that this was an almost unconscious biological process, like a scab forming over a cut or hair growing from a follicle. There was, of course, a powerful profit center wrapped up in all of this. This was the real stroke of genius in the De Beers approach. The cartel saw clearly that it would become extraordinarily difficult for any couple—or any broken half of a former couple—ever to part with the ring once such deep feelings had been written upon it. Such a fact helped ensure there would be no robust secondary market in diamonds. De Beers did not want to see all those millions of divorced or widowed carats cycling back into the marketplace, for the uncontrolled supplies would drive prices downward. If all diamonds could be permanently "marked" by their first users, then artificial scarcity could be preserved and the price kept comfortably high. This is why, in America today, it is almost impossible to resell a diamond for a price near its original retail value. There is no major commerce in "used diamonds." They are not supposed to be treated as investments to be bought and sold. Just as a wineglass was smashed in a Jacobean toast so that no inferior toast could ever be drunk from it again, so a diamond is forever inscribed by the love between the two people who acquire it together.

Or so we have been told.

I was in an empty research room in the Smithsonian Institution when I found this strategy paper, and I couldn't help but think of my own diamond—the one that had belonged to my ex-fiancée, Anne, and the one that I couldn't bear to part with, though the relationship was long over and I knew we would never be together again. It was the symbol of the life that I thought I was destined to live with her, and all that came with it: manhood, responsibility, children, a house, conjugal sex on laundered sheets, blue corn enchiladas in the oven, cut grass, soccer leagues, engraved stationery, love that mellowed and strengthened over the course of years.

Now it represented only my failure to move forward into that kind of life, and I *still* could not get rid of it.

The feeling I got sitting in that Smithsonian room reminded me of being left alone in the counselor's office of my junior high school after getting into some kind of trouble. The filing cabinet had been unlocked, and so I gave in to temptation and went to the *Z*s, looking for the dossier the school shrink had put together on me. To this day, I wish I had not done that. Reading that file was a singularly unpleasant experience. It was not so much what she had written about me as the feeling of violation that came from the knowledge that some abstract party—somebody I hardly even knew—had presumed to know what was happening in the core of my personality. She had used a fifteen-minute interview and some word puzzles to reach all kinds of conclusions about who I was and what I needed. Educational science had picked a lock and stolen a piece of my innermost thoughts. I had been stealthily manipulated by a stranger.

In the same fashion, the De Beers advertising team had grasped a fundamental psychological truth about the way that you and I sometimes deal with our messy thoughts of love. The possessions that always mean the most to us are the ones with a story behind them.

A diamond needs more than an individual myth to be considered valuable. It also requires a collective myth—one that all of society can buy into and understand.

In America, that's a job for Hollywood.

Ayer made an aggressive outreach to movie studios, offering to give free loans of fabulous diamond jewelry to starlets in return for an assurance that the product would be worn in a film. The agency also encouraged screenwriters to use diamonds as plot points and glamorous objects to be commented upon by the main characters. They were frequently aromatic of intrigue and danger. Diamond thefts provided narrative fuel for caper films like *To Catch a Thief* (1955) and *The Pink Panther* (1963). But no film delivered more free advertising than 1953's *Gentlemen Prefer Blondes*, which featured Marilyn Monroe breathing the number "Diamonds Are a Girl's Best Friend" as she wore a 26-carat canary around her neck.

Her gold-digging character, Lorelei Lee, had a distinguished history. She first appeared in a 1925 novel by Anita Loos, which contained the line, "Kissing your hand may make you feel very good, but a diamond bracelet lasts forever." It is not known if the De Beers copywriter Frances

Gerety had read the book before penning her famous tagline in 1948, but it is almost certain she must have seen the smash hit musical *Gentlemen Prefer Blondes*, which debuted the following year. The centerpiece song conveys a bleak message, but it was essentially a rhymed version of the magazine ads that De Beers had been aiming at the American public for the last fifteen years:

> Men grow cold
> As girls grow old
> And we all lose our charms in the end
> But square-cut or pear-shaped
> These rocks don't lose their shape
> Diamonds are a girl's best friend

The song title entered the American vernacular and is still used as a maxim today by people unaware that it was once part of a musical score.

Publicists in Ayer's New York office, meanwhile, produced filing cabinets full of press releases touting the celebrity connection with diamonds. Few, if any, mentioned De Beers. One release sent out to newspapers in the early 1950s was about the actress Merle Oberon lamenting her failure to acquire a Parisian bracelet when she had the chance. "Miss Oberon collects jewelry antiques the way that some women collect home furnishings in roadside cottages," said the release. "Her greatest treasure is the Napoleonic necklace, which she bought in a Bond Street shop in London. 'For just a little more I could have bought the bracelet when I got the necklace,' sighs Merle. "Now I don't even recall the name of the shop and we hear that end of Bond Street has been bombed.'"

Ayer paid a Hollywood press agent named Margaret Ettinger $425 a month to make sure photos of starlets wearing diamonds made their way into popular magazines. She did her job well: the Oberon photos appeared in twenty-four different publications. But Ettinger may never have known who was ultimately paying her salary—she claimed later that she knew nothing about De Beers or any of its subsidiaries.

Hoping for even more free exposure, Ayer tried to get its client's famous product mentioned in Broadway musicals. If the song was catchy enough, it could stick in the public lingo. A stage musical never did yield a line that equaled "Diamonds are a girl's best friend," but it was not for lack of trying. The agency went out of its way to suggest a glittery motif to Tin Pan Alley producers. Dorothy Digman of the agency's public relations department once sent several diamond-themed ditties to the Upper West Side home of songwriter Peter De Rose. Digman attached them to a brief note to De Rose's wife: "I hope one of them lights up the eye of your husband, gets into a show, and makes so much new De Rose money that Peter will buy *you* another big diamond."

One of the suggested songs (thankfully never produced) was called "Suzy's Got a Diamond."

> Suzy's got a diamond
> Tries to act left-handed
> Just so you'll notice
> What she's finally landed

Ayer also commissioned an impressive series of "radio features" on famous people in the news to be sent out to stations around the country. Some of them had only the thinnest of ties to the alleged subject. An August 1968 transcript began by noting the eighteenth birthday of Princess Anne of England, "a blue-eyed blonde who projects the informality of today's teenager," but then quickly segued into the clips and brooches the princess received from the court, as well as a description of the diamond honeycomb watch still worn by Queen Elizabeth II. "Just how much of a change will take place in Anne remains to be seen," said the broadcast in closing. "In her public role, amid the traditional pomp and circumstance, she very well may create her own youthful brand of diamond-bright royalty." Nowhere did the feature mention its true sponsor.

Press releases for newspapers were equally shameless. One February 1944 offering for lazy feature editors related an Irish "tradition" supposedly instituted by St. Patrick—that unmarried girls had the opportunity to propose to their boyfriends every Leap Year Day. It suggested several ways for girls to propose to their overseas G.I.s, all with the objective of receiving the all-important rock. "You may have to pop the question halfway around the world, by wire, V-mail or parcel post, but if he pops a diamond right back at you, it's worth it," gushed the release.

More sleight of hand was accomplished through the thousands of independent jewelry store owners across America at the end of the supply chain. They were the passive beneficiaries of hundreds of millions of dollars of free advertising from the South African cartel, which, in turn, urged them to target the local teenagers. Jewelers were encouraged to give speeches at local high schools extolling the history and science of diamonds. Youth groups, women's service clubs, and all-girl schools were considered prime recipients for the "educational" presentations. "When you deliver a lecture, take a selection of modern diamond engagement rings with you," urged a 1974 booklet. "The girls, particularly, will find them irresistible."

The De Beers magazine ads, meanwhile, grew more and more explicit with their appeals to greed and sex. The language of sensuality may have been deeply encoded in the World War II–era messages, but the ads grew bolder and hotter as the nation's morals loosened during the sexual revolution of the 1960s and the questioning of traditional marital values.

This represented a tricky pirouette for De Beers. How could it reflect the times, but also sell the same institution of marriage it had been relentlessly promoting for the past thirty years? How could diamonds simultaneously represent fidelity *and* sexual liberation, tradition *and* the Age of Aquarius? Engagement, therefore, had to be made an expression of rebellion as well as conformity. A magazine spot from the early 1970s tried to have it both ways, with mixed results. A picture of a blissful couple reclining in a meadow was accompanied by this contradictory ramble in the man's voice: "Freedom . . . no strings . . . live for the moment. That was always me. But today this ring says that freedom means being able to be more myself with her than I ever was with me. That no strings means soaring higher and higher together with nothing to tie us down." A more blatant appeal to hippies—and one just as unconvincing—was made in a 1971 ad that ran in *Life, Look,* and *Seventeen.* "My church may be a meadow. And my wedding won't be my mother's. But when it comes to my man and the diamond his love gives me, I want all things that women have always dreamed of."

De Beers further tried to distance itself from its own heritage in the 1970s by commissioning a series of Peter Max–like psychedelic images and changing Frances Gerety's famous tagline into something that might stand less for fidelity and solidity and more for impulsiveness, flash, and conspicuous consumption. "A Diamond Is For Now," blared a series of ads that tried to promote "self-gifts" of jewelry to successful women. A spot that ran in *Cosmopolitan* and *The New York Times Magazine* showed an infant in a harness fastened with a diamond-encrusted safety pin, beneath a mother's coy smile. "The rule book is torn up," said the ad. "Now you can be as spontaneous as a baby in when and where you play with diamonds." Another ad featured a woman's foot dangling halfway out of a black high-heeled pump. A jeweled brooch clung to her fishnet stocking. "Why walk when you can strut?" asked the ad. "Diamonds that shatter all the rules."

But some rules could never be broken, especially the one hammered at men throughout the twentieth century: *Diamonds will help you seduce.* The sexual bargain around the stone emerged almost completely from its subtext in a 1987 ad that featured an exhilarated young couple frolicking atop a floating pool toy. They are dripping with water and he is lying between her legs in an unmistakably copulatory position. "Once she said 'yes,' I wanted her to have a diamond that would make her say 'wow,'" said the ad. In other words, she has agreed to sleep with him, but now his potency is on the line. Her bliss—and his worth as a man—are dependent on his ability to whip out the stone.

In the midst of a recession in 1993, De Beers reverted to the more classic contours of its earlier campaigns with the long-running—and much-parodied—"Shadows" campaign, which featured darkened silhouettes of couples progressing through monumental life events with a rising violin score in the background. The only splash of color in these ads was the diamond itself. Marketing professionals praised it highly. "Because the silhouettes did not allow the viewer to see distinguishing physical traits, viewers could fill in the details or substitute themselves for the actors," noted one assessment. It also reaffirmed the close connection between strong feelings and diamonds (as well, perhaps, as the agency's belief that buyers were mere dark blobs who needed the luminescence of a diamond to get their emotions in order).

Despite the commercial and critical success of "Shadows," De Beers decided to sever its fifty-seven-year relationship with N. W. Ayer in 1995. America's oldest agency was beginning to lose its touch, some felt. It was too conservative, too slow to adapt to the changing culture. The divorce was a hard one. Ayer tried to file a series of trademark applications on some of the choicest intellectual property: "A Diamond is Forever," "diamond anniversary ring," "diamond anniversary band," and "The 4Cs." All were denied.

That same year, De Beers shifted its American account to the J. Walter Thompson agency, which already handled all its overseas marketing, and had performed so unexpectedly well in 1960s Japan. In the year that campaign began, imports of diamonds into Japan were less than 100,000 carats a year. Thirty years later, imports stood at 4.1 million carats. It was, in the words of a top jewelry executive, "like a miracle." It may have had more to do with the special character of Japan than the special character of the diamond, but no matter. What had happened there was still held up— wisely or not—as a signature example of how a well-marketed product could ingratiate itself into the culture, even more completely than it had in America.

De Beers had proposed a revolutionary concept in Japan—that a man needed a stone to get married—but it stayed conservative in at least one critical area. Fidelity to social expectations is a watershed matter in Japan, and so a strong link was forged between the purchase of a diamond and the perception that society would approve.

To balance out the heavily Western images in the advertisements, the cartel produced exactly the right "tradition" to introduce to a new generation of Japanese men. A Victorian-sounding custom had already been concocted for the United States: A young man is expected to spend the equivalent of two months' salary on his sweetheart's ring. There was a place on this sliding scale for anybody with a job—from the grocery clerk to the investment banker.

But the guidelines differed by nation. A "two months' salary" equivalent was touted in the United States, whereas men in Great Britain got off the hook with only one month. Japan's expectation was set highest, at three months. I asked a De Beers representative why the Japanese were told to spend so much compared to the Americans or the English.

"We were, quite frankly, trying to bid them up," he answered.

The "three months" guideline was drummed home so incessantly in Japan that it eventually became a part of the brand. "A diamond engagement ring: Worth three months' salary" was a tagline of most of the print advertisements distributed in the 1970s. One black-and-white magazine spot depicted a young office worker in a cubicle, staring philosophically into the distance. "Tell me," said the caption. "Do you think it's manly to spend three months' salary for my own ideal woman?" A man in another ad asked a slightly different rhetorical question. "Teach me," he said. "Are there any rumors about happiness if I give three months' salary for a diamond engagement ring?" For Japanese readers, the subtle message was clear. If you don't spend at least three months' salary on her ring, not only have you failed to live up to expectations of the national family, you are also effeminate and will be unhappy.

The message was delivered with a lighter touch in a 1984 spot, which gently lampooned the well-known Japanese reluctance to display strong emotions. The ad, entitled "Zoo," was shown to movie audiences before the main feature. A cute young couple is shown sitting on an outdoor bench at a zoo, while folksy Carpenters-type music plays in the background. They are both fidgety and both clearly attracted to each other, though they do not touch. The man is speaking meaningless palaver—"The elephant is big, isn't it?"—while a subtitle appears underneath—"I spent three months' salary to buy this"—to indicate what he is really thinking. This goes on for a while ("The cheetah is purring," she says, while his subtitle betrays, "I have to say it!") before he yanks out a diamond engagement ring and blurts, "Can you take this from me?" The spot was remarkable not only for its use of American situation comedy technique but also for depicting a heartfelt marriage proposal—a custom not widely practiced in traditional Japan.

A similar chord was struck in a print ad the same year. A solitary man stands in a meadow holding a giant inflatable heart with an arrow through it. "I give you the me that's just for you," said the caption, with the inevitable tagline: "Because I love you, a diamond engagement ring worth three months' salary."

The "three months' salary" guideline plucked a key chord in the consumer personality of Japan—the tendency toward things perceived to be approved by the society at large. "It is very difficult to get the Japanese to buy into anything new," one marketing executive told me. "But when you can finally get them to adopt something, they all run toward it." This was the critical balance that needed to be tipped, and it required a special understanding of the Japanese character.

Where outsiders might see a herd mentality, the Japanese see personal honor. This is an idea drenched in Confucianism, the spiritual import from the Asian mainland that has done more to profoundly influence the character of Japan than any other thing, person, or idea.

Confucius was a minor court official in the Chinese region of Lu in the fifth century B.C. whose followers regarded him as a model of courtliness and good judgment. In middle age, he claimed to have developed a spe-

cial understanding of man's relationship to Heaven. Confucius placed a
high premium on decorum and lack of pretense. Social rituals were to be
respected at all costs, even at the expense of individual desires. But the
point was not to extinguish the self. The point was to bring the self more
into harmony with the world at large, as represented by family, community, and the company of one's fellows. His sayings—though often paro-
died for their seeming opacity—are often reminiscent of the paradoxical
message of Jesus: that true glory comes through self-abasement rather
than self-adoration. "He who wants to be first must be last" from the New
Testament comes close to the spirit behind Confucius's "Since you yourself desire standing, then help others achieve it. Since you yourself desire
success, then help others attain it." Korean immigrants brought these
texts into Japan in the sixth century and the ideas found expression on
the then lawless feudal island, where the help of one's fellows could make
the difference between life and death.

Central to the Confucian code of ethics is a concept of deep selfless-
ness call *chu ko*, or "loyalty and devotion." It says that a samurai should
first be loyal to his local lord, and then to the emperor, and then to his
family. The idea extends to all members of society, from the strongest
warriors to the frailest elderly: sons are to be devoted to fathers, wives to
husbands, salesmen to their division managers. It is the invisible social
contract that binds modern Japan together. The "samurai way" so often
used to describe Japanese ethics is derivative of the old Confucian code,
in which personal discretion is paramount. An individual never puts himself forward unduly, expresses a radical opinion, or starts a quarrel that
tears apart the group dynamic. To do so is to be disloyal and endanger the
social fabric.

The consequent Japanese dedication to consensus-driven thinking
cannot be overstated. The nation's deepest image of itself is that of an extended family. In the military buildup to World War II, the emperor was
the unseen head of the nation-family and the one who demanded fealty
of all his children. During the industrial recovery of the 1950s, the corporations took the emperor's place as surrogate parents, but the concept of
kazoku kokka, or "family state," remains strong. It sometimes results in
decisions that do not always make rational sense to an outsider. I once
asked a Japanese friend why the government in Tokyo was spending outrageous sums to build a bridge to a remote island where only a handful of

elderly people lived anymore. Why not just move them off the island? Would you kick your grandmother out of her house because it suited you? he asked me. No, probably not, I said. Exactly, he said.

When the family makes a decision, the individual responds. In his book *Something Like An Autobiography*, the filmmaker Akiro Kurosawa writes of the day of Japan's surrender in the Great Pacific War. It is worth quoting at length:

> On August 15, 1945, I was summoned to the studio along with everyone else to listen to the momentous proclamation on the radio: the Emperor himself was to speak over the airwaves. I will never forget the scenes I saw as I walked the streets that day. On the way from Soshigaya to the studios in Kinuta the shopping street looked fully prepared for the Honorable Death of the Hundred Million. The atmosphere was tense, panicked. There were even shopowners who had taken their Japanese swords from their sheaths and sat staring at the bare blades. However, when I walked the same route back to my home after listening to the imperial proclamation, the scene was entirely different. The people on the shopping street were bustling about with cheerful faces as if preparing for a festival the next day. I don't know if this represents Japanese adaptability or Japanese imbecility. In either case, I have to recognize that both these facets exist in the Japanese personality. Both facets exist within my own personality as well. If the Emperor had not delivered his address urging the Japanese people to lay down their swords—if that speech had been a call instead for the Honorable Death of the Hundred Million—those people on that street in Soshigaya probably would have done as they were told and died. And probably I would have done likewise.

The word of the emperor made all the difference here. With diamonds, it was the word of the popular media driving the boat. *Chu ko* has influence not just over personal ethics but consumer behavior. The Japanese were told over and over that "three months' salary" was a social expectation and the right thing to do, and they agreed. It was an appeal to a deep quasi-religious meaning—to them a concept as profound as the "true value" idea promulgated in America that I had unconsciously adopted. The campaign was a smashing success. Japanese diamond sales exceeded $2 billion a year at the peak in the 1990s. It was, as that top executive put it, "like a miracle." The tradition had caught hold forever, or so it seemed.

Numbers being what they were, nobody recognized at the time how weak that hold really was.

The bottom has fallen out of the Japanese diamond market in the last eight years—a reversal as stark and abrupt as the overnight creation of the demand. It was the miracle in reverse. More than half of the market for engagement rings has simply evaporated. About $1 billion in value was lost. At the peak of the "tradition," nine out of every ten marrying couples in Japan had a diamond ring. Today, that number is five of ten, and falling, according to statistics provided by the Japan Jewellery Association. Some brokers are leaving the business entirely.

"This is all going bust," one prominent wholesale dealer, Rakesh Shah, complained to me. "Completely flat. I'm thinking of selling everything and going into computers."

The main problem was engagement rings, Shah told me. It used to be that 60 percent of his sales were in solitaires—the classic betrothal setting. Now that number is less than 20 percent. Japanese couples are simply not buying them anymore. Total diamond sales are now just one third of what they were at the peak in 1990, with the market continuing to lose a reliable 7 percent each year. Barely anybody pays attention to the "three months" guideline anymore, and those advertisements have largely disappeared from the media.

I went to the Tobu Department Store at the beginning of the summer wedding season. The place is one of the busiest retail outlets in the northern part of Tokyo—five stories of polished granite stacked high with clothing, furniture, shoes, bedsheets, and all manner of middlebrow goods, perched strategically atop the Ikebukuro commuter rail station. Shoppers glided easily between the floors on a latticework of escalators. Except for the Japanese signs and faces, it might have been a Macy's or a Nordstrom. But there was one design peculiarity. In an American department store, the glass jewelry cases would likely have been positioned near the center of the first floor. Here they have been tucked away into a hard-to-find corner of the second floor. It took me fifteen minutes of wandering to find them.

A newly married couple, Noritsugu and Emi Izuka, had the displays all to themselves that afternoon. They asked to see a ring with a tiny wink-ing diamond set into the band. Emi tried it on. Then she handed it back to the clerk. They were daydream shopping, nothing more.

"It's not very important to us," said Noritsugu, when I went up to talk to them. "It doesn't mean our marriage isn't strong if we don't have a dia-mond."

Emi added: "None of our friends expect us to have a diamond ring."

This is a widespread attitude in Japan among the younger generation. Diamonds are seen here now as a bit fuddy-duddy, slightly uncool. "There's a lot of cute jewelry out there that's more stylish," one young woman, Kazumi Murata, told me. "I wouldn't say it's unpopular, but it's not the best thing out there."

I went to see Hidetaka Kato, the chairman of Kashikey Co., Ltd., and a legendary figure in the business. He was a leading importer of the first wave in the late 1960s and is still widely regarded as the grand old man of Japanese diamonds. On his office wall, opposite a bank of windows, is a framed medal of commendation from the emperor. Around the industry, he is known simply as "Chairman Kato."

He greeted me with a shy smile full of teeth and showed me a picture of Maria Menounos, a reporter for the American show *Entertainment To-night*, who had worn a $2.5 million evening gown covered in diamonds to that year's Oscars. The dress was dotted with more than two thousand brownish diamonds—"champagne diamonds" is the preferred term. It was a publicity gamble dreamed up by the Natural Color Diamond Asso-ciation, which Chairman Kato helps lead. The emphasis is now on selling brown stones to wealthy middle-aged Japanese women because diamond engagement rings have virtually disappeared.

"It is the ladies," he said, when I asked him why. "There was a survey on this. If you asked them before the bubble burst what the number-one thing to buy was, the diamond was the number-one answer. Now the top answer is 'travel to foreign countries.' Number two is good food, good cui-sine. Even mobile phones and computers are outpacing diamonds in the surveys."

Chairman Kato's thoughts were echoed by any number of people I spoke with in Tokyo, both in and out of the industry. Japanese women were discouraging the purchase of engagement rings in favor of more practical goods.

"There are so many other things I'd want us to spend money on when

I get married," said Kumiko Igarashi, a twenty-six-year-old woman. "Something useful, like a new kitchen, for instance."

"The diamond is viewed as too traditional these days," said Hirsako Noriko, a jewelry wholesaler and one of the very few people in Tokyo I saw actually wearing a diamond. "People seem more interested in watches now."

I thought I saw them in another place—on the shoe buckles of a twenty-three-year-old woman crouching next to a concrete pillar outside a train station. She wore a foam trucker's hat marked CAMBPELL'S SOUP that would have blended just fine in a hipster bar in New York or Los Angeles. She told me her name was Reeka Oyma and that she worked as a salesgirl in a clothing store and that the little sparkly things on her shoes weren't diamonds.

"I don't like them so much," she said. "I don't even want one. There's nothing at all special about it."

What happened? It appeared the demand ignited in the late 1960s was ultimately effervescent—much like that urge to mass suicide at the end of the war. The creation of the diamond desire in Japan was remarkable for its speed, but also remarkable for its superficiality. One stock market correction was enough to wipe it away.

Kotaro Okamura looked slightly embarrassed when I started to bow to him. He gave me his hand instead and shook briskly. We were standing in front of a mahogany table on the thirtieth floor of a skyscraper in the financial district. He was the managing director of the JPMorgan Chase Bank in Tokyo and he had agreed to see me to explain what had happened to Japan after financial markets crashed all around Asia in the autumn of 1997. He ordered coffee for us, and then began to speak slowly and deliberately.

"We had previously been driven by very Japanese values—long-term profit, loyal customers, harmony among employees, the long-term escalation of a man's career path. But this has changed. Our notions of corporate stability have eroded," he told me.

The problem started in the mid-1990s in Thailand, where real estate companies discovered they could borrow U.S. dollars from overseas banks at a much better interest rate than the baht at home. Construction boomed in downtown Bangkok as investment groups looked for places to park the money, and many of the gleaming towers sat barely occupied.

Foreign lenders began to worry and began to shift money away from the country. This triggered a run on Thai banks as panicked citizens rushed to convert their bahts into dollars. The lack of confidence in native currencies spread quickly to the Philippines, Malaysia, Indonesia, and Korea. Japanese banks had been liberal about lending money to neighboring countries—$37 billion was tied up in Thailand alone—and they found themselves in trouble. The Nikkei stock market lost a quarter of its value, the nation's biggest securities firm went bankrupt, and workers were laid off in droves. Unemployment hit record levels of 3.5 percent—a mammoth figure by the standards of paternalistic corporate Japan.

"Many people started to change their workplace, which was unusual in Japan before," said Okamura. "Factories closed. Jobs were outsourced to China and India. There became a tendency to treat the junior staff—the younger men—like an 'instant workforce' instead of a future workforce. It was the American way of the temp, you might say."

This was a big part of the reason why diamond rings had passed from the scene almost overnight, he told me.

"Your job was not so secure anymore, so committing with a diamond ring would not please a girl the way that it used to. It might even be considered foolish. It would be so much better to spend it on a nice hotel for your honeymoon. That would be something meaningful."

The idea of marriage, too, is not what it used to be in Japan. Cohabitations are on the rise and marriage rates are stagnant. Like women in America and Europe, Japanese wives no longer feel strong pressure to take their husband's surnames. The *yuino* ceremony, once such an important part of betrothal, is also on the decline, regarded as a slightly musty anachronism on the level of a debutante ball or a telegram.

I asked Okamura if he had given his own wife a diamond ring, and he acknowledged that he had indeed. He was married in 1986—one of the last generation of Japanese men to feel an imperative to devote a sizable amount of their annual salary on their fiancée's ring. There had been a *yuino* ceremony in a banquet room at the Hotel Okura, which was then the nicest hotel in the city. Their respective parents had exchanged gifts. He had given his fiancée a diamond engagement ring. She had given him a slim leather wallet.

"Why did you feel you needed to buy her a ring?" I asked him, and he paused for a long time before cocking his eyebrows up at me. It was the only time in our two-hour conversation that he seemed at a loss for words.

"That is a very good question," he said. "There is an indication that the man was really committed if he did it. He was pouring so much money into one ring that it was something that women could really buy into. We liked the three months' salary guideline. If the Japanese all share a standard, it becomes much easier to adopt. They set a ceiling and so we didn't have to worry."

He smiled slightly, and added, "You know, as soon as we were married, my wife forgot all about that ring. But I think she needed something she could *materialize*."

I wondered about the orthodoxy of his grammar at first, but then I understood him perfectly—as any man who has ever been swept up in the thrill of surrender does on some level.

You can almost spy the ocean from the J. Walter Thompson offices in Tokyo, which occupy a floor near the top of a skyscraper in one of the city's most fashionable business districts. It was built on the site of the old redbrick Sapporo factory, where one of the top beers of the nation was once brewed. I went there on a May afternoon to see the two men charged with the task of reinflaming the Japanese desire for diamonds.

Peter Brodnitz is a New Jersey native who bears a strong resemblance to the actor William H. Macy. He wore a tie with colorful etchings of puppies on it. He was accompanied by his much older boss, Shimao Ishihara, the director of the Diamond Promotional Service, but Brodnitz did almost all of the talking during our two-hour meeting. Ishihara spoke only when he was asked about the nuances of a certain Japanese word.

"We know we're going to have to rebuild the values of the diamond engagement ring market," Brodnitz told me. "But that's not where the lowest hanging fruit lies. You first find a cultural need, create a product type around it, and get the trade to support it. This is the way you create a wave."

The "cultural need" he spoke of was the increasing willingness of older Japanese women to give themselves a *gohobi*, or a self-reward, with their household savings. To fit this need, De Beers was introducing the "Trilogy" brand, which featured three diamonds set in a row, either on a necklace or a brooch. The pattern of three is meant to symbolize past, present, and future. Women in middle age are not an insignificant market in Japan, where gender roles are more complex than they appear on the surface. Women are generally subservient to men in public, but inside the walls of the home, wives are usually in control of the household finances and do the books. It is customary for Japanese husbands, for example, to receive an "allowance" from their wives at the beginning of the week. The decisions of women are estimated to affect 70 percent of all individual consumption spending.

In fact, said Brodnitz, the agency is hoping to trigger a complex chain of events within a household. The woman sees the De Beers ad, decides she wants a diamond, increases her husband's allowance with a subtle suggestion, and the man will respond by "gifting" her with the desired diamond.

"Our utopian vision is for this to become as culturally imperative as the diamond engagement ring," Brodnitz said.

This is not the first time De Beers has tried to push a product that might recapture the early fire. One magazine spot from 1996 tried to start a new trend among high-end consumers. "Nature has perfected a number of beautiful shapes," said the ad. "The square-shaped diamond is one such shape. For you to appreciate its mysterious beauty to your heart's content, it is best to appreciate a caratage of one carat or more. Only a handful of women can enjoy this supreme delight." (That nature does not, in fact, create diamonds shaped like squares was a point of geology left unmentioned.)

White faces and Western celebrities—as always—played a prominent role in these late-1990s efforts to bring women back into the fold. A television ad featured the model Kate Moss wearing a solitaire around her neck, something that De Beers called the "simple diamond" necklace. The voice-over said: "I've captured the brilliance. My diamond is a reflection of me. I work hard to advance the things I have." Another television ad, shot in heavy blue tones, encouraged the recipient to think of diamonds as a divine entitlement.

The message: "God. Selected diamonds. For you now. With you forever."

Today's advertisements for the Trilogy jewels repeat this basic subtext: diamonds are what you deserve because they are a perfect reflection of who you are inside. One television ad depicts a woman in her graying years opening a new neighborhood café. Another shows an attractive woman of ambiguous age taking ballet lessons, and ends with the opening of a curtain as she toe-steps out onto the stage in warm yellow light to make her debut. There was a vigorous debate within the agency about the choice of this actress, Brodnitz told me. She had to be like Diane Lane or Julianne Moore—young enough to be intriguing to the viewership, but old enough to occupy the target market for Trilogy.

De Beers was trying, once again, to move diamonds into a place harmonious with the times. The philosophy behind the switch to middle-aged women—and away from newlyweds—was expressed in an internal strategy document that Brodnitz shared with me. "There are two elements accelerating these [sic] shift on focusing on the self," it said. "Youngsters denying any behavior embraced during the bubble economy. Older generations redefining their 'second lives' in retrospect to the life they had during the past."

In other words, the desired results were to co-opt the rising sense of "self" in Japanese women in a way that remained true to the old Confucian ethic of *chu ko*. Trilogy was one possible way for Japanese women to express themselves individually, but not *too* individually. The ads sought to steer a course through the narrow passage between the Japanese id and ego. According to the memo, this particular three-in-a-row arrangement of jewelry "is a subtle way to express a personal style & set of values that mildly stand out without conflicting with the social circle which she belongs to."

What was ultimately remarkable about this latest campaign was the way it did not depart from what De Beers has always said about diamonds: that they were a surrogate heart outside of your real heart. The first ads of the 1960s had captured the nation as if in a photographic flash—telling Japanese they could be everything they were supposed to be; they could have the bright life and the social approval all at once; they could be American and Japanese at the same time; they could look into the empty chamber of the diamond and see their own projected self, whether into manhood or marriage or ballet lessons.

I asked Shimao Ishihara if there was anything in particular about the shape or the appearance of the diamond that had a resonance in classical Japanese aesthetics and he grew animated for the first time in the conversation. The very colorlessness of the stone had a special appeal to the Japanese mind from the start, he told me, and had been a contributing factor to the wild success of the early campaigns. He likened the diamond to a "Zen temple" of symmetrical lines and harmony.

"There is a break in all of our minds," he went on. "That is the spirit of the Japanese mentality."

There is a word called *ma* often used in conjunction with Japanese art and literature. It literally means "interval," but is often translated as "negative space." It is the emptiness between two points or the quiet between two musical notes. *Ma* is what the painting does not depict or what the haiku does not say—it is the blank white area on the canvas or the complexity of emotion lurking in between simple words. A Western literary critic might call it "understatement" or "minimalism," but that is an incomplete definition. *Ma* is silence full of sound. In a classic Japanese painting, a depiction of a tree next to a river might be made with just seven or eight slashes of brushstroke. The resulting image may look like the crudest skeleton, ripped away from almost all narrative, but the drawing becomes rich and fascinating because the viewer's mind cannot help but supply the leaves, the water, the sky, and the emotion inside the empty places. This is what Ishihara meant by a break in all of our minds. What separates a good painting from a masterful one is the degree to which the artist has subtly encouraged the projection of the viewer's own mind onto the *ma*.

An entire world of color and meaning and desire is constantly wiggling within the break in the mind, requiring only the proper blank white spot on which to pour itself.

Four

THE STRONG MAN

Brazil

On the highway above the valley of the Rio Jequitinhonha, near a hill where trucks downshift in a blatting of exhaust, there is an open-sided shack made out of poles and cardboard. A traveler may spend a few cents here to buy some cheese bread or cakes or a block of peanut candy wrapped in a plastic bag. The man doing the selling has bright, arresting eyes and stands just over five feet tall. He wears a fedora over gray hair, which gives him an oddly formal look. On his cracked feet are sandals with a Brazilian flag on the strap.

His name is Geraldo de Santos Nunes, but everybody in town knows him as *"Murrudo,"* which rhymes with "voodoo" and means "strong man" in Portuguese. Despite his small frame and ropy muscles, he does not view the name as a joke, as a fat man might be called "Slim" or a tall man "Shorty." It was what people called his father, and he always liked it and adopted it for himself when he got old enough.

Strong Man pulled out a wooden bench for me when I went to visit him at his cookie stand on an October afternoon. The traffic was light that day and he had no customers. We talked for several hours as the sun slid down over the western edge of the valley and the trees on the hills faded to dark smudges.

"My father would be proud of me today, even after all that has happened," he told me. "I know that I was always his favorite son."

Ask anybody around the Jequitinhonha Valley about Strong Man and they are likely to have one of two reactions. The first is a pleasant chuckle, and then silence. The second is a pleasant chuckle and the start of a story.

"You know what this guy did? This was just after he got rich. He was driving his new pickup truck around town, showing it off. It was a new Chevy D-20 with a wide bed. A man in the crowd decided to have some fun with Strong Man and he began to criticize the color. He asked: 'Why did you buy a green pickup truck, when everyone knows that blue is the best color for a truck?' Strong Man tried to pretend that it didn't bother him, but the next week, he traded in his green pickup truck for a blue one, though it was used and had seventy-five hundred miles on it."

People who have never met Strong Man have heard variations of this same story for years. The essentials happen to be accurate, but the story is important not so much for its details, or what it says about Strong Man, but for its power to reinforce a long-standing truth about the Jequitin-honha watershed. It has been a part of the local narrative for as long as anyone can remember that this is one place in Brazil where it is possible for a very poor man to become very rich in the course of a single after-noon. And then he always finds a way to lose it in the end.

Strong Man is part of a marginal class of Brazilian workers who look for di-amonds using diesel pumps and shovels. They are known as *garimpeiros*. Although the profession is regarded as a low one in Brazil, they wear the term with pride.

The name has been associated with stealth and piracy for more than three centuries. When Portuguese explorers discovered diamonds near the Jequitinhonha in the 1720s, mining was barred to all but a few well-connected merchants licensed by the king. The hardy few who snuck into the valleys liked to say they avoided royal patrols by hiding in the cracks of the many jagged rock formations in the area. *Garimpeiro* means "a person who hides in the cracks," but eventually became accepted as a term to describe anyone in Brazil who pumps sand out of a riverbed in hopes that a diamond might be somewhere inside all the muck.

The name is also used to describe freelance gold miners, who wash their ore with mercury and leave a trail of environmental wreckage in their wake. For environmental officials and some of the larger mining companies, the work of the *garimpeiros* is like that of a swarm of termites: quick, clandestine, and costly. There may be as many as 300,000 of them now at work in the Amazon basin. Mining for diamonds is a cleaner activity by comparison, but it also lives in a shadow world of legality. The vast majority of it is done outside the scope of Brazilian law, and many of the stones are smuggled out of the country to avoid taxes.

I went to go visit some of the diggings in the company of a man everybody called "Tou." He owns a set of pumps, which makes him a boss. His house in town has a wood-burning kitchen stove and interior walls that don't quite reach the ceilings. When he smiles, dark wrinkles fan in the corners of his eyes.

He climbed into the passenger seat of my rented car and directed me down a dirt road outside the town of Diamantina in the landlocked state of Minas Gerais. The region reminded me a little of central New Mexico, with highlands of grass and volcanic red earth and *pau d'oleo* trees rounded by mountains covered with granite rockfall and cut with deep gorges. On the high ridges, it was possible to see for fifty miles.

The landscape on either side of the road was littered with gashes and withered piles of slag, the remnants of played-out diamond mines. Some of them were more than three hundred years old. Tou has made some of the more recent gashes himself. We crossed a dry channel he identified as the Rio Caldero and then he motioned for us to stop.

We walked up the sandy river flats for about ten minutes until we heard the sound of a two-stroke engine *putt-putt-putting* in the still desert air. There was a large pit dig in the north side of the dry riverbed. It was half full of dirty water. Floating inside was a strange contraption—a pair of metal tanks bridged by a diesel engine and connected to a flexible hose leading up the pit wall. The pump vibrated and smoked in the water. I followed Tou up the side of the bank where three men wearing shorts and T-shirts were adjusting the other end of the hose. A mixture of gravel and muddy water was cascading out of the end of the hose into a basin. The overflow ran down a metal ramp, where the water fed into a sluice pit and then back into the first pit through a steel pipe. There were mounds of gravel that had been shoveled off to one side. This was where the money was.

Every Saturday morning, the miners wash the week's accumulation of gravel at the side of the river. They use steel pans to sort through the quartz-rich sediment, and the ritual—known as the *lava*, or wash—is always a source of great tension because if no diamonds are found, nobody gets paid.

Garimpeiros never work for a wage. Instead, they get a percentage cut of the diamonds, which works as both an incentive and a noose. The usual arrangement is for the owner of the pumps to keep half of the profits, with 10 percent going to the owner of the land (if anybody bothered to notify him), and the remainder split among the work crew. If a particular pit is barren of diamonds, the miners go home empty-handed. An especially unlucky *garimpeiro* can work for months without earning a thing except a daily lunch of rice and beans.

This sharecropperlike system of payment devolved from the time of legalized slavery in Brazil. Most of the original Portuguese colonists in Minas Gerais allowed their slaves to keep a portion of a particularly large find. Slaves could eventually buy their freedom this way, and work their own river diggings. The profit-sharing model of compensation has survived into the modern era with some modifications. Today, the element of involuntary servitude is gone, and the gasoline-powered water pump has been added; but the essential form of the enterprise—in both engineering and economics—has remained intact.

So, too, has the aspect of piracy. Virtually all the diamond mines in this area are outlaw enterprises. This was because of a sweeping philosophical change made to the Brazilian constitution in 1988. Stated simply, mineral rights were decoupled from land ownership. The federal government took "eminent domain" possession of all the valuable metals underneath the soil—under office buildings in cities, under private farms in the countryside, under the jungle in the Amazon, everywhere. Anyone who wanted to mine a piece of land for zinc or gold or copper or diamonds had to fill out a stack of applications and permits before turning a single spadeful of dirt. A miner also had to submit a detailed report, usually more than five hundred pages long, on how he planned to repair the environmental damage he would create. It was a noble attempt to reverse a long legacy of environmental damage, but its effect has been minimal. The change in land policy, naturally, seemed both confusing and ridiculous to the *garimpeiros*. Who was to tell a farmer that he couldn't look for diamonds under his own soil? Land was land and its diamonds had been feeding poor families here for generations. And filing all those reports cost a minimum of $50,000—more than any low-level miner could afford to pay.

Thanks to badly funded and poorly trained police, the mining law is enforced sporadically, and then usually as a response to a specific complaint from a powerful mining company that wants to harass some *garimpeiros* off of a claim. "The authorities generally look the other way on the small guys," Mario Vasconcelos, a trade representative in the U.S. Embassy in Brazil, told me. "How can a group of five men with no money do any meaningful remediation work? They leave the land in a shambles."

If the law is followed at all, the standard scam is to obtain an "exploration permit" and start mining under the fiction that the hole is for research and assessment purposes instead of actual diamond production. All of the other mining permits—and the costly environmental repairwork they require—are then ignored.

"If you want to mine legally, it is virtually impossible," one experienced geologist told me in the town of Patos de Minas. "It is simply too expensive to comply with the law. And these men need to survive. Plus, there is big money involved. It is like no other business in Brazil, except for drugs. In one afternoon, your whole life can change."

Tou greeted the miners, who briefly stopped their work to talk to us. They were five days away from washing their ore. One miner had a torn shirt and huge misshapen toes poking out of his sandals. He said his name was Marcello Silva and that he was sixteen years old. "The wash day is like lottery day," he said. "Every time is a big excitement." He has drunk beer on occasion, supplied by older friends, and the feeling of looking through the gravel was like drinking a few beers. His biggest diamond thus far was about a carat in size, for which he was paid $39. It was the finest feeling he had ever had, he told me.

"It gives people a reason to throw a party for me," he said.

His two companions were both older, but they hadn't lost the thrill. "Addiction" was the word both used to describe it. "There's nothing better in the world—better even than getting paid," said Jose Pereira, a thirty-five-year-old married father of six. "The more you find, the more you want to get lucky. All the girls will come around to you."

His job was the best in the world, he explained, even though work in a bakery or a gas station would be physically easier. He earns enough off the small diamonds to equal an ordinary laborer's salary, but he gets a bonus—a weekly burst of pure adrenaline. It was the old gambler's thrill, the dopamine rush.

We hiked back down the Rio Caldero and Tou directed us to the rim of a box canyon about a mile away. At the bottom, forty feet down, was another diamond mine. This had been nothing but a small, shallow creek up until a few years ago when it had been widened and deepened by blasts of water shot from high-pressure hoses. The banks had been ripped apart to expose the diamondiferous material inside. A floating pump sat unused in a pit of sickly water colored like cream-of-tomato soup. Several miners rested below us in the shade of the cliffs. The scene looked like an eerie version of a Thomas Cole painting; *The Grand Canyon of the Yellowstone*, perhaps, only with alkaline walls and piles of rock waste instead of pine trees and clear water.

Tou took us down a narrow footpath to the mine floor. "You see that?" he said, pointing at a layer of white quartz known as *cascalho* in the cliff wall. "That's the good stuff. You see the variety in the color? From here," he drew a line with his finger, "to about here, that's where the diamonds are. They'll make a hole with a compressor, pound in some dynamite, and take the cliff down. This will probably yield about one hundred fifty carats a week." He picked up a chunk of unprocessed rock from a nearby pile and showed me a fruitcake of black crystal rocks interspersed in the silicate and quartz. "This is where they hide," he said. "We call this the *bosa*, the suitcase."

One of the *garimpeiros* was cooking a lunch of spaghetti and beans over a fire and I went to talk to him. His name was Marcelo Santos Gomez and he, like everybody else, was working on a percentage arrangement. Unlike the other miners, however, he hated his job.

"What we go through here isn't worth it," Gomez told me. "We get a lot of abuse from the buyers. They cheat us. We get fucked in the ass for the work we do. One carat makes us a hundred reals." This was an amount equal to about $30. And it had to be split four ways.

This was a frequent complaint in the mines—the gap between what a crew earns from a diamond and its eventual price on the retail market. When a Saturday wash yields a stone, the miners and the boss immediately take it into one of several unmarked buying offices in the nearby town of Diamantina. There is cursory haggling over the price, and the crew is paid in cash, always U.S. dollars. Few diamond buyers record their transactions on paper, and this is fine with the miners, who are the last people who want any documentation. The buyers keep a separate set of books, never disclosed to the government, to record the actual flow of money through their offices. There is a local expression for this: *caixa dois*, or literally, "cashier number two." The true pulse of the business beats here.

The illegal mines, meanwhile, can be abandoned as quickly as they are dug, only a hole and some waste rock left as evidence. "It's gone, the stones are in the pockets, and nobody saw anything," one gem dealer told me. "That's the Brazilian way."

Despite the low pay, Gomez said he couldn't quit mining because there were no other jobs for him and he had two children to support. He was in his early forties and too old to try something new. He pointed at a ridge on the other side of the canyon. "Over there, a hill of dirt collapsed on me last year. The first thing I thought was that I was going to die. The dirt covered me up to the neck. They dug me out and I went right back to work." Wall collapses are an everyday hazard in river mines. Two of Gomez's friends have been killed this way.

But then I asked him about the Saturday morning wash—the moment when diamonds appear—and Gomez admitted with a smile that he enjoyed it as much as everybody did. It was like a rushing sensation in his head, he said, and an intense concentration of energy in his heart. A feeling almost like sex.

"You can feel the wind leave your voice," he said.

Like most children in rural Brazil, Strong Man was put to work at an early age. His father was a hard man. Antonio de Santos had been upright and proud and suspicious of nearly everybody. He was in many ways the perfect expression of a native of the state of Minas Gerais, known throughout Brazil for their stingy ways, emotionally and otherwise. They wouldn't throw bread away until the end of the week. *Pão duro*, these people were called. Hard bread. Antonio had put his sons to work alongside him in the riverbeds, where they worked long-handled hoes, scraping the sand flat. Their hands became scaled with hard skin.

After his father died of a heart attack, Strong Man married a woman whose family lived near one of his pirate mines. Her name was Candida and they had flirted on the sly when Strong Man's father wasn't watching. She was pretty and shy and more than happy to help Strong Man work the pumps as he searched for the diamonds that had eluded his father.

"There weren't that many women in the village," he would say later, when things were quite different between them. "She was my only option." But in the early days, he was proud of her. She wasn't with him on the day seven years into their marriage, in 1991, when he and his crew were mining a site six miles upriver from Mendanha. It looked as promising a spot as any. Like the rest of the valley, it had been combed over several times—you could tell by the lines in the earth where the *cascalho* had been shifted around years ago—but there was always the chance they could have missed some gem-bearing pockets. Lazy miners sometimes hit false bedrock and thought it was true. There were also pockets of untouched gravel hidden under folds of limestone where water had eroded a hole—"devil's kettles," they were called.

This upriver digging was, of course, illegal. But this was the Rio Jequitinhonha. It was *their* river—the place where they had a right to poach stones to feed their families. Nobody was around to say differently.

The way Strong Man always told the story, he made a prayer to Our Lady of Aparecida at midday. "Please help me find a stone," he asked her. "I want to buy a chicken lunch and a glass of rum for my friend." As supplications went, this one was fairly mild and routine for Strong Man, who talked to the Virgin like he talked to his wife in the kitchen. But the prayer was quickly answered in a way that he did not bargain for. He was washing a tray of gravel about an hour later when it winkled from the slush like a sleepy insect: an octahedron bigger than he'd ever seen before. He let out a strangled whoop. His friends carried him back across the Jequitinhonha on their shoulders that day like a groom at a wedding. They were afraid he would stumble and lose the treasure in the current. Strong Man kept it clutched tightly in his right fist as they crossed the water.

The diamond assayed out at 11 carats and sold for $20,000—paid directly to him in American hundred-dollar bills. "So many bills that I could have woven a rug out of them," he told anybody who would listen. His friend got a chicken lunch and the rum the next day.

When a Brazilian miner turns on his gasoline pumps and sinks a hole, he is attempting to find a section of diamond-bearing gravel that had somehow been missed by slaves brought over from Africa in the eighteenth century. This is not an easy task because the slaves did a remarkably thorough job.

The Portuguese already had occupied the east coast of South America for more than two centuries before the first discovery of diamonds. They had a beautiful colonial port at Rio de Janeiro, a few filthy settlements in the interior, an illiterate class of New World tycoons, millions of acres of sugar cane under cultivation, and a thriving cross-Atlantic traffic in slaves captured or purchased from Angola, Senegal, and Gambia.

It was because of this trade in human beings that Brazil today is a nation with a racial spectrum unique in South America, a rich miscegenated stew of African, Portuguese, and Indian in which rigid definitions of color have blurred through successive generations of lust and intermarriage.

An estimated 4 million Africans were taken by force to Brazil. Many were sent up to the boom state of Minas Gerais, which means "General Mines." Placer gold had been found here in 1695 by a group of adventurers and roughnecks known as *banderiantes*, who had penetrated the deep interior in search of new slaves among the Tupi Indian villages. The news created a sensation in the royal court at Lisbon and triggered the world's first gold rush. Fortune seekers flooded into Minas Gerais, sank shafts and tunnels into the hillsides, and cut down most of the trees for smelter fuel. Hundreds of voyagers died on the six-week journey from Rio de Janeiro and a wave of famines hit the region, which was too dry and mountainous to support large-scale agriculture. At the height of one food shortage in the summer of 1700, stray cats were reportedly sold for the exorbitant price of 32 drams of gold.

History does not record the name of the person who found Brazil's first diamond, but it happened near a hillside settlement called Tijuco ("Mudhole") at some point in the late 1720s. A local story, probably apocryphal, says that a group of gold miners were using the "crystals" they had found in the streams as markers in a running card game. The local Catholic friar, who had been posted in India as a young man, recognized them for what they were and asked casually if he might save a few trinkets as souvenirs. He left for Rio with a sackful, promptly booked passage to Amsterdam, and was never seen again.

The story may have been a reflection of perfidy that actually went much higher. It seems certain that the colonial governor of Minas Gerais, Dom Lourenco de Almeida, had been quietly stockpiling some of the gems for himself before rumors of the discovery spread beyond control and he was compelled to make a report to Lisbon. He wrote a carefully worded letter to the king in July 1729 offhandedly reporting the discovery of "some little white stones" near Tijuco. With the letter, he enclosed six samples. The king's jewelers inspected the stones and proclaimed them diamonds, a verdict that did not come as much of a surprise. A steadily growing trickle of smuggled stones had been flowing into Europe for the last two years, via cargo ships returning from South America.

Once the trade was legitimized, Brazil quickly surpassed India in carat production and became the world focus of the luxurious new industry. The resulting flood of stones into the royal courts of Paris and London sent prices into a slump. Diamonds were the new fashion among the wealthy—they had first been imported by Jean-Baptiste Tavernier from Golconda only sixty years earlier—and new stones coming in from the Americas lessened their scarcity and threatened to make all of them worthless. Jewelers protested that such fine stones could never have come from such rough lands and insisted they were really India diamonds smuggled through Brazil to create a bubble. The king of Portugal responded to this crisis by sealing off the Jequitinhonha Valley to all outsiders and making it a crime for anybody to mine it except for a select few companies which had obtained special licenses from the crown. Outsiders discovered in the area were skin-searched and deported. Exaggerated stories were put into circulation that anyone who so much as washed his hands in the Jequitinhonha would see them amputated by the king's patrols. Diamonds were also taxed at a fifth of their value—a tribute known as the "quint" that was routinely dodged. These restrictive measures almost single-handedly created the *garimpeiro* class, as well as the general air of mendacity and petty corruption around the trade that thrives to this day in Brazil.

Tijuco, the town named for a mudhole, renamed itself Diamantina, meaning "Diamondlike," and began erecting double-steeple churches and paving the twisting streets with cobbles of sandstone. It took on the air of a corpulent middle-European village in the midst of the badlands. A twentieth-century writer for *Century* magazine summarized the change: "Broken noblemen and men of education came here to make their fortunes and eventually all the province of Minas Geraes became a focus of 'civilization' as the word was understood in those days—much powdered hair, knee breeches . . . minuets and swarms of miserable slaves."

The slaves' workday lasted from sunrise to sunset. Their clothes were often little more than a cloth wrapped around the waist to cut down on thievery. Some crews were forced to work naked. When they weren't combing the river valleys for shallow-lying rough, they were made to line up and wash gravel under the eye of a supervisor holding a whip. This frequently took place in an elongated thatched structure with a line of metal bins. When a slave found a diamond, he was supposed to clap, stand upright, and hold the find high in the air for everybody to see. Each was laid carefully in a bowl of water next to the bin.

The object for the slave, of course, was to quietly tuck a diamond inside his mouth or between his toes. A fence market for these stolen goods thrived among all classes in Diamantina, respectable and otherwise— "They are easily sold to the huckster, the pedlar or the keeper of the nearest groggery," one visitor reported—and so the overseers developed a system of inventory control that relied on twinning extremes of harsh punishment and great reward. If a slave was suspected of having stolen a diamond, he was confined to a jail cell for several days until his feces could be examined. But slaves could literally buy their freedom with found diamonds if they stayed honest.

A dramatic description of this practice comes from the British geologist John Mawe, who obtained a special dispensation from the king of Portugal to tour the region and make recommendations. His account of the journey provided some of the only details about the region available to the outside world at the time.

"When a Negro is so fortunate as to find a diamond of the weight of an *oitava* [17.5 carats], much ceremony takes place; he is crowned with a wreath of flowers and carried in a procession to the administrator, who gives him his freedom by paying his owner for it," wrote Mawe. "He also receives a present of new clothes and is permitted to work his own account." Goods and praise were also distributed to finders of lesser stones. The opening leaf of Mawe's book, published in London in 1812, bore a depiction of this scene. A line of slaves is stooped over their bins, but in the middle, one stands triumphant, his right hand extended skyward, his chest swelling like a victorious Greek soldier. His posture suggests that sweet freedom itself is clutched between his thumb and index finger.

This etching was to make a great impression on Richard Burton, who read Mawe's book as a child and would later grow up to become one of the most renowned explorers of the Victorian era, credited with helping discover the source of the Nile. Burton had a taste for forbidden areas and

obtained permission to traverse the regions around Diamantina on a canoe expedition in 1869.*

Though laced with insults directed toward his Indian porters ("I secured a sober start from Bom Successo by sending forward my Calibans to
bivouac at a place beyond the reach of liquor"), Burton's published journal offers several keen insights into the mechanics of diamond mining, or
the lack of it. Teams of slaves were made to clear vegetation, scrape away
surface clay, dig pits, and haul away waste rock. They stacked logs to
sluice away water, and hunched to sift gravel. The sole technology was
human.

"I found in the most civilized diamond diggings of Minas Geraes no
trace of kibble, crane and pulley, or rail, no knowledge of that simplest
contrivance, a tackle," wrote Burton. "[T]he Negro was the only imple-
ment and he carried as much as a schoolboy would stuff into his pockets."
Many slaves who obtained their freedom through escape or pilfering or
lucky finds became *garimpeiros* themselves, working illegal mines in ways
they had learned under bondage.

For the slave, the diamond was both the object of misery and a cherished token. It embodied freedom and captivity all at once. This duality
can be witnessed in the following story which Burton heard from several
people on his canoe journey:

Three men from the coastal regions committed a serious crime and had
avoided execution only by agreeing to a permanent banishment into the
wilderness of Minas Gerais. They were prohibited from entering any
town and had to sleep under the stars. For lack of anything better to do,
the men became *garimpeiros,* working freelance gold diggings along the
banks of the Rio Abaete. In the midst of a drought, the water level
dropped and exposed some untouched gravel. In it, they found one of the
biggest diamonds Brazil has ever produced—a stunning piece of 144-carat
rough. The men were now in a quandary. They could not hope to secretly
fence a gem this large without inviting arrest, for what they had done was
blatantly illegal. Under Portuguese law, the stone belonged to the government. Rather than give the stone back to the river, the men at last took it
to a country priest, who interceded for them with the governor. The dia-

---

*He could not have known it at the time, but it was the same summer that diamonds were dis-
covered near the Vaal River in South Africa, a development that would spell the end for Brazilian
dominance of the industry and plant the seeds for the De Beers cartel.

mond itself—its sheer size, its brilliance—was a powerful argument in their favor. The men were pardoned on the spot and received a full restoration of their civil freedoms. As for the diamond, it was shipped to Lisbon and wound up on the neck of King Dom João VI.

This is a narrative that lives on today in the Jequitinhonha Valley. A man can buy his way to freedom, if he could only find a big enough diamond.

The place where Strong Man found the first diamond got a special name: *Mina Domato*, "The Mine of the Forest." It kept blessing him with stone after stone. There was never one bigger than the original, but the stream of lessers was enough to make him the richest man in Mendanha. "You couldn't fit any of them into the top of a Coke bottle," he liked to brag, though it wasn't true.

He bought a five-room house for his mother. A house for Candida's family. A fast car for himself—the green Chevy pickup truck that didn't last a week after he was teased about it in Diamantina. He thanked the Virgin of Aparecida for his fortunes, lifting his fedora off his head every time he mentioned her.

His luck defied basic geology. The diamonds he was digging up were alluvials—the kind that had washed out of the cores of dead volcanoes centuries ago. Pipes of the mother rock kimberlite had to be somewhere in South America, but nobody had ever found anything conclusive. The dispersion of river diamonds was inherently chaotic and it was unusual to find such a rich concentration of them so close together. It was the luck of the *garimpeiro*. There was a saying about them: "One year they are in Heaven, the next they are in Hell." Or more to the point: *"Calca de veluda ou bunda de fora"* ("Either in velvet underwear, or with your ass hanging out").

A professional mining engineer in Diamantina heard the story of Strong Man and laughed.

"Geologists have always had a problem in this country," he said. "They can't find diamonds in the usual ways, so they need the *garimpeiros* to show them the best alluvial sites. In this sense, Strong Man was a brilliant geologist."

People began to notice new women around Strong Man. This was his velvet underwear time and the women often came away with jewelry and other gifts. There were whispers about prostitutes and girlfriends in other cities. He and Candida began to fight. He threatened to divorce her. "Go ahead and try," she told him. "I won't give you one." They had been married in the Catholic Church by a priest, so that was the end of that. The most he could do was buy her a new house across the highway from the gas station and tell her to stay away.

Strong Man's fame had spread. People he hadn't seen in years came back to Mendanha to party with him. He was known as a rich man who kept the common touch and he always picked up the bill for drinks. The stones from *Mina Domato* began to peter out, but he still had some cash on hand to pay his debts. At least half a million American dollars had passed through his hands over the life of that mine, and it seemed plenty was left. There was the matter of the pumps, for example. Strong Man needed to dip into his savings to pay for the newer ones he bought on credit.

One day, a man arrived from the nearby city of Teofilo Otoni with an offer. Strong Man had accumulated a large amount of U.S. currency from his diamond sales. Would he be interested in converting it into Brazilian cruzeiros at a highly favorable rate?

This was a common underground business in Brazil. The legal place to change money was at a bank, but their rates were always terrible and their commissions high. Illegal money changers were like clandestine diamond mines—they were everywhere. Strong Man held a meeting of his family and some friends where the offer was discussed. The decision was made to accept it, and some friends even chipped in their own stashes of dollars to be changed along with the remainder of the profits from the depleted *Mina Domato*. It had been a good run, but now it was time to invest in some new equipment and go looking for another pocket that the nineteenth-century slaves had missed. Strong Man took the bus to Teofilo Otoni with the suitcase of dollars riding on his lap.

The rendezvous with the money changer seemed to go too quickly, but Strong Man was too intimidated to say anything. He did count one wad of bills before he was hustled out of the room, and everything seemed to be in order. When he reached the men's room of the airport-sized bus station in the state capital of Belo Horizonte, he reached deeper into the bag of money and pulled the paper strip off one of the stacks of cruzeiros at the bottom. It had been covering up a large stripe running through the midsection of each bill. *"Não tem valor,"* they all said in red letters—"nothing of value."

The bills had been printed as teaching tools for bank clerks. Official fakes. Strong Man went though all of them and discovered that only one of the packs was real. Their total face value didn't even add up to the amount he was supposed to have received. He had been cheated even in counterfeit.

That was the last of the *Mina Domato*. Strong Man called the news home. And then he sat down on a bench next to the departing buses and cried.

If a river is too wide to be dammed, there is another way to get at the rich sand at the bottom. A man must dive to the bottom with a breathing tube in his mouth and a suction hose in his hands. This is one of the more dangerous methods of diamond mining known in the world, but there is a class of men in Brazil who embrace it and think nothing of spending four hours every day under a river so opaque that a hand cannot be seen an inch in front of one's face.

These miners call themselves the *balseiros*—the "boat people"— and, like their fellow miners, they get no wages and are paid only in percentages. A typical day starts at sunrise, when a three-man crew shoves off on a river in a pontoon boat made out of two hollow metal tanks bridged by a metal platform. On board is a compressor pump, a collection tank for the gravel, a jig to sort the rocks from each other, and a cheap blue plastic tarp to provide shelter from the sun. This crude barge is a slightly more sophisticated version of the gasoline pumps used to dig holes in the dry rivers. The *balseiro* typically wears a foam wetsuit and wraps tape around his fingers to protect against the sharp rocks on the river floor. He then puts the breathing mask over his face, makes the sign of the cross, and goes under. In one hand he carries a crowbar and in the other is the suction hose, which he is seeking to ram into the bed of the river. Visibility is often poor, or nonexistent.

"My hands are my eyes—they can touch and recognize everything," a thirty-year-old *balseiro* named Rubens Francisco Calixto told me. "I am not afraid of this work."

Like all of the divers, he wears a 53-pound lead belt around his waist. If a problem develops, he simply unbuckles the belt and floats up to the surface. There is also a universal system of signals made with tugs on the breathing tube. If the *balseiro* pulls twice, he's telling the crew on the deck that the suction is at a good level. If he pulls three times, he needs more slack in the hose. If the men up above pull four times, it means it is the end of the shift. A series of frenetic tugs from up above means that a large diamond has turned up in the jig and that a payday is imminent.

"Sometimes you get a diamond every day, other times it is impossible to find a stone," Calixto told me. He is a divorced father of two, with compact muscles rippling under a damp soccer jersey. The work has been good to him, he says, and he has never run into danger in his four years of diving.

"I can't feel the time running when I'm down there," he said. "It's kind of like what it must be like to fly. I try to watch everything around me when the water is clear. The feeling is even better when we're mining under a waterfall. I feel the water swirling all around me."

For others, the daily dives are tedious, and occasionally terrifying. "We do it because we don't have anything else," a diver named Jose Wilson told me. "Many of us don't even know how to swim." Crippled men are said to be especially good at the job because their constant use of crutches supposedly builds upper-arm strength. This is important underwater, where the diver uses his hands and the crowbar and occasionally a hammer to break apart rocks and move debris away. Large boulders are shoved to the side, and smaller ones are sometimes lifted to the barge above in a metal box. But the most important tool is the suction hose, which is fitted with a triangular iron cage over the mouth. The diver is supposed to use it as a coal miner uses a pneumatic drill. The end goal is the same: a wall of ore must be broken apart. He kneels on the floor of the river, jams the end of the hose into the ground, and starts vacuuming out a tunnel—known as a "road"—underneath the surface of the riverbed. This is where most of the danger lies. Miners have been killed in these tunnels when large boulders shift and collapse on top of them, pinning them underwater. Other hazards include a sudden loss of suction in the hose, which can send a shower of rocks down onto the diver.

This happened once to a man named Djavan Pereira, a middle-aged Afro-Brazilian with matted dreadlocks. He had just finished digging a road under the Madeira River and his boatmates had pulled the hose back to the surface when something compelled him to look up. In the haze of the water, he saw something he will never forget—an avalanche of rocks and debris streaking toward him like a dirty rain. Pereira's reflexes were good, even in the slow-motion gel of the water, and he twisted out of the way of the rockfall's center. If he hadn't looked up, he would have been killed.

"I thought I was gone," he said. "My adrenaline skyrocketed. When I got to the surface, I took a long, deep breath."

In deep rivers, he has seen friends die from the bends when they ascended too quickly, the pressure in their blood too unequal to the surface pressure. They perished quietly on the deck of the boat, their arms and legs drumming softly on the wood like a caught fish flopping its last moments away. Pereira told me his own system for avoiding the bends—rise until you can feel the temperature change, stop, remove the mask, take a sip of water, relax a few seconds. Then replace the mask, go up a little more, stop, sip. Repeat until surfaced.

We were squatting together in the shade on a Sunday afternoon in front of a four-dollar rooming house in the town of Patos de Minas. Pereira was in a cheerful mood, despite being low on cash, because he was heading to the city of Boa Vista where he had a special fondness for one of the brothels there. He had been mining gold and diamonds for twenty-three years, had traveled all around South America, and he named for me the rivers that he had vacuumed: Araguaia, Paranaiba, Abaete, Iapok, Madeira, Tres Rios. In his luggage, he carried a small flute and a book of photos. Among the snapshots of various girlfriends and flings, there is one of himself standing nearly naked in the mud in the remote jungle state of Rondonia. He is holding a hydraulic hose, and is in the process of blasting apart a riverbank.

"I'm addicted to this. It's the only way I really feel like I'm living," he told me. "My life is on the water."

Pereira was not a typical *garimpeiro* whose life is hemmed by the demands of family and imminent poverty. He was more of a mercenary who listened to his own whim. But what he wanted was the same.

"I live from diamond to diamond," Pereira said before he went back inside the rooming house. "It's the best thing there is. There's cars, booze, and women. Good hotels and good restaurants. A regular job? I'd have to be crazy."

Calling the police was out of the question for Strong Man because the money changing had been illegal from the start. It would have been like complaining of being ripped off in a drug deal. Not only would he never see his dollars again, he'd likely be arrested. There was always the possibility of seeking independent revenge, but Strong Man wasn't that type of person and he would have no idea how to find the money changer again anyhow.

Without any funds left to pay his debts, he was forced to sell his pumps and his pickup truck. In the slang of the miners, Strong Man had "broken the face"—that is, he lost everything and had to quit mining. He took a job chopping wood on a farm six miles away, and he had to walk there on the days when he couldn't get a ride. Around town, he would see the girls who had flocked to him when he was rich. They still had the jewelry he had given to them.

He began to hate himself for his pride. He knew he had been arrogant in his wealth and he sought to atone. Strong Man began to mortify his own flesh. He walked barefoot to his farm job to make himself hurt and humble. He grew his beard down to his waist. Then he got the idea of making a *promesa* to Our Lady of Aparecida.

This was serious business. It would be a personal vow to the Virgin of Brazil, who was the confirmed appearance of the Mother of God in his own country. Everyone knew the story—it was also about hunting for something elusive, and seeing bad luck turning good: Three fishermen were having a bad day on a river near São Paulo in 1719 and were ready to turn home when they captured a headless statue of a Madonna in their net. The next cast turned up her head, and the one after that returned a huge haul of fish. It was a miracle, the fishermen decided, and the priests agreed. A chapel was built in her honor. Our Lady of Aparecida was black of face, just like the Virgin of Guadalupe in Mexico. Strong Man would walk to Diamantina for her, not once but three times, barefoot, just as he had been walking to cut wood, and then pay his respects to her at the parish church of São Antonio. He would try to walk away the greed that had led him to the money changer. He ended each journey on bleeding feet. But he did not get rich again. In fact, he sunk deeper. He carried a few of the *não tem valor* bills around in his wallet just to have something inside, and to show those who thought he had blown everything on prostitutes.

One good thing did come his way. He had at one point agreed to be the godfather for the son of a friend in the nearby village of Cuoto Magalhaes. A young daughter there named Josemary caught his eye. She was a bit on the fleshy side, but she was loving and generous and accepted Strong Man for all his faults, his pinwheeling extremes of carnality and pious resolve. This may have been because of the depth to which she shared these extremes herself.

They could not marry, thanks to first wife Candida's intransigence, but they could "join themselves" as so many couples in rural Brazil call it when they live together in a common-law state outside the blessing of the church. She moved into his small house at the top of the hill and together they opened up the roadside cake stand to make a little money. "The only thing wrong with you is you're too humble," she liked to tell him.

Strong Man's fall was enjoyed by some. "He used to go barefoot to be holy," laughed a gem dealer. "Now he goes barefoot for real."

For all their ingenuity and hard work, the *garimpeiros* find only about a half-million carats every year, which is less than 1 percent of total global production. This makes Brazil a minor player on the world diamond stage today; but the nation has been of perpetual interest to multinational mining companies because of the undiscovered kimberlitic resources. If anybody found a rich pipe, Brazil could very quickly become a serious bonanza.

The diamonds that had delighted the eighteenth-century court at Lisbon had to have come from a subterranean source, probably a series of volcanic complexes in various places around Minas Gerais and neighboring states. They had avoided detection, either because the pipes had completely washed away after eons of rain and wind, or because the kimberlite had changed to a material unrecognizable as kimberlite, or because they were capped over with hundreds of feet of sandstone. Several barren pipes had been located—there was one strip of black clay near Brasilia that you could see in a roadcut from the highway—but "the mother of the diamonds" remained elusive.

In 1975, a team of French geologists from the company BRGM followed a trail of alluvial diamonds to a hillside near the São Francisco River and took core samples from the summit. What they found was paydirt—kimberlite with a sprinkling of microdiamonds. Further exploration revealed shallow pipes containing gem-quality diamonds. By African standards, it was a pittance, but it qualified as a revolutionary discovery in Brazil—the very first contender for the legendary mother of diamonds.

De Beers quickly learned what was happening, purchased the claim through a front company, and did its own slow geological work on the hillside for several years. This was a move consistent with the cartel's practice of grabbing or co-opting every new find before the production could throw off the artificial scarcity in the market. It looked like a fairly rich lode—a bulk sample of 20,000 tons of ore yielded a respectable 5,000 carats—but there was no rush to put it into production.

There was another factor working against development. The plateau was less than three miles from the source of the Rio São Francisco, a legendary river of Brazil to which many residents felt a strong emotional tie. The worldwide publicity given to the depletion of the Amazon rain forest in the 1980s had breathed life into the environmental movement in Brazil and a whole new host of nonprofit organizations stood ready to create obstacles. The De Beers cartel, meanwhile, had done little to win over popular opinion with its new neighbors, and had probably poisoned relations from the start. "You had these secretive, tight-lipped British and South African guys coming in and out of there creating all kinds of speculation and they would never say what was up," one observer told me. Given Brazil's historic preference for progress over preservation, these factors might not have gotten in the way. But in this case, the kimberlite pipes happened to be located in an extremely inconvenient place—right outside the western border of the massive Serra do Canastra national park created by the Brazilian government in 1972. Environmental activists and one powerful faction within the federal Environment Ministry wanted to see the borders of the park pushed even farther west, sealing off this mother of diamonds forever. It would be a knotty problem.

But not for De Beers. After the cartel made a monumental shift toward retail sales at the turn of the twentieth century, it began to reevaluate its mineholdings throughout the world. The pipe in Brazil was deemed to be a salable asset, and was acquired in 2002 by a Canadian junior mining company called Black Swan Resources. Black Swan changed its name to Brazilian Diamonds, Ltd., and began trying to persuade the federal government to issue a license that would allow it to mine the hilltop before the park could be enlarged. Production could not go forward otherwise.

"When people think of a mine site, they think of a whole mountain being washed away," said Lucio Mauro de Souza Coehlo, the finance director for Brazilian Diamonds, Ltd. "But this is 1.5 hectares big—no more than a soccer field. The government can't afford to not know what's in there."

While the Canastra lobbying effort dragged on, the company sought to stop the pirating of river diamonds in its other claim sites. One of them was in the western part of the state, in the basin of a serpentine creek called the Santo Antonio do Bonito. A team of military police had been called in by the state's attorney to crack down on illegal mining. The *garimpeiros* were angry. It seemed to them yet one more case of high-level machinations depriving them of their rightful diamonds, with environmental laws a convenient cover. Tensions were high.

I went out for a look and met up with the operations director for the area, a former Portuguese Special Forces trooper named Mario Freitas. He had been a De Beers man before the cartel abandoned Brazil. He had a potbelly and a cell phone and a spiral notebook with page after page of tight lettering. We got into his Mitsubishi pickup truck and we went bouncing out along a dirt road that led into the diggings. The countryside looked a little like Sonoma County, California, with coffee bushes in place of the vineyards. There were gentle green hills dotted with faraway cattle, and combine tracks in the undulating loam. Soybean sprouts would be coming up in a few months.

The mines might be dangerous, Mario told me. He had not been directly threatened, but everybody knew his truck and knew he had the power to send the police to break up an illegal mine. He sometimes carried a pistol into the fields and was ready for trouble—he had been on duty when the Portuguese were preparing to evacuate their colony in Angola in 1975 just ahead of the brutal civil war.

"I keep my eyes open around here," he said. A smiling pumpkin deodorizer hung from his rearview mirror.

We went over a series of ridges and came to a cement farmhouse in a broad river valley. "I know the people here," Mario said. A woman came out and invited us into a kitchen full of smoke and houseflies, where she poured us thick sweet coffee out of a yellow thermos. Her name was Alice Borges. She and her husband had bought the farmhouse with the profits from an 87-carat diamond he had found in a streambed a few years earlier. Money was not so easy these days, she told Mario. The waste rock from that digging was still there and she had been pestering her husband to go wash it again to look for more diamonds, but he had delayed and now the rains were coming in.

Mario told Alice he was going to have a look at her land, which was technically inside the claim boundaries of Brazilian Diamonds, Ltd. It was a wide sweep of shortgrass cradled in a bend of the Santo Antonio, crisscrossed by barbed wire and speckled with cattle. A lone palm tree stood in the middle of the biggest pasture. The land was prime diamond turf, Mario told me. The 90-degree bend in the river and the flatness of the Borges farm hinted at a lot of untapped *cascalho* under the grass. The river had almost certainly flowed over the farm centuries ago and changed course.

We passed through a series of wire gates and rattled over the fields toward a digging near the edge of the river. A middle-aged *garimpeiro* was standing inside the shallow gash, swinging a pick at the earth. A small battery-powered FM radio at the lip of the digging was tuned to samba music playing from Coromandel. The lone miner put down the pick and introduced himself as Lazaro Nunes DaSilva.

"Nothing yet," he told us. "I'm waiting for the time chosen by God."

Mario hunkered down and looked at the wall of his digging, which went three feet deep. Sure enough, there was a layer of chunky gravel below the topsoil. He withdrew a device that looked like a tire gauge from his breast pocket. It was a slim metal pendulum attached to a wire. Mario held it close to a dirt clod from the ore pile and the pendulum swung slightly toward it. The pendulum was magnetized and would be attracted to kimberlitic rock, he told me. More geological work would be necessary, but this did not look like good news for the Borges family.

We shook hands with DaSilva and left for another digging, this one a few miles upstream. It was in a valley cluttered with piles of waste rock. Many of them were long grassed over; this bend in the creek had been worked ever since colonial days. Mario inched the truck over the river crossing and pulled up next to a deep pit on the other side. I got out and stretched and looked over the hood to see a young man with a long fishing knife walking toward us. Mario flinched, and then put on a huge smile. "*Ola!*" he said, and the young man smiled back. He was wearing a filthy shirt and jeans with one leg cut off. The fly was open and his penis hung halfway out, red, wrinkled, and forgotten. He held the knife at his side while we conversed.

His name was Jose Machado Neto and he told us he and a companion were cutting hose to fit the pump aperture. Their two pits had yielded about eight good-sized diamonds in the last few months, but none over a carat. Jose had been a miner ever since he was six years old. There were calluses on his hands that looked nearly half an inch deep.

"The *garimpeiro* is a drunk man and mining is like rum," he told me. "Once you start, you never want to stop."

Jose's companion came over and Mario—relaxing after his initial look at the knife—asked them what they were doing. The companion crouched and began drawing a map in the dirt. There had been violence in this valley seventy years ago, he explained. Two crews of miners had each moved inland from their respective parts of the streambed and had met in the middle. They had both laid claim to a spot under a farmer's land where a giant diamond had been unearthed. Words were exchanged, and then gunshots. The farmer had told both sets of miners to fill in the hole and get lost. The promising claim disappeared, and nobody was sure exactly where it was today. Jose had seen lightning over this particular spot and took it as a sign from God.

What was going to happen? Jose asked Mario. Would they be evicted? "There was a guy downstream who got shut down by the cops, but he has started up again," said Jose. He was clearly worried the hand of the law was about to descend on him and his pirate operation.

"You shouldn't worry," said Mario. "We have no complaint with you. You're not excavating a whole lot. It's the guys who operate the big jigs who don't respect the environment."

Once we were back in the truck and rolling away, Mario muttered in English. The two *garimpeiros* had excavated a pile of gravel that would take at least six months to wash, he said. They would never get it done before the police arrived.

"It's only a matter of time," he said.

Strong Man gets a certain amount of business at his cake stand from people who have heard the story of the green pickup truck. He happily talks about the diamonds with those who are curious, skipping over the parts about the wild living and the illegal diggings and emphasizing his uncanny streak of luck in the 1990s and the barefoot walks to fulfill his *promesa*. Truth and mythology blend together in an indistinguishable pudding as he tells his story. He has become the central actor in his own legend, his life a moral theater for his neighbors. Though he is now too poor to afford electricity for his house, he is happy with Josemary and feels anxious and melancholy when she is away. "She is more than a wife to me," he says, and considers for a way to describe her that wouldn't be blasphemy.

He finally says: "She is like a mother."

If he could, he would go back to mining. Josemary had a dream the other week where she was sitting on the shore of a river, playing with handfuls of sand. In one handful, she found a 6-carat diamond. "These diamonds have a force of their own," she says. "For you to find something in the ground that you didn't put there yourself—there is something religious about that."

Others in the village think Strong Man is better off selling peanut candy. "He's a nice guy, but he went and got cuckoo with miner's disease," said the owner of the local tavern, João Barboza. He was using the local term for the binges in spending and sex that often accompany the discovery of a large diamond. "I will say this about him, though," Barboza continued. "A lot of these guys forget their friends during the time they are rich. Strong Man never did."

His ex-wife Candida still lives in town, in the house built by Strong Man's diamond money. I found her across the highway from the gas station, gathering firewood outside when the sun was low over the ridge of the Serra do Espinaco Mountains to the west. Well into her forties, with rings of graying hair wrapped into enormous cardboard curlers, she was still a strikingly beautiful woman. Candida worked as a janitor at the local elementary school. She was putting one of her sons through college at the University of Diamantina, where he was studying to be a protector of the environment.

I asked her about Strong Man, and she smiled tiredly. "He went berserk," she said. "He changed completely. The first thing he did was abandon his family. He got plenty of girlfriends and gave them all jewelry."

But she did not hate him. Whether it was from her Catholicism or her peaceful repose in life was hard to say. Candida knows that she has done much better than her ex-husband, with her house that had a green metal gate, and electricity, and a flowering plant in the front yard.

"I feel pity for him," she said. "For all that has happened, he was never an awful man. He never raised his voice to me in all the years we were together. I raised his three sons. I gave him everything that I had. I am grateful for him."

None of Strong Man's sons would become *garimpeiros*, she told me.

"Money from mines is cursed money. If you don't manage it well, it slips through your fingers. But we have done well. What we could have gotten, we got. It's all done. No more diamonds."

Then she picked up her sticks of wood and went into the house.

Five

THE CARTEL

South Africa

Near the open-air butcher stalls of Smithfield Market in central London, a five-story office building stands on a slope. The address is 17 Charterhouse Street. The concrete and glass exterior gives off a sense of bland British discretion, and offers no indication as to what goes on inside, only that it must be something that requires tight security. A nattily tailored guard stands in a bulletproof booth near the entrance. There is a high iron gate and a ramp into the basement for armored cars.

Ten times every year, approximately eighty of the most powerful men of the diamond world meet here for a ritual that would be alien to almost any other commodity trade in the world. Each client is led into a second-floor room where there are white tables and flex lamps and a carpet bearing a muted blue pattern of squares and ovals. Coffee and tea is offered. Pleasantries are exchanged in Oxbridge-toned accents, but the atmosphere is hushed. An attendant goes to a window at the end of the corridor and comes back with what looks like a yellow-and-black plastic lunchbox. Inside are gem diamonds of all varying types and sizes, and the mixture may or may not resemble what the client had ordered several weeks beforehand. The client is handed a loupe and is invited to inspect the collection. There are no negotiations over the price, only an implied choice: Take it or leave it. Few ever leave it.

These events are called "sights" and the host is De Beers Consolidated Mines, Ltd., the corporation that has maintained tight control of the supply of diamonds for more than a century. The stones passed out here represent slightly under half the total carats released to the world every month. To be invited to a De Beers sight is the pinnacle of a career in the diamond industry. It means your firm has been rigorously evaluated for financial standing, marketing acumen, and proven ability to distribute the stones to a wide network of wholesale buyers and boutique customers. To be a "sightholder" also means you have convinced De Beers you will not make waves by selling too much of the box at wholesale, or by protesting the quality of your allotment. In exchange for docility, you are virtually guaranteed to make a healthy profit from your box, whose cost can range from $1 million to $30 million.

Clients are permitted to quibble about parcels within the box, but never the box itself. That invites swift punishment. The last man said to have refused a box was the legendary New York dealer Harry Winston, who had once called the sightholder system "vicious" and always hated De Beers' arrogant ways. He was promptly uninvited from the next sight and he soon found himself at a severe disadvantage, having to acquire his supply at a markup. He tried to build a relationship with a remote mine in the Portuguese colony of Angola, but the deal was quashed after a British cabinet official telephoned an official in Lisbon with the news that any arrangement with Winston would be regarded as "an unfriendly act." How De Beers engineered this act of brute diplomacy was never disclosed. Chastened, Winston returned to the sightholder list and never again complained about his regular ration of diamonds.

A former high-ranking De Beers official told me that every box was calculated to release exactly the right amount of stones onto the market. They had to be enough to meet consumer demand, but not enough to cause the price to fall. This was a matter of utmost importance, because fluctuations of supply and demand—the normal dynamic of every other metals exchange in the world—are not tolerated in the diamond industry.

"Keeping the balance was everything," said this official, who asked that I keep him anonymous. "We would check the price of rough in Bombay, Antwerp, Tel Aviv, and New York. We knew whatever we did would have a huge effect on the marketplace."

Outsiders usually aren't permitted on the sight floor, which represents a kind of inner temple of the diamond world. But I was in London in the dead week after Christmas and managed to speak with an executive in a generous mood. His name is Andy Bone and he wore a tidy button-down shirt under a sweater. We shared a lunch of lobster bisque and coq au vin in the cafeteria and then he took me up to the suite where the gems are distributed to the elite every fifth Monday.

I wasn't sure what I was expecting to see, but the sight rooms looked like an ordinary set of 1980s-style conference rooms. The only thing that would have set them apart from the architecture of a middlebrow law firm was the presence of square lamps and electronic scales next to the windows, and an eye-in-the-sky security camera bubble mounted on the ceiling. It looked disappointingly ordinary. I sat in one of the padded chairs and said as much.

"Kind of mundane, I agree," said Bone. "But I suppose it *is* an important thing, in its own subdued way."

He wasn't kidding. Three floors beneath us were a series of vaults that contain the world's largest stockpile of unpolished diamonds. The exact value of this reserve is a source of some speculation, but the best estimates put it at half a billion dollars. These gems are doled out in the sights at a controlled rate, but to De Beers, they remain much more valuable right where they are. The continuing stability of the diamond industry depends on an artificial scarcity which De Beers has worked hard to create, all the while spending billons in advertising to maintain the image of a diamond as the ultimate token of love. The De Beers organization is now in the midst of trying to reinvent itself as a vendor of specially branded diamonds rather than being the custodian of the trade, but critics contend that it remains a cartel in the classic sense—an interlocking web of corporate interests designed to regulate production. De Beers has managed the remarkable feat of operating a seventeenth-century economic model in a twenty-first-century world, thus ensuring that a mineral not so rare in nature fetches a price far beyond what its value would be in a truly free market.

Nobody knows that value. And that is because the trade in diamonds has not been free for 118 years—not since the De Beers cartel was born in a semidesert, in a corner of the British Empire that had previously been viewed as worthless.

Every civilization needs a founding myth, and this is the one of modern South Africa. On a spring day in 1867, a teenager in a remote part of the grasslands went out to repair a clogged water pipe on his father's farm. Erasmus Stephanus Jacobs was the son of a Boer, part of the tough group of sodbreakers who had trekked up to the dry fields on the edge of the

Kalahari Desert to escape British rule at Cape Town. They spoke a lilting dialect of Dutch called *Afrikaans* and believed in a literal interpretation of the Bible. Many believed the earth to be flat. In the sere plains of the African desert called the Great Karoo, they tried to scratch out a living among the scrub grass and the camel-thorn trees. Jacobs was an ordinary farmer's son, but this afternoon proved to be unlike any other.

"Having secured what I wanted and feeling somewhat tired, I sat down in the shade of a tree when I suddenly noticed in the glare of a strong sun a glittering pebble some yards away," he recalled years later. "I became curious and went and picked up this *mooi klip* [Dutch for "pretty pebble"]— it was lying between some limestone and ironstone. The spot was quite a distance from our homestead, but only a couple hundred yards from the bank of the Orange River. I, of course, had no idea that the stone was of value. I was at the time wearing a corduroy suit and simply put the pebble in my pocket. I did not feel at all excited at finding such a beautiful stone."

Jacobs later gave the *mooi klip* to his young sister, who used it in a game called Five Stones, similar to jacks. One stone was tossed in the air and the player had to scramble to pick up other stones scattered on the ground in time to catch the falling stone. A neighbor named Schalk van Niekerk came by to visit and interrupted a session of Five Stones in the dooryard. He professed admiration for the shiny pebble and tried to scratch a windowpane with it. Van Niekerk asked if he could buy the child's stone and Mrs. Jacobs told him she wouldn't think of charging him for a rock. Van Niekerk sold it to a traveling salesman named O'Reilly, who was laughed out of the pubs of Hopetown after he displayed what he was certain was a diamond. The gamepiece wound up in the office of an anesthesiologist who scratched a pane of glass with it and proclaimed it a genuine diamond. Stories of other *klips* being picked out of the Orange River were circulating, meanwhile, and the anesthesiologist forwarded the promising news to merchants in London.

A universal truth of the diamond business is that discoveries are almost always greeted with skepticism that masks dread of a price collapse. This time was no exception. A Bond Street jewel merchant dispatched an agent named James Gregory down to South Africa for a look at the supposed diamond fields. Gregory toured the countryside, inspected some surface geological features, and issued a damning verdict in the journal *Scientific Opinion*: "I can now only conclude by expressing my conviction that the whole diamond discovery in South Africa is an imposture—a bubble scheme." The *mooi klips*, in short, had been imported from India or Brazil and salted into African soil by unknown persons trying to make a quick buck. It seemed to fit the general impression of South Africa at the time, a place of thin anemic rivers, swarms of sandflies, and endless plains of grass.

Gregory was dead wrong. Soon after his report was released, a sheep-herder found an 83-carat stone in the sands of the Orange River. It was later polished into a brilliant jewel called "the Star of South Africa." In a possibly apocryphal story, Colonial Secretary Richard Southey made a speech in the Parliament at Cape Town using this gem as a prop for a grandiose statement. "Gentlemen," he is supposed to have intoned, "this is the rock upon which the future of South Africa will be built." A merchant who kept a careful diary of the first stones to show up in Hopetown offered a similar appraisal: "In spite of Mr. Gregory's attempt to decry our diamonds, he will not succeed in putting an end to their existence along the Orange and Vaal Rivers, but I venture to predict that they will in the future bring immense wealth to our hitherto unfortunate country."

This turned out more correct than the Victorian hyperbole suggests. The word "gregory" became South African slang for "gigantic mistake." News of the big diamond's discovery went off like a cannon shot in the summer of 1870. Prospectors from all over the world flooded into South Africa to join the potential bonanza. There were veterans of the California gold fields and the American Civil War, and the recent Australian gold rush, as well as country bumpkins from Essex and Nottingham. Sailors deserted their ships off the coast of South Africa and jumped on wagon trains while still wearing their gumboots and oilskins. The emigrants formed a scraggly line of carts and oxen across 500 miles of dry veld up from the port at Cape Town. Above the plains of the Karoo, a giant pillar of dust and smoke marked the place where a clamoring tent village of gem hunters, prostitutes, thieves, and swarms of Zulu and Griqua villagers* was excitedly digging into the river sands. There had been a herd of ostriches who gathered at the edge of the river to water themselves, but they were quickly shot and their entrails combed for diamonds they might have swallowed.

The work was dirty and hot and mostly unrewarding, though occasion-

---

*The Boers called the natives by the insulting name *kaffir*, a corruption of the Arabic *qafin*, which means "infidel." The name, unfortunately, stuck.

ally thrilling. Loads of sand and gravel were hauled up from the river, washed through swinging sieves called "cradles" or "babies," and then poured onto flat wooden tables. The wet ore was said to be a vibrant casserole of greens, yellows, and reds—"a medley of worn and rolled chips of basalt, sandstone, quartz and trap, intermingled with agates, garnets, peridot, jasper and other richly colored pebbles," reported one mining engineer, calling it the prettiest he'd ever seen. The prospectors used a knife or a flattened piece of tin to sort through the colorful ore, before raking the batch off to one side and taking on another. Speed was of the essence, for the more a man sorted, the more wealth he chanced to find. Experienced hands bragged of their ability to quickly spot the wink of diamond among the rocks; reexamination of the waste piles more than a century later proved that thousands escaped their eyes. A miner named Fred English reported the following incident: "Old R—— has found a stone at last; he nearly scraped it off the table, but his son, a mere kid spotted it, a fine 26-carat stone. He is offered £2,600 for it and there is joy and will be liquor in the tent of R——."

A fortunate few emigrants got rich. But the vast majority came up empty, or nearly so. Typical was a young man named John Thompson Dugmore, who wrote letters home about the new frontier to his wife Sydney back in England. In one of his first, dated September 9, 1870, he described the country around the diggings:

> The appearance was one of the most dreary and barren you could imagine, my spirits fell to zero at the very appearance. Not a vestige of grass and the few bushes almost all leafless and scarce but a gravel free from stones with the exception of a bed of sand so deep that the oxen could barely tow the wagon through.

Dugmore spent a month washing gravel and eating sheep meat and porridge. They found nothing.

> I cannot say I am disappointed for I was never very sanguine, but as far as the paying prospects of the speculation is concerned it is, in my opinion, as complete a sell as you ever heard. I do not think the prospect is worth four shillings. There are hundreds of people here working hard from day-to-day and from month-to-month without the least success. The whole is a lottery in the strictest sense of the word.

By autumn, Dugmore got even more frustrated and moved to a new spot. The diamonds always seemed to be coming up on the opposite side of the river, he complained, even though he spent six days out of every week in the backbreaking task of building dams and washing gravel. But Dugmore had clearly been stricken with that universal fixation of diamond fields everywhere—"miner's disease"—even though his total haul had been three stones of no more than a carat each.

Thousands of others were just as dauntless. A man named J. E. Fannin saw constant disasters—locusts ate through his food supply and his tent was blown over by windstorms—while constantly worrying his young daughter would not even remember him when he returned. He promised to come home by the spring of 1871, but then sold his tent and oxen in April for just one more try. Near a spot called Dutoitspan where some stones had been found, a digger named Richard Jackson came across a tall, laconic Boer on the weedlands. The stranger said his name was Cornelius and showed Jackson his small collection of diamonds. He had been given permission to search by the dour brothers who owned the land—Johannes and D. A. De Beer—in exchange for a quarter of what he found.

Did anybody else know about this? Jackson asked.

No, said Cornelius, he was the only one.

Jackson dashed back to the river camp, threw his equipment into the back of the wagon under a tarp, and announced loudly to anybody who would listen that he was taking a break from mining to go hunt game. He must have been a bad actor, for the next day, a column of ox-drawn wagons was roaring toward the De Beer farm as if the demons of hell were at their tails. Jackson arrived too late to get a good stake. Cornelius grew frightened by the mob and abandoned the area. The De Beer brothers—long-jawed Boers with muttonchop whiskers—watched with disgust as their land was trampled, their vegetables plundered, and their farm covered with thousands of rowdies in search of the next big strike. They tried for a time to collect royalties and finally sold out to a group of investors from Port Elizabeth for £6,000 and left their mud house on the veld forever. It seemed like a sweet deal, for they had purchased the farm for a mere £50. Johannes De Beer would say later his only regret was not asking for a new wagon and some yokes.

The De Beer brothers then disappeared into obscurity, leaving only their name behind on the pit that had swallowed their farm. It was a historical accident that surely would have irritated them. They had cared little for money, but their name would soon be applied to the most ravenous capitalistic empire that Africa had ever seen.

But that was not their doing. That would be the work of a great empire builder.

Cecil John Rhodes, whom Rudyard Kipling would eventually call "the greatest man now living," was born on July 5, 1853, the anemic son of a Hertfordshire minister. He was a desultory student, prone to long periods of silence and dreaming. An early silver nitrate photograph of him at Bishop Stortford School in Essex shows him in a starched cricketer's uniform, sitting on the grass apart from his classmates, staring at the camera with a wan expression. After he suffered a heart attack at seventeen, his parents allowed him to join his brother Herbert on a cotton plantation in South Africa in the belief that the climate would improve his health. Africa did more: the relentless sun and open grasslands had an intoxicating effect on the young Cecil, who saw in them wild and untapped horizons.

Herbert left him in charge of the cotton plantation and thirty natives and departed for the De Beers' farm, where hopeful prospectors were swarming like fire ants. The reports were encouraging and Cecil set off with an oxcart to join his brother. His first job was selling ice cream to the miners. By this time, there were four major digs in the vicinity and the greatest of them was on a low hill to the east of the De Beer brothers' abandoned mud house. In a replay of Erasmus Jacobs's chance find of a *mooi klip*, a Griqua servant named Damon, who had been sent to herd some cows on the hill, stopped to rest under a tree and noticed a glittering stone nearby.

It was as if another cannon shot had gone off. Within two days, more than eight hundred claims had filed on the new hill. Stones of unbelievable size turned up under only a few inches of red earth: 21 carats, 37 carats, 14 carats, 28 carats. Nobody realized at the time that the hill was the top of a volcanic tube carrying some of the most diamond-rich ground ever discovered. The miners took the hill apart by hand and then chased the diamonds downward. Narrow roads bisected the diggings and then collapsed into the ever-widening pit, which soon became known as the "Big Hole." The terraced claims began to resemble the high walls and ladders of a Southwest Indian pueblo. The inevitable saloons sprung up amid the hurdy-gurdy of canvas tents and shacks made of packing crates: Kings Bar, the Old Cock, Cut and Gridiron, Uncle Tom's Cabin. Among them were the stands of the "*kopje* wallopers"—diamond buyers whose stands often masked large-scale fencing operations for stolen goods. The frontier boomtown acquired the name New Rush, and then, in a touch of politically minded class, renamed itself Kimberley after the sitting colonial secretary in London.

At sixty feet down, the loose yellow soil of the pit gave way to a harder "blue ground." A new method of mining had to be developed. Wooden platforms were built around the lip of the pit and buckets made of rawhide were taken up and down from the individual claims by pulley mechanisms. The cobweb of lines extending into the hole resembled the strings of a gigantic shimmering harp: it was said to be an unforgettable sight under the moonlight. Hundreds of tons of rich "blue ground" were hauled up painstakingly by hand. But there was no reliable water nearby, so the diamond hustlers had to sort through gravel without washing it. A small creek called the Dutoitspan became severely overtaxed. One miner reported that a body was discovered floating upstream; the color of the unfortunate man's skin had changed from black to white after nine days of submersion. "Imagine our feelings when we reflected on the pollution of the water we had been drinking with enjoyment for over a week," he said. Soda water hauled in from Cape Town became cheaper than real water, and some went so far as to bathe in it.

Cecil Rhodes had been traveling between Europe and South Africa, but in the midst of the chaos, he now saw an opportunity. He had already made himself a tidy profit renting out the only machine pump during summer floods and had bought up some claims of his own in both the De Beers and Kimberley mines. He saw that amalgamation of the checkerboard of mining claims into one giant company could bring huge benefits: lowered labor costs, greater machination, and vastly increased production. In 1880, Rhodes formed the De Beers Mining Company out of a stitchwork of claims, many of them choked by wall collapses and flooding. The days of the wildcat mines were coming to a close; what was now needed was a strong infusion of capital to build shafts and plants. Rhodes and his partners laid out a grand plan with two key features: They would rip all of the pulleys and wires out of the pits and replace them with more efficient underground tunnels; and black workers would be confined to on-site barracks to cut down on the illicit diamond trade thriving in Kimberley.

With £2.5 million in financing from a Paris bank, they set about trying to buy out all the claims. But nothing went right. Squabbles erupted over the valuation of different parts of ground and the scheme collapsed after the French backers grew wary. Rhodes, undaunted, continued his buying spree of smaller companies and plotted his comeback.

One other would-be diamond lord stood in his way. Barnett "Barney" Barnato, the chairman of Kimberley Central, was a character every bit as cunning as Rhodes, though from a notably different background. Rhodes had come from stilted Anglican bourgeois, whereas Barney was a street tough and bartender from London's East End who had come to Kimberley with forty boxes of cheap cigars he sold fraudulently as "Havanas." He loved boxing and crib, hookers and dirty stories, and could recite Hamlet's entire "To be or not to be" soliloquy while standing on his hands. But Barnato's real passion was diamonds.

His key insight concerned the unstable "blue ground" turning up at sixty feet. It was not as rich as the topsoil and claim prices began to fall amid a general belief that the hole was playing out. But Barney tended to believe a new theory—later proved correct—that volcanic soil was a host rock for diamonds. All those stones in the Big Hole must be coming from a "tube in the earth," reasoned Barnato, and he quickly raised £3,000 to buy as much of the unseen tube as he could. By 1887, he and Rhodes had emerged as the two strongest players in Kimberley. A fight between them was guaranteed.

"Externally, the difference between Rhodes and Barnato was most marked," wrote Gardner Williams, an American mining engineer and the longtime general manager of De Beers, who knew both magnates in their youth. "The little, chunky, bullet-headed, near-sighted Hebrew taking a hand in current sport or traffic, and the tall thoughtful young overseer, sitting moodily on a bucket, deaf to the chatter and rattle around him, and fixing his blue eyes intently on his work or some fabric of his brain, were as unlike as two men could possibly be."

What followed for these two towering personalities was a race to buy out the other. It was high-stakes opera buffa for nearly everybody in South Africa. With the assistance of his canny manager, Alfred Beit, Rhodes traveled to London and solicited the help of the venture capitalist Nathan Rothschild. His target was the one unsecured concession in Barnato's Big Hole, which was owned by an outfit called Cie Française des Mines de Diamant du Cap, but known to all as the French Company. Barnato was able to make a higher offer and Rhodes suggested a unique deal: Rather than engage in a destructive bidding war, he, Rhodes, would buy the French Company and then sell it back to Barnato for a paltry £300,000. All he asked in return was a fifth of the outstanding stock in Barnato's company. Barnato couldn't see the downside and agreed.

He hadn't counted on Rhodes's overpowering thirst for control. De Beers' brokers were told to snap up all the outstanding shares in Kimberley Central regardless of cost. The price quadrupled in a month, but Rhodes had now acquired a majority interest and Barnato conceded defeat rather than continue the ruinous competition which had driven down the price of diamonds. One thing stood in the way: a disgruntled group of Kimberley stockholders tried to oppose the sale in court on the grounds that its charter permitted merger only with a "similar company." De Beers, they insisted, was anything but similar. By Rhodes's own admission, the company aimed to do more than mine diamonds. In fact, it aimed to annex other African nations, conduct diplomacy with local chiefs, build railroads, raise a standing army, and even wage war. De Beers, argued the shareholders, was pretty much a law to itself and accountable to no one. The judge agreed and blocked the sale.

Rhodes's response was classic brute politics, South African style. He and Barnato simply dissolved Kimberley Central and immediately reacquired its assets under the umbrella of De Beers for a staggering sum. The £5,338,650 check to the liquidators of Kimberley Central was the largest ever written up to that point. It was the keystone moment of the diamond trade; nothing forward would ever be the same, nor would the market for stones ever be as unencumbered. De Beers now aimed for nothing less than to become, as Rhodes told his shareholders on March 31, 1888, "the richest, the greatest and the most powerful company the world has ever seen."

With 90 percent of the world's diamond supply under his thumb, Rhodes threw thousands out of work. Nearly a quarter of Kimberley's white workers lost their jobs, and half of the blacks. More important, he and the De Beers directors instituted two policies that would define the way diamonds were sold for the next 125 years—policies that continue to echo today. First, he cut mining production by nearly half, creating an artificial scarcity that sent the price of diamonds climbing skyward. Second, De Beers instituted a single channel for distributing the world's stones: they were sold exclusively to a small ring of selected middlemen in London known as "the Syndicate." It was the forerunner of today's sightholder system. The price of diamonds nearly doubled within a year.

At the mines, meanwhile, labor policies began to crystallize that would play a fundamental role in shaping the apartheid society of twentieth-century South Africa. The British colonial authorities were persuaded to enact a Pass Law in Kimberley—officially color-blind, but enforced only against blacks—requiring all "servants" to carry a document stating their legal right to work in a particular area, their wage, their work history, and their current employer. Any white or policeman could see it on demand; violators were jailed or fined. Black miners were forced to strip nude at the end of their shift to have their orifices probed for stolen diamonds, an indignity not forced on their white colleagues. When the managers felt the stealing had gotten too rampant, compounds with iron-barred walls were built next to the mine shafts. Black diggers were forced to live inside for the length of their contract. Conditions were predictably miserable: twenty men to a room, filthy latrines, cold slop eaten out of wooden buckets. The son of a compound worker remembered the dismal scene at one of Rhodes's mines in 1901: "My father was serving a term in a Kimberley mine, which meant he remained in the compound for at least six months, never emerging until his term was over. Once a month, he would come to the gate to see relatives, but at a distance across a fence, as in a prison."

Rhodes was burned in effigy by unemployed miners in Kimberley and cursed in the local newspapers. "He takes no interest in the community whatsoever, except where his selfish interests are concerned," fulminated one. But it did not hurt his political clout in Cape Town, or at Westminster. He was held up as a model imperialist and a favorite of Queen Victoria. When he visited Windsor Castle, she asked him: "What are you engaged on at present, Mr. Rhodes?" His answer was of the first water: "I am doing my best to enlarge Your Majesty's dominions."

He was good for his word. Having made a fortune on the vanity of others, he now sought to expand his own vanity, under cover of the British Empire, into the heart of the African continent. He convinced Parliament to let him charter a company to acquire mining and farming rights in a region to the north called Matabeleland, near the ruins of a vanished city the natives called Great Zimbabwe. Gold reefs had recently been discovered there. Rhodes promptly secured the new territories by dispatching a column of troops to clear the area of restive natives and establish the out-post capital of Salisbury. "Please understand that it is no personal avarice which desires this," he wrote to a London newspaper, "but, as you know, gold hastens the development of a country more than anything." In more candid moments, he dismissed his critics by saying, "I prefer land to nig-gers!"

Three years after the invasion, the chief Lobengula—who had been duped into signing away his own lands—died in the midst of an uprising against the mercenary forces dispatched by Rhodes. One of his last acts was to send his pursuers a bag of gold sovereigns along with a note: "White man, I am conquered. Take this and go back." There was no chance of that. Matabeleland was now an undisputed possession of the British. Settlers poured in and railroads and telegraphs were quickly built to link the colonies with the outside world. The newspapers started call-ing the new region "Rhodesia" for its conqueror. The name stuck. Cecil Rhodes had become one of the only people in world history to stamp his name on a sovereign nation.

He found this immensely satisfying, for nothing concerned Rhodes more than his legacy. The man so critical to laying the foundation for the twentieth-century tradition of the diamond engagement ring never got married himself and may even have died a virgin. "I hope you will not get married," he once wrote to a friend in Hertfordshire. "I hate people get-ting married. They simply become machines and have no ideas beyond their respective spouses and their offspring." Rhodes's real passion in life was the extension of the British Empire; the diamonds were only useful tools. A map of Africa hung in the head offices of De Beers and Rhodes used to stare at it intently. To one visitor, he proclaimed: "I want to see all of that red," meaning British red. To another visitor, in a moment of worry about his beloved Rhodesia, he plaintively inquired: "They can't take it away from me, can they? You never heard of country's name being changed?" In his will, he set aside part of his fortune to endow the famous scholarship program at Oxford for students who showed both intellectual and physical prowess—future imperialists, in other words. He once told a friend he expected to be remembered more than four thousand years af-ter his death. In his private letters, Rhodes's thoughts ricochet wildly from one grandiosity to the next, with barely time for explanation, or even coherent grammar. In one, he fantasized about bringing England's lost colonies back into the fold, and outlined what was perhaps his ultimate vision:

> After my death still perhaps if that name is coupled with the object of England everywhere and united the name may convey the discovery of an idea which ultimately leads to the cessation of all wars and one language throughout the world the patent being the gradual absorption of wealth and human minds of the higher order to the object. What an awful thought it is that if we had not lost America or if even now we could arrange with the present members of the United States Assembly and our House of Commons the peace of the world as seemed for all eternity—we could hold your federal Parliament five years at Washington and five at London—the only thing possible to carry this out is a secret [society] gradually absorbing the wealth of the world to be determined to such an object.

What he had in mind was nothing less than a new world order financed by diamonds and other mineral wealth—a kind of *Pax Diamantes* that would bring all mankind under the sway of a small circle of elite men who had hoarded all the claims. He failed to achieve that, but diamonds had helped him create the modern nation of South Africa, as well as the colossus of De Beers that lives on today with much of the imperialist spirit he breathed into it; the philosophy of a roaring camp applied to the rest of the world. Rhodes died of a heart attack at his house in Cape Town on March 26, 1902. His true monument is not Rhodesia—a name now vanished from the map—but the twinkling rocks sold at outrageously inflated prices at nearly every jewelry store on earth.

As for Erasmus Stephanus Jacobs, the Boer farmboy who started it all, his find of the *mooi klip* was as close as he came to getting rich. He worked in the fields during the Kimberley rush, found nothing but dirt, and then went on to father eight children, only four of whom survived. One of his sons got a job tending black prisoners for the De Beers cartel. When Jacobs was in his eighties and in poverty, the citizens of Kimberley took up a collection for him totaling £30. He wound up telling the story over and over of the day when he became curious at the sight of a glinting pebble spotted from under a tree. Diamonds had brought him nothing at all, he said in a statement dictated at the end of his life, in 1934. "I have not received anything whatsoever from the Cape or the Union government or from any company or person as a reward for my share of bringing to light the presence of the diamond fields in South Africa, which I am told have already produced gems of a total value of over £300,000,000."

Somebody once asked the longtime twentieth-century chairman of De Beers, Harry Oppenheimer, if he had any preference between gold and diamonds. "Yes, diamonds every time," said Harry. "I think people buy diamonds out of vanity and they buy gold because they're too stupid to think of any other monetary system which will work—and I think vanity is a more attractive motive than stupidity."

De Beers' lock on the world's vanity could only be kept intact through a strict policy of either co-opting or sabotaging new diamond mines. In fact, throughout the twentieth century, the cartel spent almost as much energy *suppressing* production as it did actually producing. "Whenever you hear that a new mine has been discovered, if De Beers are not there, they are very near," Cecil Rhodes once said. He did not mean that company geologists were looking for neighboring kimberlite; he meant that De Beers' agents were trying to seduce or intimidate the owners into selling out.

Nobody forgot the lesson of the Premier Mine, one of De Beers' greatest early failures. In 1902, a bricklayer named Thomas Cullinan claimed to have found a deposit outside the gold rush town of Johannesburg. The cartel's official posture was one of skepticism. Rhodes's replacement as chairman, Francis Oats, went so far as to accuse Cullinan of the oldest mining scam in the book—"salting" the ground with diamonds to make a barren property look fertile. When Alfred Beit went out for a closer look, however, he saw immediately the gravity of the situation. The pipe was gargantuan and Tom Cullinan was obstinate about selling to De Beers. How did he know he'd be getting a fair price from the cartel, given its well-deserved reputation for deception? He made an independent marketing deal with a pair of young diamond dealers named Bernard and Ernest Oppenheimer. Soon the recalcitrant mine was producing 1.9 million carats a year—almost equal to the output of *all* of De Beers' South African mines put together.

The deposit even yielded a magnificent surprise: a chunk of pure diamond the size of a softball. "The Cullinan Diamond," as it was called, remains the largest ever discovered. A decoy was sent to London on board an ocean liner amid much pomp and press coverage while the real one was quietly sent in an unmarked package through the regular mail. A Belgian craftsman studied it obsessively for nine months and, after he struck the first chisel blow, fainted dead away. The mammoth rock was cut and polished into nine jewels. The largest, the 530-carat "Great Star of Africa," is now set into the royal scepter of the crown jewels of Great Britain. Further damage to De Beers' position was headed off only by the outbreak of World War I. The Cullinans' share price fell as the appetite for diamonds evaporated in a darkening Europe. De Beers was able to finally absorb its rival in 1914 after being forced for more than a decade to cut its own production to keep prices stable.

The Cullinan episode was not the last piece of trouble that Ernest Oppenheimer would mete out to De Beers. The shrewd young negotiator had been born in Germany, the son of a cigar manufacturer, and had found his calling as a teenager when he took a job sorting diamonds. Unlike Cecil Rhodes, who saw the stones merely as gamepieces for the expansion of empire, Oppenheimer caught a little of the romantic dream that De Beers was working so hard to promote. The gems had a hold on him and he worked through the night peering at each one through a loupe, watching them twinkle and fire under gaslight. "To him, each had a personality of its own," wrote his biographer, Anthony Hocking. "No two were the same. He literally fell in love with diamonds."

The boss was Anton Dunklesbuhler—"Old Dunkels," as his protégés called him—a member of the powerful London Syndicate; a man of large girth and titanic temper who once bawled out Ernest for spilling a pot of ink on his head. But he took a liking to the young gem sorter nevertheless, and when it came time to replace the firm's agent at the mouth of the mines in Kimberley, it was twenty-two-year-old Ernest who got the job. The senior man he was replacing, Leon Soutro, got a taste of Oppenheimer's confidence in a curt telegram sent in advance of his arrival: "Meet me at the station to look after luggage."

In the boomtown atmosphere of South Africa, where politics and mining have always been close cousins, if not actually interchangeable, the good-looking diamond man from London won a reputation for exacting speech and manners, as well as having what was said to be the most muscular pair of arms in town. He was cut from different cloth than the schemers and glad-handing strivers who had dominated Kimberley since the time of the rush on the Big Hole. Oppenheimer got himself elected mayor within a decade. He also displayed a firm grasp of the principle that had made De Beers into a giant, and had lifted South Africa to unlikely prominence. "Common sense tells us that the only way to increase the value of diamonds is to make them scarce, that is to reduce the production," he said in 1910. But Ernest Oppenheimer understood that the flip side of this maxim was De Beers' greatest weakness: any new diamond deposits operating outside of the cartel's control could spell disaster.

World War I ended the Cullinan threat, but helped create a new one. The Germans abandoned their colony in Southwest Africa—a sandy coastal region now known as Namibia—and the nation of South Africa wasted no time in claiming it as a protectorate. Inside the colony, near the mouth of the Orange River, was a sere alluvial plain approximately the size of South Carolina which produced remarkably transparent diamonds. The Germans had called this area *Sperreegebiet*—"the Forbidden Area." Ships were prone to wreck here on their way around the Cape and their curved skeletons rotted on the shore amid millions of buried carats. After the war, the German owners of the field found themselves in an awkward position. Their possessions were certain to be annexed by South Africa and their claims forfeited. They needed a friendly buyer who could liquidate them quickly. Oppenheimer stepped in ahead of De Beers with the right mechanism in hand. With the help of the U.S. secretary of commerce, Herbert Hoover, who had introduced him to the powerful financing house of J.P. Morgan, he had formed a gold-mining company called Anglo-American which could tap deep wells of ready cash. The Namibian fields went to Oppenheimer for the bargain price of £3.5 million. The Forbidden Area was soon funneling a huge stream of gems to the London market outside of De Beers' control. It was the Cullinan fiasco all over again.

In 1921, Ernest was knighted by George V of England and three years later he won election to South Africa's Parliament. His Anglo-American company prospered in the booming 1920s and spun off a web of subsidiaries so varied that the organization came to be known by investors as "the Octopus." But Sir Ernest had one ultimate objective in mind. Using a favorite tactic of Rhodes, he mopped up all the outstanding shares of his enemy that he could find. By the end of the decade, he was too strong and his target was too weak. The De Beers board of directors relented on December 20, 1929, and elected Sir Ernest Oppenheimer their chairman. He wrapped his Anglo-American company into the De Beers cartel. Once again, virtually the entire output of diamonds in the world was in the hands of one man.

Only one thing could challenge the supremacy of De Beers and that was the discovery of a new vein of diamonds in a place it could not reach. Just such a lode had been found in 1906 by a farmer in an Arkansas hog pasture. But a series of strange events retarded its development as a mine and it never produced more than a trickle of diamonds, despite its potential. This was a source of great mystery and frustration to its investors. The events led many—including the U.S. government—to suspect that De Beers had sabotaged the development of the best pipe of diamond-bearing magma ever found in America.

The story began in the railroad town of Murfreesboro, Arkansas, where a jug-eared farmer named John Wesley Huddleston signed with an *X* to buy a patch of undulating land along a creek. He was putting out some salt licks for his hogs one morning when something caught his eye: flecks of what looked like gold winking in the ground in front of him. Huddleston washed a load of the dirt at the house and came up not with gold, but two transparent pebbles. When he put them to his knife-sharpening wheel, he couldn't put a scratch on them. Instead, the stones carved a deep groove in the metal. Whatever they were, they were harder than any rocks Huddleston had ever seen. Excited, he showed them to a clerk at the local bank named Jesse Riley, who offered him fifty cents for the unusual stones. "Hell no, Jesse," replied Huddleston in his reed-voiced twang. "These are deemints and I got a whole field of them!"

The state geologist came out for a look and told the local newspapers that perhaps $100 million worth of diamonds were in the ground near Murfreesboro. It seemed that Huddleston's hog pasture was atop a volcanic tube perhaps 100 million years old. It was the rarest of geological formations—the type of kimberlite that contains diamonds. The pipe was said to have a surface expression almost as good as anything ever seen in South Africa. After the findings were confirmed by scientists from the U.S. Geological Survey and the Smithsonian Institution, a group of Arkansas investors led by a banker named Sam Reyburn bought the farm for $36,000. Huddleston insisted on being paid entirely in twenty-dollar bills. With this windfall, and with the later sale of a Bull Durham tobacco pouchful of diamonds, he bought a new Model T Ford and married a blond woman described only as a "carnival girl from Arkadelphia." One evening while she and Huddleston were out driving, he stopped off at the drugstore to buy a cigar and she took off in the Model T, never to be seen again. The rest of his money, he put in a safe that he never figured out how to work; when somebody accidentally shut and locked it, Huddleston simply drew his pistol and shot the dial off.

The prospects looked boundless for America's only diamond pipe. Ten thousand prospectors flooded into the area and pitched their tents all along Prairie Creek. The state of Arkansas went so far as to incorporate the shape of a diamond in a redesigned state flag. The farmer next door, a man named Millard Mauney, found part of the ore body on a wedge of his property and started charging onlookers fifty cents to hunt for diamonds in the black gumbo topsoil. He also laid out a townsite with street names like Topaz, Ruby, and Garnet, and advertised lots by having a small diamond embedded in one of his front teeth. He had a dentist take it out after he grew tired of people asking him to smile.

Reyburn and his partners, meanwhile, formed the Arkansas Diamond Company and hired a former De Beers engineer named John T. Fuller to run their operation. Things went smoothly at first. They built a pump station and a boiler, drilled test holes, scraped away soil with railroad-grading equipment, and recovered more than 1,400 diamonds from the top crust. Then the trouble started. The processing plant, for one thing, was letting thousands of diamonds go unrecovered because it was pushing the ore through too fast. Better equipment was needed and most of the best technology was in South Africa. Early in 1910, Reyburn sailed to London for a fund-raising trip aboard the ocean liner *Kaiser Wilhelm*. He was approached by a pair of South African bankers named Isaac Lewis and Samuel Marks, veterans of the Kimberley rush, who, Reyburn noted, "wined me and dined me for three weeks before telling me they wanted full control" of the Arkansas mine in exchange for their financing. The proposal began to look stranger when Reyburn learned that the mining director for the firm Lewis & Marks was none other than Bernard Oppenheimer, brother of Ernest. The bankers finally suggested a deal: They would buy a $250,000 option in the mine and pay Reyburn a $50,000 salary if he would only shut the property down. Reyburn felt strongly, however, that a working diamond mine would be a boon for poor Arkansans and declined the offer. He said years later he believed Lewis and Marks to be "agents for De Beers."

What happened next, however, has fed suspicion in Arkansas for generations. John T. Fuller—the former De Beers man who couldn't seem to build a decent washing plant—resigned his position. Reyburn said he was unable to raise any money for better equipment and closed the mine in 1912. And then his career took off. He was hired for a highly paid executive position at the Lord & Taylor department store on Fifth Avenue in Manhattan. The store was then owned by the textile firm Claflin Co., which had been bankrolled by J.P. Morgan, the primary financier for Ernest Oppenheimer's Anglo-American company. Reyburn wrote a book called *Selling Home Furnishing Successfully* and ran the fledgling Arkansas mine out of his office in the department store in midtown Manhattan. If he hadn't been bribed, it sure looked like he had.

When the price of diamonds climbed after the end of World War I, Reyburn hired a geologist from the Michigan College of Mines named Stanley H. Zimmerman to restart the operations in Arkansas. Zimmerman had thin lips and rarely smiled and he immediately rubbed the locals the wrong way. They derided him as a "Yankee" out to enforce his own ideas, and he did seem like a man in a hurry. He helped build a five-story main plant, an oil house, a machine shop, and a water tank. But once again, mechanical problems intervened. The plant seemed incapable of breaking down the hard clay where the diamonds were embedded. Dirt was balling up and passing over the grease tables in great clumps and unknown thousands of diamonds were being lost. A mining engineer named George W. Vitt complained that the mill was of an inefficient type that had long been phased out of use in South Africa. The waste rock coming out of the plant was incredibly rich in diamonds, he said.

On the neighboring plot of land, meanwhile, things were going no better. Mauney had leased his chunk of the diamond pipe to a father-and-son team of amateur geologists from Minnesota named Austin and Howard Millar. They worked their plot for all it was worth, building a small mine railroad to take their ore for washing in Prairie Creek and recovering thousands of quality diamonds. But mysterious fires kept erupting in their facilities, enough for their insurance policy to be canceled. Somebody poisoned ten of their chickens. Blasts of gunfire kept coming from the nearby woods and narrowly missing Howard Millar. And on the night of January 13, 1919, their nightwatchman was lured away from his post by an attractive woman. "She wasn't a native of the area and her reputation wasn't good," wrote Howard Millar later. "We did not doubt that she was paid to entice the watchman to leave the plant so the arsonists could set fire to it." Four separate fires were lit in different parts of the mine, destroying the entire complex. Suspicion fell upon Mauney, with whom Millar had tangled repeatedly in court. But Mauney received a 25 percent royalty on all the diamonds recovered, so he would have been acting in severe opposition to his own interests by torching the plant. The loss was total. Nobody was ever prosecuted for the crime and the Millar family never again tried to mine diamonds on a large scale.

The Reyburn plant was also taken out of commission the next year, and also under suspicious circumstances. In March 1921, Zimmerman was summoned to a meeting at the J. P. Morgan offices in New York. Among those present were Sam Reyburn, J. P. Morgan's mining administrator, and Sir Ernest Oppenheimer himself, recently knighted and a close ally of De Beers, though not yet its chairman. What was said at this meeting has never been revealed, but as soon as it was over, Zimmerman sent a telegram to his chief engineer in Murfreesboro that read: "Developments this evening lead to closure of the mine for awhile. . . . Have Scotty put things in best shape for long shutdown. . . . Get all records and other data in good shape so I can quickly go over them." Work stopped immediately, and sixty-five men were promptly fired. Zimmerman reviewed the written records at the mine site and told his remaining employees to burn them all. He then traveled to England and South Africa for several months, where he met once more with Ernest Oppenheimer. Asked what he was doing there, he claimed to have been studying De Beers' mining techniques for later use in Arkansas. But they were never put into practice. Fires leveled the facility and Zimmerman later took a lucrative job with J. P. Morgan.

Things lay quiet in Arkansas until the outbreak of World War II, when diamond-tipped tools suddenly became crucial for cutting parts for tank engines and airplanes. With the German invasion of North Africa and U-boats prowling the shipping lanes, it appeared that the United States was in danger of losing its primary source of industrial diamonds in the Belgian Congo. De Beers had control over these deposits through marketing deals made through a tangled web of subsidiaries, including shadow companies like Koffiefontein Mines, Cape Coast Exploration Company, Premier Diamond Mining, and New Jaegersfontein Mining & Exploration Company. More than 40 million surplus carats had been hoarded to keep prices high during the depression. The strategy had been wildly successful: De Beers was able to resolve all its bond debt and pay huge annual dividends to its investors after being in arrears for several years. It entered the war years in splendid financial health, with direct control of 95 percent of the world's diamond supply.

Those stockpiled gems were now considered critical to fighting the Nazis, but the cartel refused to sell them to American arms factories. Its logic was this: If the United States was allowed to build up a reserve and the war should suddenly end, all those diamonds would be sold off as surplus and crash the market. This was intolerable.

In 1940, as the Nazis overran the diamond-trading centers of Europe, Sir Ernest Oppenheimer traveled to New York to make an offer to the Army-Navy Munitions Board. De Beers would agree to sell 1 million carats, an amount far below the original request for 10 million carats. In return, Oppenheimer asked for an exemption to prosecution under the Sherman Act and permission to form a branch of his London Syndicate to do business in the lucrative American market. But Oppenheimer balked at allowing a cache of diamonds inside the borders of the United States. He would agree only to create a reserve under its own control in Canada in case London should fall to the Germans. The meeting resolved nothing. De Beers continued to dribble out a limited supply of industrials at sky-high prices. "The Diamond Syndicate will not sell us a stockpile because it will not tolerate large stocks outside its monopoly control," concluded a U.S. government memo.

A series of advertisements ran in American magazines to ensure a steady business in romantic diamonds through the war. The hypocrisy was nothing short of breathtaking. Women were told that they could actually help the war effort by continuing to ask for diamond engagement rings. Any impediment in the flow of diamonds to the United States must be due to the fact that Americans simply weren't buying enough jewelry, according to one 1943 ad in the *Saturday Evening Post*, which said this about industrials: "The occasional gem diamonds found among them help defray production costs for all these little 'fighting' diamonds. Consequently, there are no restrictions on the sale of diamond gems." In the trade magazine *Department Store Economist*, store managers were advised to reassure women that buying a diamond was not an unpatriotic act: "To the chagrin of our enemy, our side controls almost the entire supply of another kind of diamond to do the countless jobs of speed and skill in pouring out armaments. . . . Your lovely gemstone has helped put them to work!"

President Franklin D. Roosevelt became angry with the foot-dragging and ordered the Justice Department to investigate possible violations of antitrust laws. And thus commenced a long period of antagonism between De Beers and the U.S. government that has had profound effects on the way diamonds are sold today. Finding a way to nail the Syndicate, in fact, became something like a religion in the Justice Department, where De Beers was regarded as both arrogant and deceptive. But in order to make an antitrust case stick, the government first had to prove De Beers was "doing business" within the borders of the United States. It was a hard burden to overcome, as De Beers had skirted antitrust penalties for years by simply using the sightholder system to sell gems to independent wholesalers. *They* were the ones bringing the stones into America—not De Beers. There seemed to be nothing the federal government could do about it.

It was soon learned, however, that the advertising agency N. W. Ayer & Son did more for the cartel than just create sentimental advertisements. Justice attorneys found a gem dealer named Louis Baumgold who told them he had secretly purchased a large quantity of cut diamonds out of the Ayer offices in Rockefeller Plaza. Ayer also purportedly leased office space for the cartel on the eleventh floor of the RCA Building and furnished regular reports to Johannesburg about the state of the U.S. diamond market. Moreover, De Beers maintained dozens of accounts under various names at American banks and stored millions of dollars' worth of gems at the Chase Safe Deposit Co. Harry Winston told investigators that "a most vicious system was operated by the London Syndicate, but that apparently nothing could be done about it in this country." The government thought otherwise. In January 1945 it filed suit, charging De Beers with "conspiring to restrain and monopolize the foreign trade of the United States."

In the course of gathering information for the lawsuit, the Justice Department sent investigators down to Arkansas to learn why the best opportunity to create a homegrown diamond source had been botched so thoroughly. They found a pattern of events that seemed to suggest foreign sabotage, but came up with nothing definitive. A Justice lawyer named Herbert Berman examined the closest thing the government had to a smoking gun—a letter sent by Stanley Zimmerman after that suspicious meeting with Oppenheimer in March 1921. "Several strange things have occurred which I will relate *personally* to you on return," Zimmerman had written to one of his employees. "I am sure you will be surprised and intrigued to hear Sir E.O.'s views which I feel are extraordinary and unique."

Berman had no insight on what those "views" might have been, but as he concluded in a January 6, 1944, memo to his boss: "An inference could be drawn from Zimmerman's letter, the order to destroy the records and Vit's [*sic*] testimony regarding the mill, that the property was sabotaged and then closed at the insistence of Sir Ernest Oppenheimer." But Berman added a qualifying statement that admitted the case for dirty playing in Arkansas was not airtight: "On the other hand the facts are consistent with an inference that the company sought financial assistance from Oppenheimer which was refused and the mine closed because operation was unprofitable." It is difficult to believe, however, that Oppenheimer would have bankrolled any mining endeavor without demanding total control; such a move would have gone against every principle that had made the cartel what it was.

Nothing about the murky situation in Arkansas was ever proved. A federal district court ruled against the claim that De Beers was, in fact, "doing business" in the United States and the lawsuit stalled. But the threat lingered. De Beers' executives were barred from entering the United States under threat of being forced to answer questions under deposition. The Arkansas pipe, meanwhile, never did become a mine. A series of investors, including an airplane manufacturer and a Texas oil field baron, tried and failed to make a profit on the site after the war. No serious attempt to strip away the surface layer of lamproite was ever made. The best way to make money out of the Murfreesboro lode, it turned out, was to do what farmer Mauney did and simply charge amateur rockhounds a few dollars to pick around in the topsoil.

The Millar family tapped into the honky-tonk roadside culture of the 1950s and put up a forest of highway signs advertising their "Number One Tourist Attraction of the World." The rule was simple: What tourists found, they could keep. Fox Movietone came out and shot a newsreel of the grand opening. Things really took off after Mrs. Arthur "Winnie" Parker of Dallas found a gorgeous 15.31-carat stone casually exposed in the top layer of dirt. She had it polished and called it "the Star of

Arkansas." Howard Millar was invited to be a guest on the national TV show *I've Got a Secret* and twice on Johnny Carson's *Who Do You Trust?* The failed diamond mine became Arkansas' version of the alligator-wrestling dens that populated Florida's highways in the same era. Despite his success as a roadside entrepreneur, Howard Millar never gave up his belief that De Beers had sabotaged the property by buying off Sam Reyburn in London and ordering Stanley Zimmerman to build a faulty mill. Amid declining attendance at the "Number One Tourist Attraction" in 1972, the state of Arkansas bought all the land surrounding the pipe and turned it into a state park. The rule remains the same: finder's keepers. And suspicion lingers today among some people in Arkansas that shadowy forces from overseas had cheated them out of something wonderful.

One evening in March, in a convenience store across the street from the squat Pike County Courthouse, I met with someone who thinks the sabotage theory is ridiculous. Dean Banks is a man nearing seventy, with a pencil mustache and long fingernails. He once wrote a long academic paper on the pro-fascist propagandists of the 1930s and he has no tolerance for what he calls "demagoguery." He believes Howard Millar and others were exploiting the native insecurity of rural Arkansans by pointing to De Beers as the reason why the diamonds never showed up. Geology alone was to blame, he told me. Test bores drilled in 1993 seemed to indicate the pipe was shaped like a champagne glass—wide on the top, but tapering down to a narrow shaft. This created what Banks called a "surface bonanza" and explained why the commercial operations always failed.

"There's hard evidence that Howard Millar was a promoter and a mythmaker and his primary obligation was promoting his own interests," Banks said as we sat at an orange booth near the soft drink section. "The diamonds were never there in great numbers."

There are many people who disagree with this assessment, however, and one of them is J. Michael Howard, who has worked for thirty years as a geologist for the state of Arkansas. He wrote a report in 1999 that condemned most of the bore testing as superficial. The champagne glass analogy doesn't hold up, he told me. The lower regions of the deposit are much bigger. "There has never been a proper bulk sampling test out there," he said. "Parts of that pipe could be very lean, true, but parts could be very rich. We'll never know because the state of Arkansas has passed a law stating that there will never be any commercial exploration out there again."

I went out to the Crater of Diamonds State Park for a look and was shown around by the park's assistant superintendent, a genial man named Bill Henderson who used to teach earth science and coach football at Murfreesboro High School. We walked past furrows of black soil where dozens of tourists in T-shirts and knee socks were picking at the ground with rented shovels. "I'd say the average time that people spend here is about two hours," said Henderson. "They don't find anything and then they get bored." The park sees the occasional hard-luck visitor come in complaining about a mountain of debt, and voicing the hope that a big diamond score will solve their problems. They invariably get nothing but dirty.

Henderson showed me the skeleton of a processing mill that had been built in 1946 and shut down shortly thereafter because of disappointing results. It was now surrounded by a second-growth forest of oak and pine. I stood on a barren concrete platform and asked Henderson why he thought the lode had never amounted to much, despite all the geologic promise.

"Was there sabotage out here? Oh, there's no question about it," he said. "Who did it is anybody's guess. But De Beers had the most motivation of anybody."

Sir Ernest Oppenheimer always had a love of detective stories and spy thrillers. One of his favorite authors late in life was Ian Fleming, the creator of the James Bond series, who had traveled to Africa to research a new novel. The resulting work, *Diamonds Are Forever*, told the story of a criminal mastermind smuggling diamonds to Las Vegas with the help of a shady dentist and a femme fatale named Tiffany Case. It was standard Bond fare, heavy on the gimmicks and the girls, but what most readers didn't know was that Fleming's inspiration came courtesy of a real-life intelligence network set up by Sir Ernest himself.

Diamonds have always made attractive targets for thieves and smugglers: they are easy to conceal and even harder to trace, and can carry value more densely than any other substance on earth. Nearly half the output of the Kimberley mines had been lost to "illicit diamond buying," or what the locals called IDB, and circumstances in the new century were not significantly more honest. De Beers' mines in Angola, Congo, and Tanganyika were primary sources for the black market and it appeared the inventory loss went beyond the occasional stone tucked under a tongue or inside an ear. The sheer amounts pointed to a pattern of sophisticated inside jobs. Even worse, the illegal stones competed with the legal ones and drove prices downward—a state of affairs that could not be brooked. Entire milk bottles full of West African diamonds wound up in Belgium at prices as low as one-twentieth of what De Beers was asking.

Ernest's son Harry thought he had the answer. He had served in a British intelligence unit during the war and had helped unravel coded Nazi cables sent from Rommel's front lines in North Africa. Harry had also made the acquaintance of Sir Percy Sillitoe, the legendary pipe-smoking head of MI-5, who had recently retired. Why not recruit England's master spy to run a secret squad of diamond police? Sillitoe was tracked to a country town in Sussex where he was selling toffee and chocolates to suburban housewives over the counter of a sweetshop. The shop belonged to his son, explained Percy, and he had pitched in for something to occupy his time.

Sillitoe was persuaded to come out of retirement and work for the Octopus. He toured some of Africa's worst thieves' kitchens and identified Dakar, Antwerp, Beirut, and other cities as key smuggling junctions. In English old-boy style, he recruited some MI-5 colleagues and formed a private agency called the International Diamond Security Organization (IDSO) to crack down on the leakage. Job number one, he decided, was tightening security at the mine sites. X-ray machines were installed at the perimeters and anyone leaving was subject to a scan. One IDSO hand described the process: "If the machine operator saw a black spot in your stomach, for example, he might tell the mine manager and then you'd be put in the hospital and very politely but thoroughly purged." Some of the miners reportedly took to swallowing buttons, pebbles, and other hard objects just to test the efficacy of the machines. Other IDSO agents were sent out to infiltrate the smugglers' networks and figure out who was running the gems to Antwerp. In a case that would foreshadow the "blood diamond" wars of the 1990s, Sillitoe's team tried to figure out how so many gems were mined illegally and shipped out of Sierra Leone bearing false paperwork.

Fleming found all of this irresistible, and after seeking permission from De Beers, was allowed to meet for a week at the fly-specked Minzah Hotel in Tangiers with a top IDSO operative identified only by the pseudonym "John Blaize." The two had plenty to talk about. Fleming was a

neocolonialist of the Cecil Rhodes variety and had served in a naval intelligence unit during the war; Blaize had read and admired several of the
James Bond novels. He regaled Fleming with several stories of midlevel
De Beers employees who had fallen prey to temptation. The lure of
riches, to Blaize, was quite mundane. "He's got no criminal record, but
suddenly he likes the idea of having £50,000 in the bank and perhaps a
Cadillac and a girl-friend in Paris. One day he's honest and during the
night, he suddenly decides to be a crook." One such man was a De Beers
geologist working along the Skeleton Coast of present-day Namibia. The
anonymous agent decided to call the man "Tim Patterson," perhaps to
highlight his point about the banality of evil. At any rate, Patterson was
out there working alone and he started squirreling away some of the best
diamonds in holes he dug next to the shore. He would come back at night
to retrieve them in either a seaplane or speedboat. After he resigned from
the cartel, IDSO was tipped off and began to investigate. When Patterson's plane crashed one night, nearly killing him and the pilot, his racket
was up. Investigators found a buried canister near the beach that contained a stash of 1,400 purloined diamonds. He was sentenced to nine
months hard labor; a relatively light sentence that probably owed a great
deal to the color of his skin.

Fleming produced a quickie nonfiction book entitled *The Diamond
Smugglers*. It must have pleased Sir Ernest enormously, for not only did it
tout the invincibility of the diamond police; it also added to the aura of international glamour and intrigue around diamonds that never hurts the retail price. Fleming even allowed his world-weary hero to feel it. In
Diamonds Are Forever, James Bond examines a polished stone and has an
epiphany: "Now he could understand the passion that diamonds had in-
spired through the centuries, the almost sexual love they aroused among
those who handled them and cut them and traded in them."

The men of the IDSO were not choirboys. Many had come from the
police forces of colonial Africa, where due process was often not high on
the list of priorities. A former South African policeman reportedly wire-
tapped the phones and broke into the houses of suspected smugglers in
the Congo. When these methods proved too subtle, he would beat them
severely. There was also a Liberian shopkeeper named Fouad Kamil,
who had grown angry with the diamond smuggling around Liberia and set
up a vigilante squad to mete out a rough kind of justice. He later claimed
that De Beers had paid him through an intermediary to become a merce-

nary soldier for the diamond empire. Kamil was known for laying mines along smuggling routes and wiping out the survivors with hunting rifles. But De Beers always denied that Fouad—nicknamed "Flash Fred"—was on the payroll, and his credibility was damaged when he tried to hijack an airplane in an attempt to force De Beers to pay him what he said was back wages. He served twenty-one months of hard labor in a Malawi jail for the stunt.

Smuggling was not the only trouble coming from inside the continent. South Africa's leadership had become bitterly divided over the question of its exploding black majority and the shantytowns that ringed the cities and the mine shafts. They were, in large part, the legacy of Cecil Rhodes: diamond and gold mining had done more than any other social factor to destroy tribal life for hundreds of thousands of Zulus, Griqua, Xhosas, and Bechuanas who had been pressured out of their villages to take up the white man's burden of hauling ore. "The native is to be treated as a child and denied the franchise," Rhodes had once told the legislature. "We must adopt a system of despotism, such as works so well in India, in our relations with the barbarians of South Africa." He had laid the foundations for the harsh legal system that later became known as apartheid, if he had not actually created it. With nothing left to exchange but their labor, the blacks of South Africa became virtual slaves to the diamond. Cash wages replaced an agrarian barter economy and squalid brick compounds replaced the mud-and-pole villages. There was no hope of any real advancement in this new world. Miners' pay was usually a third of what the whites received, and they had little chance of promotion to a managerial level or using capital to start their own enterprises.

Segregation had been a fact of life since the first diamond rushes in Kimberley, but apartheid was enshrined into law after the victory of the Afrikaners-dominated National Party in the 1948 elections. The new government convinced whites they were on the brink of a racial emergency and rammed through a package of legislation designed to strengthen the minority's shaky hold on power. Typical was the Prohibition of Mixed Marriages Act, which accomplished exactly what it sounded like, and the Immorality Act, which forbade sexual relations of any kind between whites and nonwhites. Existing marriages and romances were forcibly broken up. Blacks and mulattos were forbidden to own property in most areas, and stripped of the paltry representation they had enjoyed in Parliament. In return, they were given ostensible control of "homelands," a series of districts that comprised less than 13 percent of the nation, and often represented some of the worst real estate available. Frequently they were no more than dry fields with a few water taps poking up from the ground.

Though the De Beers company had unquestionably been the one to benefit the most from cheap black labor through the decades, the Oppenheimer family positioned themselves as liberals on apartheid. Harry Oppenheimer's objection was based on eminently practical grounds: South Africa had simply come too far as a multiracial nation, he said, and to split it up into racial fiefdoms would be suicide. In the last year of his life, 1957, Sir Ernest Oppenheimer took it upon himself to tour a slum community on the edge of Johannesburg and was appalled at the conditions. Knifings and robberies were ordinary; babies were born in the dirt streets; "houses" were shacks of wood and rocks and scrap metal thrown up in concentric mazes, usually around a single filthy faucet. Shocked at a side of his country he was seeing for the first time, Sir Ernest secured a £3 million loan from the Bureau of Mines to build decent housing in one of the worst areas on a patch of gentle hills to the southwest of the city, far from the glass skyscrapers of downtown. "These native people are, in general, the employees of European citizens," he told the newspapers. "It is no more than enlightened self-interest that we should do what we can to ensure that the conditions in which they live should make for healthy, efficient, law-abiding and contented service." From the stones of the cleared shanties, a tower was built near the center of the new housing development to resemble a ruin of the ancient city of Great Zimbabwe, in the neighboring nation that was still called Rhodesia. At the base was a plaque bearing Sir Ernest Oppenheimer's name. It was the tallest structure in the desperate area that took its name from a government acronym: SOuth WEst TOwnship, or Soweto.

Meanwhile, Harry Oppenheimer got himself elected to Parliament and irritated the National Party with speeches that called for a gradual withering of the apartheid laws. Altruism was not his motivation; this was sheer economic survival. "It is plain that, in Africa, we have reached a stage where further physical progress, which is certainly possible, is going to depend more and more on solving the human problems that have been created," he said in one speech. To another audience, he used the word "revulsion" to describe his feelings about the racial repression, and said the government's policies were "in ruins." But critics remarked that De

Beers' policies at the mine sites hardly lived up to the rhetoric, even late into the apartheid era. *Fortune* magazine pointed out in 1982 that blacks at De Beers facilities were not allowed to polish any stones over 1.19 carats, "a typical absurdity of apartheid." Black miners were paid significantly less than whites for the same work, the magazine noted. They were also kept inside compounds, where the conditions were reasonably livable, if humiliating. "The boys had lives of what must have been intense boredom in the isolation, but they are kept clean and well-fed and, by South African standards, well-paid," reported a writer for *The New Yorker* who was given a De Beers–sponsored tour of a compound in 1956.

The segregation was bringing the nation an increasingly bad name on the world stage; but De Beers—part of the mining colossus known derisively as "South Africa, Inc."—still found ways to mop up diamonds from nations that would have otherwise been hostile. Deception was a necessary element, and dummy corporations provided the answer. Marketing agreements were signed with the governments of Angola, Sierra Leone, and Ghana, and the gems funneled though innocuously named outfits in Europe, which turned around and sold the gems back to De Beers at cost. An instant company named Willcroft was set up in the Bahamas to assume a half-ownership of a huge mine in Tanzania. The other half belonged to the black-led government, which could not afford to be publicly linked with a prominent symbol of apartheid. Most spectacularly of all, when geologists in the Soviet Union came across a huge diamond pipe in the Siberian tundra, a De Beers representative flew to Moscow and offered an unprecedented deal: De Beers would buy the entire run of the mine at a guaranteed price for years to come. The transfers would be concealed through a web of holding companies.

The Soviets found the offer too tempting to refuse. The sons of Lenin were in bed with the most antediluvian capitalist enterprise on the planet, true, but the profits—estimated at $25 million a year—bolstered the Kremlin's treasury and helped fund the buildup of nuclear arms and other military technology. The Russian gems went into the vaults under Charterhouse Street. And everybody's hands were clean, at least in public. "This arrangement would give the Soviet delegate license to pound his fist on the tables of the United Nations, denouncing monopoly, condemning the racist capitalists of South Africa, and urging a boycott of the country's exports—even as his country was wholesaling its stones to the enemy," wrote the historian Stefan Kanfer. When the Soviet Union unraveled in 1990, De Beers went back to Moscow, offering the transitional government $1 billion in ready cash in exchange for a part of the nation's large stockpile of Siberian diamonds. It was a collateral arrangement—the Soviets sent the gems to London to be held until the loan was repaid. De Beers was not as much interested in selling the diamonds as it was in keeping them out of the hands of others.

The myth had been saved once again. Diamonds are not particularly rare in nature, but De Beers had made them rare in the world. The hyped association with love and the controlled trickle from the vaults virtually guaranteed that the business would always be profitable for those willing to play the game. Diamonds were a $40 billion retail business by the 1990s and De Beers entered the decade in fairly robust health. Only one thing could threaten its position, as always, and that was the possibility that somebody, somewhere, might find the core of a diamondiferous volcano and produce a large supply of stones outside the grasp of the cartel.

In a corner of the Australian Outback, it finally happened.

Six

THE NEW ERA

Australia

The old religion of the Australian Aboriginals says that the world was literally sung into existence by the creator gods. Everything that makes up a landscape—rocks, trees, rivers, coast—is the physical manifestation of millions of songs composed during the time before humans were around, a preexistent state known as the Dreamtime, when the land was formed out of a void through the playing of music. A traveling Aboriginal had a ritual obligation to repeat the Dreamtime songs as he walked from place to place because if the world was not continuously sung, it would cease to exist. The landmarks in the desert were not just associated with lyrics, they were *made* of lyrics. A riverbed might be the tracks of a trickster snake, a pile of stones is the resting place of a chief, a copse of gum trees is the vagina of an old woman, and the music was their whole substance. The tracks across the land were called "songlines." They made excellent navigational aids, because you knew exactly where you were as you unspooled the story in time with the passing landscape. When you finished the song, you were at your destination. If you took a tradition-minded Aboriginal on a Jeep trip with you down the songline, going 25 mph, he would sing the song five times as fast to keep the music in time with the land. Australia is knitted together with countless songlines; not even the oldest Aboriginals can name them all. The earth is a cloth of holy sound.

On a ridge in the northwestern Australian Outback on the edge of the Great Sandy Desert, two ridges come together in a saddle. The Aboriginal songline associated with this place concerns a barramundi fish named Daiwul who swam in the waters of the Indian Ocean to the north. Three women tried to catch the fish in nets made from the fiber of spinifex trees. The fish escaped through a hole in a net and fled inland, where it tunneled into the spot between the two granite ridges. The fish lives in the ground today at a place called Barramundi Gap. The women became despondent over the loss of the fish, walked into a seasonal river, today called Cattle Creek, and died.

At the bottom of a tunnel near Barramundi Gap, warm water was seeping from the rocks and the air was as hot and suffocating as a car trunk in August. I was down here under the outback floor, half a kilometer deep, wearing a miner's lamp and coveralls and listened to a mining engineer named Ian Bell talk about the upcoming assault on the cone of diamonds somewhere in front of us. The tunnel, now about half complete, is aimed at the lower depths of the Argyle lamproite structure, which already produces about 100,000 carats of dull brown rough every day and has approximately 1 trillion carats left to give. In terms of the sheer number of stones inside, the Argyle Diamond Mine is the richest in the world.

"If you come back here a few years from now, you'll see much more activity in here," said Bell. He aimed his flashlight at a movable drilling mechanism in front of us, at the very end of the tunnel. The drill was standing idle, but would be rattling again in a few hours. The tunnel was advancing on a downward angle at a rate of 4.5 meters per day and was expected to intersect the diamond pipe in about six months. "Drilling and blasting," said Bell, as we stood in the dripping darkness, "is a mining technique that's been around since the invention of gunpowder in the fifteenth century. And before that, they used to build a fire against a rock wall and then throw cold water on the wall so it would crack." The walls around us were coated with a spray-on substance called Shockrete and reinforced with eight-foot-long steel bolts.

This tunnel was being dug in hopes that the owners, the board of Rio Tinto, Ltd., in London, would decide to extend the life of the mine for the next twenty years by attacking the diamondiferous soil from underground. All indications were that they probably would. The mine has been fantastically profitable for Rio Tinto since it went online in 1985, despite the poor quality of its stones. By the mid-1990s, it was producing a half-billion dollars of rough every year.

As large diamond mines go, Argyle's products are among the worst in the world. The stones are small and dingy, most of them the color of breakfast tea. They seemed destined for knife blades, dental tools, and drilling bits, until a remarkable new business partnership was forged across the Indian Ocean. It would come to change the modern consumer's concept of what makes a diamond pretty.

When it was all over, De Beers emerged as the big loser. In fact, Australia was a disaster on the level of the loss of the fabulous Cullinan mine a century before. It forced De Beers to rethink its core business philosophy and triggered major changes in the diamond industry that are still being sorted out today.

All of this happened not because the Australian stones were so radiant, but precisely because of their gloomy tint.

The Argyle deposit is shaped a little like a human molar, with a wide top and a bottom that descends in a forked shape. On geological cutaway maps, these forks look like the roots of a tooth. This pipe is loaded with diamonds that probably emerged from the earth's mantle around 16 billion years ago. But unlike almost every other diamond lode on earth, it is not made of kimberlite. It is a volcanic rock named lamproite, which is a close cousin to kimberlite. There was a large concentration of nitrogen in this lamproite that turned all the diamonds a yellowish color, and gave a few of them a weird pinkish cast.

After several of these were found in outback rivers in the 1960s, a team of geologists decided to start looking for their source. They followed a trail of smoke-colored diamonds up to Barramundi Gap and realized they had a bonanza. The Ashton Mining Company entered into a joint venture with Rio Tinto, Ltd., made a land-use agreement with some local Aboriginals, and started peeling away the overburden.

Along came a historical accident. The discovery of the Argyle mine happened to coincide with the emergence of a cutting and polishing industry in India. With lax labor laws, some ready capital, and millions of people willing to work for about $2 a day, the northern India city of Surat was emerging as a strong competitor to the shops of the old masters in Tel Aviv and Antwerp. Here was a place where you wouldn't lose money by polishing a diamond the size of a caraway seed. Indian jewelry manufacturers arranged these tiny dull stones by the hundreds into bracelets and necklace settings and found a ready market among American discount stores such as Target, Wal-Mart, and Kmart.

Argyle was the perfect supplier for these diamonds. Like every other new diamond mine of consequence, it had been co-opted almost immediately by De Beers, which was having difficult times already when news of the discovery in the Australian desert leaked out. The price of diamonds had tumbled in the early 1980s, forcing De Beers to stockpile well over half of its annual production in the vaults of Charterhouse Street. The cartel lost nearly a billion dollars just keeping diamond prices stable during this period. And so the Australian threat had to be contained, even though only 5 percent of the stones were suitable for gem mountings. De Beers made a deal with Ashton and Rio Tinto to become the primary buyer for 4.5 tons of diamonds every year, most of the mine's total output, trash and all.

Trouble erupted almost immediately. Australian politicians fulminated in Parliament about such an all-encompassing deal with a company based in apartheid-controlled South Africa. De Beers made things worse by displaying a heavy hand. The cartel's directors started telling Argyle to stockpile a good portion of its diamonds to counterbalance a wave of smuggled stones coming in from the Angolan civil war. The agreed price-per-carat also dropped from $12 to around $9 in the first year of the partnership. The reason? De Beers claimed the stones were getting worse and worse as the pit deepened. Argyle's executives secretly hired the outside accounting firm Coopers & Lybrand to confirm this assessment. Instead, they were told the stones were no different than the ones close to the surface. The reaction from De Beers to this news, wrote one observer in Melbourne, "was similar to a naughty boy being caught with his hand in the lolly jar." De Beers told Argyle chief Mike O'Leary his behavior was "ungentlemanly," and threatened to withdraw its team of twenty diamond sorters from the mine site. O'Leary shocked them by telling them to do just that, giving the crew two days to pack up and leave. For the next four months, there were no De Beers sorters at Argyle.

The rift was smoothed over, but it set the tone for what was to follow. Output at the mine was doubled to compensate for the low price. This was the last thing that De Beers wanted—more gems in the world to vacuum up. By 1996, the Australians decided they had had enough of lowball prices and high-handed ways. When they started to make noises about not renewing their marketing contract with De Beers, the cartel made public signs of not taking them seriously. Managing director Gary Ralfe told a reporter he was "fairly relaxed" about the squabble. "They would not want to disturb the world market," he said to suggestions that Argyle would try to sell diamonds on its own. It then came as a surprise when Argyle did just that, announcing it would sell its gems directly to the Indian manufacturers through a Bombay office and a previously existing group called the Indo-Argyle Diamond Council.

"This was a rather selfish act," complained De Beers' chairman, Julian Ogilvie Thompson. "If everyone did this, there wouldn't be a diamond market at all." The statement revealed perhaps more than he had intended. The cartel, chagrined, tried a power play that would have made Cecil Rhodes smile: it dumped $400 million of cheap rough into India in an attempt to force down the price of Argyle's diamonds and bring the rebels back into the fold. The cartel also told bankers to expect large-scale business failures among Bombay cutters. It took a reassuring visit and a factory tour from two Argyle executives—both bearing red "third-eye" dots on their foreheads—to keep the banks from calling in their loans on the Indian polishers.

There was a larger reason why De Beers' fear tactics failed. During their years of acrimony with the cartel, the Australians had managed to create a new branding identity for their brownish stones—enough to build a demand that De Beers could not challenge. Attractive phrases were coined to describe previously unappealing goods: "champagne diamonds" and "cognac diamonds" were heavily promoted to individual jewelers and in magazine advertisements that were invariably designed with a rich chocolate hue. A simple color scale similar to the famous 4Cs was developed to give consumers a sense of control over their purchase. The new paradigm even took hold inside the mine, where the term "industrial quality" was no longer applied to 75 percent of the pit's output. In its place came the term "near-gem quality."

This was an ironic rehash of an unsuccessful De Beers campaign in the 1940s to unload brown diamonds on the American market. A 1941 ad in *The New Yorker* had extolled the spectrum of dull diamonds "from the lightness of champagne to the richness of cognac." This resurrected campaign was not at all in De Beers' interest this time and the cartel offered no cooperation. But it didn't matter: a globalization drama was being played out on a grand scale as millions of low-quality gems from Australia were pressed into necklaces and rings in Indian factories and shipped to America, Japan, and elsewhere. They enjoyed unexpectedly brisk sales. A "champagne diamond" was an ideal way for a customer of modest means to feel like he (or she) was part of a luxury class, but at a price he could afford. *Entertainment Tonight* host Maria Menounos helped reinforce the image by showing up on the red carpet at the 2003 Oscars wearing a dress studded with more than two thousand smoky stones that previously would have been ground into dust and embedded on a saw blade. She was reportedly rendered speechless when the actor Owen Wilson looked at the front of her dress and asked, "Are those real?"

In fact, the redefinition had succeeded so well that Argyle's U.S. agent, MVI Marketing, recommended in 2002 that the retail price of brown goods be raised several price points because—astonishingly—surveys showed most of the U.S. buying public thought the rarity of "champagne diamonds" was equal to or greater than that of colorless diamonds. In other words, Argyle had developed a new story around its stones; another way to sing "The Diamond Song" to the world's consumers. De Beers' loss of Argyle shook the cartel to its core, and only reinforced the truism that in the diamond business, as in so many other aspects of life, controlling the narrative means controlling everything.

The odds were excellent that the diamond I gave to Anne had passed through the De Beers chain. At the time I bought it in 2000, the cartel controlled up to three-quarters of the world's rough diamonds. But tracing it beyond that point was simply impossible. The most likely point of origin—statistically speaking—was the mine at Orapa in Botswana, the largest source nation for De Beers and a model of self-sufficiency. At the time I bought the ring, Orapa was putting out 12 million carats a year. But the symbol of my love also could have come from the Internatsionalnaya Mine in Russian Siberia, or the Premier Mine in South Africa or the Skeleton Coast deposits in Namibia or even the Rio Jequitinhonha in Brazil, or from the war spoils of Angola or smuggled out of the Central African Republic. There was no way to trace its history, except to say De Beers' office in London was the probable point of transfer to America.

The cartel's executives have always disliked the term "monopoly" as a description for the way they do business, and technically, they have a point, for they never controlled the world's *entire* supply of diamonds for

most of the twentieth century. There would always be smuggling and illicit diamond buying and small secondary trickles into Antwerp and New
York. But generally speaking, if you wanted to buy a diamond, you were
buying from De Beers, even if you weren't aware of it. It was the ele-
phantine middle junction that stood between the mine and the mall.

De Beers had tried mightily to shield its name from the retail world,
particularly in the United States, where free market competition is an article of popular faith. It also tried to deny its own nature when put under
scrutiny.

"If this is a monopoly, it is a monopoly based on the popular support of
its consumers," said an internal memo at one of De Beers' advertising
agencies suggesting ways to talk around the issue. "The facts in the diamond industry are that all producers of diamonds are free, *if they so wish*
[their italics], to market their own diamonds. De Beers has no actual
power to coerce these producers to sell their diamonds through De Beers
or the Diamond Corporation organization. This so-called monopoly is
therefore a free association of producers who enter into contracts with De
Beers because they appreciate the benefits of collective marketing."

This was laughably untrue. Economic coercion has not just been a last
option for De Beers—it has been common business practice. In 1981, the
impoverished nation of Zaire became unhappy with its deal with the cartel and sought an agreement with three independent European companies to sell its relatively modest output of industrial diamonds. De Beers
took revenge by deliberately releasing a flood from its stockpile, driving
down prices and forcing Zaire's diamond industry into a state of near collapse. When it was in league with the cartel, it was receiving about $3 a
carat for its industrials. On its own, it received less than half of that. This
punishment was inflicted on a place with one of the worst rates of poverty
in the world, and also one of the most corrupt governments in the person
of Mobutu Sese Seko, an abysmally craven dictator even by African standards. But he was forced to rejoin the cartel two years later to save his nation's diamond industry from ruin. "Anyone want to follow Zaire?" one
De Beers executive was said to have remarked at the time. If this was indeed a "free association of producers," it was one that a member could apparently never escape.

Even so, the rewards for staying inside were undeniable. In exchange
for bartering away their independence, any person or country who signed
an agreement with De Beers was virtually guaranteed to make a profit.

The cartel would spend millions to make sure that no strong competitors ever popped up outside the single channel to steal a jeweler's business. Harry Oppenheimer had a saying he repeated countless times: "There is no one concerned with diamonds—whether producer, dealer, cutter, jeweler or customer—who does not benefit from it."

That customers benefited from the inflated prices was a debatable point, but De Beers' value to producers and dealers was clear. The jewelry trade was one of the safest risks around for small businesses. There were copious amounts of free advertising ("A Diamond is Forever") that promoted the *idea* of the gemstone instead of any individual jeweler. And the well-established link with love ensured a steady stream of customers through the generations. People were not about to stop getting married.

The cartel craved stability and order; it detested uncertainty and competition. It campaigned incessantly—and mostly successfully—through the twentieth century *against* diamonds as an investment commodity. The point was hard to argue. Diamonds are highly portable, but also vulnerable to theft and sudden total loss. And no two stones are alike, making it hard to create a standardized valuation, as can be done with gold, silver, or other metals. Unless you were a refugee or a criminal trying to sneak assets across an international border, diamonds were a terrible way to store wealth. "Our policy is that diamonds should be regarded for their beauty, rarity and lasting value," said chairman Julian Ogilvie Thompson in a 1988 statement to a California newspaper. He did not mean "value" of the monetary kind; the diamond's value to the consumer was supposed to last into eternity, not into the next business cycle. This was another pillar of the cartel's stability. The emotional trappings of a diamond can make them difficult for people to sell—as I well knew.

This was the beauty of the link with love, at least in a commercial sense. About 1 billion carats of polished diamonds exist in the world today, approximately enough to fill a London double-decker bus to its roof. De Beers did not like to see those gems circulating; it would like them to stay around necks or inside the hinged boxes tucked inside the closet. An active secondary market would create unwanted competition for new polished gems.

Better still, the stabilizing effect of the cartel meant that the retail prices wouldn't be swinging up or down. In exchange for playing by the rules, a diamond merchant could be assured of a reasonably risk-free profit for years to come. Being inside De Beers during a depression was like being inside Switzerland during a world war. After the U.S. stock market took a plunge in 1986, a reporter asked De Beers official Robin Walker if the cartel would be adjusting its price of rough to reflect the new realities.

"Oh, no, absolutely no," he replied. "We never reduce price, never."

De Beers had survived many things in its long history: the Cullinan fiasco, antitrust litigation, the Nazi blitz of Antwerp, the horrors of apartheid, the chaos of postcolonial Africa, worldwide depressions, bad press about "blood diamonds." Its very existence at the end of the twentieth century must be regarded as something like a miracle, in that its mercantile philosophies were more derivative of Vasco da Gama than Coca-Cola. But the pressures of Argyle and the new discoveries in the Canadian Arctic were becoming too much for the old order to bear. More than a quarter of the world's rough now lay outside monopoly control, and an increasing percentage of De Beers stock was owned by American investors who viewed the legendary stockpiles under Charterhouse Street—approaching $5 billion at the time—as nothing more than dead weight. "After the isolation of apartheid, De Beers was anxious to shed its image as a secret, sinister organization and instead move into the world as a cosmopolitan world-class firm," noted an analyst from the Harvard Business School. With the ascension of Sir Ernest's grandson, Nicky Oppenheimer, to the chairmanship, the cartel moved to reinvent itself. In 1999, the board of directors hired the Boston consulting firm Bain & Company to conduct a review of its methods and practices.

The recommendation was striking: De Beers was urged to abandon its historic role as "custodian of the industry" and focus its attention on creating branded luxury goods. Oppenheimer sent shock waves through the diamond world by adopting this idea and launching a program with the somewhat opaque name of "Supplier of Choice." "As we continued to trade diamonds, we paid scant attention to the efficiency of the pipeline, which did not add value to consumers," Gary Ralfe explained in an industry newsletter. "Instead, we ignored the needs of the consumer and what it was they required from a piece of diamond jewelry."

In other words, the real competition for the diamond empire was no longer going to be renegade geologists or starving *garimpeiros* in Angola, but fripperies like perfume, Bermuda vacations, and BMWs. Almost overnight, De Beers' obsession shifted from the supply side (the obsessive grabbing of every loose diamond in the world) to the demand side (the direct engagement of any wealthy customer who wanted a prestigious stone). It was like Cecil Rhodes proposing to strip all the pulley wires out of the Big Hole and put the entire enterprise under one grand company. This time, De Beers was trying to cut out all the confusing layers of dealers, brokers, and middlemen—known colloquially as "spaghetti junction"—who bought stones from the sightholders and sold them at a markup. De Beers aimed to cut through this knot of lesser players with a bold stroke.

The once reclusive family enterprise became more extroverted. The De Beers name, once a virtual taboo in America, began to show up in more of its own advertisements. If you could slap a brand name on drinking water and charge a premium for it, why not diamonds? The company began etching its name and a logo called "Forevermark" onto the girdle of its gems in microscopic laser print. De Beers also signed a joint venture deal with the French luxury goods vendor LVMH, which also marketed prestige brands like Moët & Chandon Champagne and Louis Vuitton handbags. At the turn of the century in London, the company exhibited a 203-carat stone it called "the Millennium Star" and received an unexpected burst of publicity when a band of thieves tried to steal it. The resulting front page in the *Evening Standard*, headlined £350 MILLION DIAMOND RAID AT DOME, is now framed on the wall of the company's public relations department in London. The mystical—and highly salable—link between diamonds and perfidy was at work once more. Nicky Oppenheimer was said to have remarked: "If we could get headlines like this all the time, we could do away with the publicity department altogether." If he didn't say it, he should have. When I asked the director of external relations, Andy Bone, at De Beers about the authenticity of the quote, he responded, with a dry smile, "Well, it was what we were all saying internally, anyway."

Other changes were on the way. De Beers took the amazing step of settling its long-running feud with the U.S. Justice Department and agreed to plead guilty to criminal price-fixing violations in a federal court in Columbus, Ohio. These charges stemmed from a 1994 allegation that De Beers had conspired with General Electric to rig the price of industrial diamonds. The deal allowed cartel officials to travel freely in the United States without threat of subpoena for the first time in a century. America's first De Beers retail store opened on Manhattan's Fifth Avenue in the summer of 2005, a spectacle that would have infuriated Franklin D. Roosevelt, had he been around to see it. The cartel also spent $17.6 billion to reacquire its own stock and become a private company again, giving it some relief from querulous investors and the analysts of Wall Street. The stockpile of gems underneath Charterhouse Street was reduced by nearly half.

The sightholder system remained, but the list of elite was trimmed from slightly over a hundred down to approximately eighty-four. Those who remained were strongly encouraged to start branding their stones with the De Beers imprimatur. One of the sightholders who lost his ticket was the New York dealer W. B. David, who responded by filing a lawsuit in U.S. federal court accusing De Beers of running a "brazen and unrepentant monopoly" and of using the new Supplier of Choice system as a ruse to actually strengthen its chokehold on the market rather than lessen it. The grand strategy, alleged David, was to establish market dominance over stones measuring 2 carats and above. Anyone competing with De Beers in this high-dollar realm, David said, was subject to being ruthlessly squeezed out. The lawsuit asserted what many in the diamond industry felt was an open secret: that the largest recipient of rough diamonds at the sights, a company called Diamdel, was actually owned by De Beers. If true, the cartel was distributing diamonds to itself, in other words, at a value approaching half a billion dollars a year. This confusing, hall-of-mirrors corporate structure had been an Oppenheimer specialty since the formation of Anglo-American.

The incestuous nature of the sights was compounded by the broker system, in which every sightholder was required to conduct its dealings with De Beers through one of six approved London companies. At least one of them, I. Henning & Co., was widely suspected to be a possession of the De Beers empire, and Nicky Oppenheimer admitted as much in 1999 in an interview with the Canadian journalist Matthew Hart. This meant that the 1 percent broker's fee was apparently being paid from De Beers to itself. The self-dealing allegation was repeated in the David lawsuit, which also quoted speculation by the respected diamond consultant Chaim Even-Zohar that De Beers was planning to make up for lost market share by simply charging more for diamonds. "That isn't so easy in a competitive market," wrote Even-Zohar in a 2003 trade newsletter article. "But it is certainly manageable in the better goods, if there are as few players as possible in that segment."

And the players had no choice but to obey, on pain of losing their place at the London sights. Even in the new climate, De Beers was still judge, jury, and executioner of the trade. The price sheet publisher Martin Rapaport put this reality in colorful terms: "If De Beers wanted its sightholders to line up on Charterhouse Street, dress in bikinis and Indian turbans, jump up and down on one foot and go 'Woo-ooo,' you'd see them all doing just that," he said. "They have to."

De Beers refused to comment on the lawsuit when I asked for a reaction. But Andy Bone told me it was "rubbish" that De Beers was trying to reassert monopoly control.

"We didn't do Supplier of Choice to screw people," he said. "That's a ridiculous allegation. Ten to fifteen years ago, marketing wasn't important. If you look at the way diamonds were traded, they were just cycling around being passed through so many hands, and nobody adding any value. We had to modernize. The railroad barons of the nineteenth century kept thinking they were in the 'railroad industry' and not in the 'transportation industry.' And so they missed the development of cars. For many years we saw ourselves in the diamond industry, but we are really in the luxury goods market. We have to become more market-savvy."

One former executive of De Beers—and no fan of his former employer—told me he thought exactly the opposite was true. The Supplier of Choice program, in his mind, was an attempt to reconstitute its lordship over the business. "What is being instituted now is a more venomous type of monopoly," he told me over the phone. "They are trying to control their clients even more. They are linking the supplies of diamond they give out to how much each client spends on advertising."

Dealers down the chain, in other words, were being ordered to promote the De Beers name throughout the world instead of trying to conceal it. The penalty for disobedience appeared to be a revocation of the sight privilege, and separation from some of the best diamonds in the world. But not the dingy stones of Argyle; those are gone from the cartel forever.

Twenty years' worth of champagne stones still lie buried under Barramundi Gap in Australia. The costs of a possible underground assault were still being calculated when I visited the mine, but Ian Bell told me the project would likely cost $500 million. The idea was to build a hollow chamber under the ore body and let it fall into piles on the chamber floor, thanks to a combination of pressure, gravity, and carefully placed explosives. Done correctly, the ore would drop as regularly as drops of sugar water from a hummingbird feeder. The ore would then be crushed by processors underground and ferried to the surface on a conveyor belt. This method of extraction, known as "block caving," had been pioneered in copper mines in South America in the 1950s. There was every reason to think it would work at Argyle, though the stability of the rock mass under the lode was one large question mark. Progress on the tunnel had halted the previous year when the drillers came across the shale lip of a volcano tipped on its side. Nobody had known it was there and the geologists had to assess it for stability before work could proceed. The last thing anybody wanted to see was a tunnel or a chamber collapse. Every attempt to raid the earth has its unknowns.

"The front end is typical of any big mining operation," general manager Kevin McLeish told me. "It's only when you get into the recovery process that you see what you're getting into." He is a tall, slow-speaking man with plenty of experience in the recovery of steel, iron, and copper at Rio Tinto's other mines scattered through Africa and South America. He would be going after these diamonds in the same relentless fashion. The variables were the same, the equipment was the same, the volumes were the same, even the language was the same: ore bodies, grade recovery, tons/week, heavy media separation, country rock, terracing, advance rate. Only the end product was different. A day's output could fit into a small suitcase and was bound not to build skyscrapers, or electrical grids, or automobiles, but for rings and bracelets sold in American discount stores. Most people who work at Argyle have thought about the irony to some degree or another. McLeish put it this way: "This is the first time I'm pushing a product that adds no value to the world."

All this empty product must pass through a room on the third floor of a glassy office building in the coastal city of Perth. Known as the Valuations and Sorting Department, this room is barricaded behind an airlock-type door and watched relentlessly by dozens of security cameras mounted on the ceilings. Every diamond recovered from the mine comes here to be sized and packaged for the polishing mills of Surat in India. That means that slightly over one quarter of the diamonds now produced in the world pass through this room, which is no larger than a suburban three-car garage. I was surprised to see plastic tubs of diamonds lying almost casually around, as if they were buckets of paint scattered in a careless handyman's tool shed. I looked closely at one. The rocks were dull and gray, like driveway salt. They were the most unremarkable-looking things in the world. But I had a sudden urge to run my hands through the rocks, to feel them falling through my fingers.

"Can I touch this?" I asked the manager, Rodney Criddle, who had been showing me around. "You can watch my hands."

"I don't think that would be a good idea," he said, a bit nervously. "Security wouldn't like it."

Dull as they may have been, these stones from under the outback had played a powerful role in the history of the diamond business. They had a story behind them. They represented the unraveling of the old Syndicate and the possible beginnings of a new one.

There is a hilltop cafeteria at the Argyle mine with a beautiful view of the termite mounds and red earth of the empty scrublands. It faces away from the diamond pit. I had a dinner of roast beef and Vegamite on bread here with a miner who had worked in the pit almost from the time of its opening. He and his schoolteacher wife were about to quit their jobs, buy a hardshell camper, and prepare to make a walkabout across the continent. Though he was looking forward to the trip, he was sorry to be leaving Argyle, which he said had treated him very well and made him feel like he was part of an adventure.

"We thumbed our nose at De Beers and got away with it," he told me. "Nobody had ever done that before. It's a great story and I'm proud to be a part of it."

Since he had been working there, the Dreamtime song about the barramundi had gone through a slight revision. The Aboriginals who lived nearby, many of whom had jobs at the mine under a land-use agreement, had expanded on their story of the fish that had tunneled underneath the ground to escape the women with the net. All those diamonds, they decided, were scales that had fallen from his back.

The comparison between De Beers and an exceedingly polite kind of mafia has been made more than once. The headquarters building on Charterhouse Street, for example, happens to sit in the same London neighborhood where Dickens set Fagin's kitchen in *Oliver Twist*. He described it then—quite accurately—as a place full of gas lamps and cutpurses and fence markets where the greasy spoils of crime were unloaded to willing customers. Right around the corner of the De Beers building, as a matter of fact, is an old hanging ground at the Smithfield Market where countless pickpockets and burglars were executed in the nineteenth century. The gang-of-thieves history of the Holborn neighborhood has been an irresistible metaphor for modern critics of the diamond empire who consider the practices of the cartel to be nothing more than theft with a pocket-square. I came across the analogy myself several times, both in and out of print. "Dealing with these guys is like dealing with the mafia, only they all have English accents," one frustrated mining official told me. And the opening lines of Stefan Kanfer's popular history of the cartel, *The Last Empire*, contains this allusion: "Here in London its executives are soft-spoken Oxford men outfitted by Savile Row. They act with the utmost discretion. But they can exhibit the cold will of mafia dons when the occasion warrants."

The analogy is entertaining, but it fails to capture the true essence of De Beers. For one thing, the cartel has not faced a credible accusation of actual physical violence in a very long time. The history of De Beers is checkered with occasional bouts of mayhem—armed strikebreaking at the Big Hole, the disgraceful conquest of Rhodesia, the jungle ambushes of "Flash Fred" in 1950s Liberia—but those belonged to a different era. Diamonds are mined today in all kinds of miserable and bloodstained circumstances, particularly in Africa, but De Beers is not directly responsible for the carnage. One might argue that the overinflated market controlled by the cartel has fueled African conflicts in an indirect sort of way, but that drifts a long way from comparisons to *La Cosa Nostra*. The muscle the cartel prefers to use is always of the economic variety, not the gunsight.

The notion of De Beers as a sinister mastermind organization breaks down on another level. It evokes images of tight-lipped emissaries able to pull off international missions with discretion and efficiency. Quite the opposite is true. One of the secrets of the diamond trade—and one that very few will talk about openly—is just how prone De Beers is to miscalculation and incompetence. There have been brilliant coups in its history, but the colossus of Oppenheimer has racked up a string of notable mistakes of late.

"This is the thing nobody realizes about De Beers—just how moth-eaten they really are," said Bruce Cox, the marketing director for Rio Tinto in Australia. "Their arrogance has bred inefficiency. They have not adjusted to business realities. They are gradually trying to catch up." Most large companies in the British Commonwealth were advertising their commitment to environmental sustainability and social responsibility by the 1980s, he told me. De Beers has only recently begun to do this. These pronouncements are sometimes hollow, but, of course, the cartel's failure to even make the attempt struck Cox as a notable public relations gaffe. It was as if they weren't reading the annual reports of anybody but themselves. "This is a corporate trend two decades old and they're just starting to do this now?" he asked.

De Beers' inability to get in front of the bonanza in the Canadian Arctic also casts doubt on its abilities, both geological and political. One of the standard ways for a big mining firm to make new discoveries is to let shoestring companies known as "juniors" do the hard work of prospecting, and then swoop in with a buyout offer once something promising turns up. De Beers not only failed to co-opt the junior discoveries of Eira Thomas and Chuck Fipke near Lac du Gras, but it sent its own geologists out to Canada with models more appropriate for the African savanna than the tundra. The models reportedly did not correct for the vast amounts of glacial till that covered the earth, nor did the geologists fully accept the idea that glaciers could have carried indicator minerals hundreds of miles away from kimberlite pipes. De Beers was finally forced to buy its way in, acquiring the company Winspear and its Snap Lake project for $259 million in a hostile takeover in 2000. But the headaches did not cease. Delays in getting regulatory approval for the mine were partly attributed to the cartel's inability to quickly reach an accord with the native Dogrib people on whose land the mine would be dug. This respect of aboriginal rights is an absolute necessity under Canadian law and one that De Beers was slow to understand. "They came in like a bully, expecting to get their way," one observer to the process told me. "They just didn't get it."

One mining official in the far north town of Yellowknife told me the following story about De Beers during the frenzy of the Canadian staking rush in the early 1990s: "They had this office in town that was completely unmarked and rigged with security cameras, although everybody knew exactly what it was. There were these guys with South African accents coming and going. It was sort of comical. I went in there one time and they had a corporate newsletter displayed on the coffee table. There was a picture of [a De Beers executive] at a cocktail party in front of a fireplace with his arm slung around the shoulder of the latest African dictator. And

I told them, 'Guys, I don't know if this is the image you really want to be bringing into Canada.'"

It was a pattern repeated elsewhere. Examining the wake of the Argyle mess, the Australian *Business Review Weekly* concluded that De Beers was simply not used to negotiating with partners it could not bulldoze. "Until Argyle hit the scene," noted the magazine, "most diamonds came from De Beers' backyard of South Africa and Namibia, Third World countries run by easily exploited dictators, or countries such as Russia, where earning hard currency displaced the need to make a true profit."

Even in Africa, where it should have been strongest, De Beers was proving itself to be less than all-powerful. The cartel had enjoyed a flow of gems from Angola for decades, even during the sanguinary civil war in which both sides used diamond profits to arm themselves with AK-47s and land mines. De Beers opened a string of buying offices in the combat zones in 1996 but was forced to shutter them two years later amid international publicity about "blood diamonds." But in 2000, there was a dispute with President Eduardo dos Santos that led to the suspension of the contract. Even more ominously for De Beers, the Russian-Israeli tycoon Lev Leviev moved in and bought a stake in a rich deposit called Catoca. He now runs the second largest diamond business in the world. The cartel, meanwhile, is still trying to recover its position in its lost colony.

I paid a visit to the De Beers handler in Angola, a trim and fastidious man named Gaspar Cardosa. He has an office in a $30 million skyscraper with the company name mounted on the top in deep blue letters, and the legend UN DIAMANTE E PARA SIEMPRE carved in a pane of glass at the entrance. The building features one of the only working elevators in the entire country. Cardosa has a whole floor virtually to himself; he is one of the only employees left here. His office has a commanding view of the harbor, but no art on the walls.

The relationship between Leviev and the government was deteriorating, Cardosa told me, and the cartel was ready to step back in as an alternative.* Only 2 percent of the nation had been properly canvassed for kimberlite pipes, and it was widely suspected that De Beers already knew where some of them were. "We want to prove things can be done

---

*The Angolan leadership might have been excused for its skepticism about De Beers; this was, after all, the same company that had helped funnel hard currency to the UNITA rebel army dedicated to its overthrow.

the right way," Cardosa told me. "We want to use the best practices of the diamond industry. We want to help. Even the government doesn't know what they have." His efforts to repair the political damage would go on, even as De Beers sought international arbitration to settle the dispute.

By the end of 2004, the legendary "single channel" instituted by Cecil Rhodes had sprung so many leaks that De Beers was in control of just under half of the world's supply of rough diamonds, down from 80 percent just a few years before. This had the ironic effect of allowing De Beers to claim even more vociferously that it was not, in fact, a monopoly. "Pushing guys out?" Andy Bone asked me. "Well, then, we've been bloody awful at it!" The cumulative effect of all the recent defeats also raised the question of where the cartel's real power had come from all this time. Did it come from a team of Machiavellian geniuses inside Charterhouse Street? Or was it from a widespread *belief* in that power?

"De Beers was always a creation of its own image," the former cartel executive told me. "It never had the control that everybody thought it did. It was an incredibly inefficiently run place. There were very low caliber people we used to [hire]. It would have shocked you. Staff morale has always been rather low at De Beers in London."

This may have been the crowning irony: De Beers was exactly like the product it pushed. Its greatest strength lay not in what it really was, but rather in the nimbus of invincibility that it was generally assumed to carry. The illusion of strength *was* its strength. De Beers had the narrative of power, and in diamonds, the narrative is everything. The cartel had begun as a vision of Victorian imperialists and morphed into a corporate octopus. Now it was seeking to reinvent itself once more as a twenty-first-century branding tool. It was quite a bit like the Coca-Cola Corporation, which sold brown water and made it the most recognized brand name in the world. All history is publicity, it might be said, and De Beers has done a magisterial job of spinning a beneficent image around a core of nothingness.

De Beers entered the new century battered but intact. It still had a half-billion of rough in the vaults, a brilliant advertising team, and the power to make its remaining sightholders bend to its will. It had the rising powers of India and China to exploit for new customers. Most of all, it had a 117-year-old name that turned out to have a surprising amount of cache in the retail marketplace. Affluent consumers recognized it the way they did Louis Vuitton or Prada.

At De Beers' glass-and-concrete office campus in Johannesburg, I spent an hour talking with two public relations officials over lunch. One of them, a burly South African named Tom Tweedy, was telling me how the company was excited about the stones that would be sold in the United States as "De Beers–brand" stones. The name and the presence of a tiny laser-inscribed mark would be a sign of quality and prestige for the American consumer, he said.

"But this is a company that, for better or worse, has an image that a lot of people associate with something shady," I said. "What would be the appeal of having a diamond with that name on it?"

"I'll tell you what it is," he said, leaning forward. "Mystique."

Seven

BLOOD DIAMONDS

Angola

Jonas Savimbi died in a way that might have pleased him. It took seventeen bullets to bring him down. He was wearing his camouflage and field boots, holding a freshly emptied pistol in his right hand.

What would prove to be the final military operation of the Angolan civil war—code-named *Kissonde* for a species of poisonous ant—had begun with an anonymous tip that the elderly rebel general was hiding in the Moxico province. Orders came from the capital: Kill Savimbi at all costs. Trees were defoliated, villages burned, and hundreds of refugees herded together and interrogated. Savimbi had tried to throw off his pursuers by crossing and recrossing several rivers, but on the afternoon of February 22, 2002, he stopped to rest in the shade of a tree. That was when the hit squad moved in.

Savimbi probably also would have been happy with the way his corpse was treated more like a statue than a casualty of war. The government soldiers laid him on the banks of the Luvuei River and called in a camera crew to film the prize for broadcast on national television. There were two rifle bullets in his head, but his beard was still black at sixty-seven years of age and his face did not seem to sag in death. It remained plump and wide. His squashed nose and characteristically flared nostrils were there to identify him as the rebel general who had kept Angola's civil war alive for more than three decades, far beyond the point of any rational political agenda. The man Ronald Reagan once welcomed at the White House, the Protestant who chose "the Black Cockerel" for his nom de guerre, the

Maoist-trained guerrilla leader who had bankrolled his army with millions of illicit diamonds, the founder, leader, and sole unifying force of the National Union for the Total Independence of Angola, was dead. The war would shortly die with him.

The government of Angola signed a peace treaty with the remnants of Savimbi's rebel army less than two months later. The news was greeted with quiet celebration in the diamond quarters of Antwerp and New York. It meant the end of what had become a massive public relations problem. Angola was the nation that had virtually invented "blood diamonds"—the headline-grabbing name for those stones used to finance civil wars in Africa. Savimbi and his movement had been responsible for up to half a million carats a year, bartered for AK-47s and rocket-propelled grenades sold by Russian arms dealers.

Savimbi's death meant that the stream of awesomely colorless diamonds from Angola would soon become more expensive. But it also paved the way for Angola's entry into the plan for gem certification known as the Kimberley Process, which the De Beers cartel and the rest of the industry had been forced to create in 2001 under pressure from the United Nations. Humanitarian groups and reporters had begun to point out that Savimbi's murderous rebels were buying their rifles and grenades with diamonds plundered from the villages they had captured. America's favorite jewelry item was also a major ignition point for the war in Sierra Leone in which troops had hacked off the forearms of hundreds of civilians to keep them from voting. For a product whose sole value rested in its association with love, these horrific pictures from Africa could have spelled lost market share, if not outright collapse.

"We didn't want to become another 'fur,'" one diamond executive told me, recalling the intimidation campaign run by animal rights activists. "This was a major problem. We're selling a dream. We don't want to sell a nightmare."

The Kimberley Process was a way to head off protests outside Tiffany's and Wal-Mart. The concept is simple: Any nation that exports diamonds is now required to seal the stones inside a tamperproof container along with a document certifying they were not mined in the midst of a war. Angola was brought into the system eleven months after Savimbi's assassination and was immediately held up as a success story. Its diamonds, regarded by experts as top quality for their transparency and brilliance, are now officially considered "clean."

But the era of blood diamonds is not over in Angola. It has only taken on a new and even more insidious shape. Violence and midnight killings are still omnipresent near the diamond mines; this time, the mayhem lacks any political agenda except greed. Soldiers are robbing and killing miners and there are multiple reports of people being thrown into jail on manufactured charges if they are suspected of possessing a diamond. Some are forced to work in a state of virtual slavery, under threat of execution if they attempt to quit. The majority of Angola's diamonds are mined in the provinces of Lunda Sul and Lunda Norte, which are also the centers of the continuing violence. For many, this is hardly a coincidence.

"The diamonds are at the root of it all. They are an attraction for people who are trying to make money in the most barbaric way possible," said Rafael Marques, a researcher with the Open Society Initiative for Southern Africa who is attempting to document the human rights abuses. "During the war, there was at least a systematic method to it. The leaders could be blamed. Now people are being killed at random. There are no sides anymore."

Today's diamonds from Angola are even more suspect, in some ways, because they carry a veneer of purity while they continue to be mined in a virtual war zone. The violent commerce Savimbi helped create is still booming. Just before I arrived in Angola, the bodies of four men were pulled out of the Cuango River bloated beyond all recognition. The only identifying mark on any of them was a tattoo on one man's arm that appeared to say *Dony*. It is unclear if this was his name. Two of the bodies were sealed in plastic garbage bags. All of them had been eviscerated from neck to crotch with a long knife or a machete. The assumption was that one of the party had apparently tried to conceal a large diamond by swallowing it and the killers—possibly police or soldiers—had been searching for the missing stone in the dead men's digestive tracts.

On a continent already full of plundered dreams, there are few wastes as sorry as Angola. It should have been one of the richest countries in Africa. The capital, Luanda, is built on one of the best natural harbors in the southern hemisphere. Pink and lemon-yellow skyscrapers were built by the Portuguese during their long colonial tenure, and they line the waterfront in a graceful urban crescent reminiscent of Rio de Janeiro. The scrublands of the west coast rise to a central plateau crisscrossed with rivers and full of rich loamy farmland in which virtually anything can grow. There is abundant sunshine and the night air feels gentle and Hawaiian on the skin. Reserves of oil are off the northern coast, and galaxies of diamonds are scattered in the rivers to the east. The well-watered meadows of the highlands used to teem with exotic animals. With peace and clean government, the place could have been a model for a rising postcolonial Africa.

Instead, Angola has been wracked by civil war, corrupt government, and appalling poverty ever since it claimed independence in 1975. Up until very recently, it was impossible to drive anywhere outside of the capital because all the roads had been seeded with land mines. So many people have lost their hands, arms, and legs that one of the only domestic industries in the country is the manufacture of prosthetic limbs. Much of Angola's rich stock of wildlife—including giraffe, elephant, lion, and hippo—has been eaten by a near-starving population. Its roll of social statistics is among the most dismal in the world. More than 80 percent of its 13 million people live in a state of absolute or relative poverty, and 13 percent of them are suffering from severe malnutrition. The average person will die before he or she reaches forty-one years of age. In 1999, UNICEF declared Angola the single worst nation on the planet in which to be born.

Luanda never saw any serious combat during Savimbi's war, but it remains a sacked and hollowed place. Those few people with money live inside houses that resemble fortified bunkers, with high pulley gates, off-the-grid generators, and private soldiers sitting outside with Kalashnikovs resting between their knees. The European-style promenades are littered with trash, pools of evil-looking gray water, and the occasional burnt slab of a car chassis. Refugees from the war have taken up squatters' residence inside many of the downtown skyscrapers, which still bear giant rusting words on the rooftops, advertising the products of forty years ago: RENAULT, SANYO, SINGER. Some of the rooms inside are lit with candles of cow fat, and the wallboard has all been stripped or burned away. Plumbing is often nonexistent in these desiccated towers and so buckets of drinking and bathing water must be carried up dark stairwells, sometimes as much as twenty flights. The elevators are all broken; there is hardly one in the entire nation that works.

I became fascinated with the elevators. Their shafts were often stuffed with garbage, their button panels torn off and wiring stripped away, the cars permanently stuck between floors, when they were there at all. In one apartment building, the sliding doors had been pried off and the shaft had been turned into a *pissoir;* the reek was overpowering. On the third floor of another I found a metal plate bolted over the shaft and a row of carefully tended houseplants set in front to liven up the bare wall. Yet another shaft had been turned into a locking storage closet for somebody's bicycle.

Some of Luanda's elevators looked as if they had once been near works of art, with Art Deco numbering and open-air cages and modish Space Age staircases wrapped around their lobby cores. I couldn't stop looking into these dead elevators. They seemed to represent a broken promise.

"Listen, my friend, there is only one word of Portuguese you need to know," said Rafael Marques as he drove me through the nighttime streets of Luanda. "You will find it a very useful word: *confusão.* It means 'confusion.' It is the embodiment of everything here in Angola."

Marques is the director of the local office of the Open Society Initiative, an organization bankrolled by the billionaire George Soros and dedicated to lobbying for transparency in government. Marques's activities have gotten him into trouble. He has spent six months in prison for criticizing the president. It is a widely accepted fact in Angola that a good portion of the nation's petroleum royalties—by some estimates, as much as 33 percent—is siphoned off for the personal enrichment of high government officials, but Marques is one of the only nonforeigners willing to say it publicly, and he paid the price.

His other focus is the bloodshed in the diamond zones. Marques made a fact-finding trip to both Lunda Norte and Lunda Sul a year after Savimbi's death and wrote a report detailing the level of control exercised by private security firms staffed by soldiers home from the civil war and without any prospects for another kind of job. These firms, often indistinguishable from the army, routinely set up roadblocks and harass the miners. That initial research has been supplemented by a registry of violent diamond-related deaths in the Lundas on his office computer. This may be as close to a permanent record of the violence as exists anywhere. Marques's information comes from the relatives of the murdered and the testimony of anonymous police officers who have fed him tips.

A sampling, paraphrased:

- August 24, 2004, a team of private security guards stole a 24-carat diamond from three miners and forced them, at gunpoint, to dig all night long at the minesite to find more diamonds.
- December 2004, exact date unknown, two miners were suspected of having swallowed large stones. They were put in jail and fed an unknown liquid designed to give them diarrhea. The medicine killed both of them and their bodies were later found floating in the Cuango River.
- December 6, 2004, in the village of Mussendi, dozens of miners were jammed into a single jail cell without any ventilation. They may have been subject to exhaust fumes from a faulty generator. A protesting crowd gathered in front of the jail the next day and the police fired into the crowd, killing two.

"This is the *confusão* at work," said Marques. "Crimes in the Lundas are never solved—there is never any investigation. Of course these are 'blood diamonds.' If somebody is cut open because he has a diamond in his belly, that's a very bloody diamond. In some senses, it is even more bloody than a war diamond. It used to be one enemy attacking another. Now you have private security firms and government soldiers literally slaughtering people."

What helped unleash the new wave of violence was a postwar military campaign called "Operation Brilliante," aimed at driving out the nearly 300,000 emigrants from the Congo who had been encouraged to come mine diamonds for Savimbi's rebels during the war. Numerous human rights abuses were reported as the soldiers carried out the expulsions—robberies, rapes, and murders of Congolese and Angolans alike. One diplomat told me he was convinced the real motivation for Operation Brilliante was to drive all freelance miners out of the diamond fields so military officials could take a greater share of the income. Ex-soldiers who have their own weapons are given free license to search citizens and roam the area. They are paid an average of $1.50 per day and fed one meal at noontime. The combination of hunger and guns—and the omnipresence of diamonds—turns many of them to robbery.

"That region is very violent and it is all because of the diamonds. The police will not take responsibility for the brutality," said João Pinto, editor in chief of Radio Ecclesia, an independent station which broadcasts reports of violence in the Lundas called in by listeners. The station has not been granted a license to broadcast outside Luanda and so the reports are routinely ferried through the miners' family and friends who have found their way back to the capital.

Luanda was a city built to accommodate, at most, a half-million people. Today it swelters with more than 4 million, most of them living in shanty-towns radiating out from the harbor in crazyquilt patterns. Many of these urban settlers are refugees from Savimbi's war who came to the capital seeking safety behind the government lines. I met more than a few in the slums who confessed active involvement in diamond smuggling—even after the conflict was over.

One of them was a thirty-seven-year-old man named Cassanga Coimbra, who now sells baseball caps, but had been the boss of a mining crew made up of children. This was a dangerous profession because of the constant threat of murder or robbery. The best way to move cash through the wilderness, he said, was to put it into your stomach.

"Take a condom," he told me. "Roll up the money very tight and put it inside. Tie it closed. You can then put it up your ass, but the soldiers may search you there. The better way is to swallow it. You tie a string to it and then tie the other end to your tooth"—he opened his mouth and showed me a rear molar—"and then try to swallow it. I like to put some Vicks on the condom, it numbs the throat and makes it go down easier.

"It took several tries for me to get used to this," he went on. "I puked several times. You can't eat anything for twenty-four hours before, otherwise you puke." Eventually he became practiced enough to swallow as much as $4,000.

If the string around the tooth breaks, he said, there is no choice but to try to pass the condom and the bills. You must drink a mixture of water and spoiled milk, which gives you diarrhea. Diamond trading in the bush is always conducted with American hundred-dollar bills—known to the miners as "Franklins"—and many of the bills in circulation around northeast Angola are hard-worn and stained vermilion from blood and shit from the various innards they have traveled through.

The diamonds, too, are often swallowed on their way to Zambia or the Democratic Republic of the Congo. The trade in illicit gems continues three years after Savimbi's assassination. On paper, Angola is the world's fourth largest producer of diamonds as measured by dollar value; but in reality, it is probably the third largest. The difference is due to all the diamonds illegally smuggled out through neighboring countries.

On the southern edge of the city is a carnival grounds called the *Féria Popular de Luanda* which has been closed for the last two years. The sign is missing several letters. Garbage clutters the midway and three cars of the Ferris wheel are hanging precariously off to one side, connected only by a few remaining bolts. There is a meat-and-clothes market across the street where I met a diamond miner with a shaved head named Jorge Valentim. The Levi's jeans logo was tattooed on his right bicep with ink that had been siphoned from a ballpoint pen.

Valentim had been working near the town of Cafunfo during the war and discovered that a diamond mine was a bad place to be. Troops could simply stand on the lip of the pit and spray machine-gun fire down at the workers below. The only place to take refuge was inside some of the tunnels dug into the sand and clay, and these, too, could be deathtraps. Soldiers would often roll grenades into the tunnels, Valentim said. If you weren't ripped apart by the explosion, you stood a good chance of being buried alive under the fallen soil.

Savimbi's death in the spring of 2002 brought no peace to the diamond fields, he said. In some ways, it made things worse. Poorly paid government troops, as well as defeated rebel veterans, were suddenly left without an enemy to fight and no clear mandate from the capital. They had their weapons, though, which made them equivalent to the law. They began to turn their frustrations on all the *garimpeiros* who had flooded into the region in the 1990s, many of whom were young male immigrants from the Congo with no close relatives in the area to protest if they happened to disappear abruptly. The soldiers often used the miners like pilot fish to find the richest diamond deposits. Those diggings rumored to be yielding the best stones were the ones most often raided by soldiers and policemen, according to Valentim and others. The only way to make any money was to have a steady—and quiet—production of small diamonds that could be sold to foreign buyers. Silence was crucial. Far from being a godsend, a big enough stone could be like a death sentence for a mining crew if anybody talked.

"You have to keep an eye on your friends," said Valentim. "The smart ones keep it to themselves. You work as a group and everybody gets a share and it's difficult to keep a secret."

In Luanda, I met a miner named Cardoso who had the bad luck to be working at such a mine the previous year. A squad of soldiers had heard about the diggings and showed up with their rifles drawn on a Friday afternoon, right when the mining crew was about to wash a pile of gravel. One of the soldiers took a length of rope and draped it down the middle of the pile. "This is yours," said the soldier, pointing to one half. "And this is ours." He pointed to the other half. Cardoso wasn't sure if the soldiers had been watching from the brush all along or if somebody among them had let the wrong word slip in a drunken moment. Whatever: the result was the same. The crew was forced to wash half their gravel at gunpoint and surrender all the diamonds that appeared in the sifts.

"There is nothing you can do about it," said Cardoso. "If you take part of what they say is theirs, they will beat you or kill you. You cannot complain to anybody. These soldiers are not attached to a unit. If you can't come to an agreement, all you can do is run away." He had once lost a 15-carat stone to soldiers, but told me he didn't regret it so much as he dreamed only of finding another just like it someday.

While we talked, I began to get the impression that Cardoso had thought all along that I was a buyer wanting to smuggle some stones back to America. At one point, he sent a friend into the house behind him to fetch a small plastic bag of garnets to show me. These were the indicator minerals he had collected over the years. Did I want to see something else?

I said no, I only wanted to hear about diamonds, not buy them.

"The real way to make money in Angola is not to mine diamonds but to rob the miners," he said. "When you're mining, everybody takes advantage of you. Even the people among you."

Then he asked for my cell phone number. Since he left the diamond fields, he was working at a nearby store that sold fruit and soda pop, but it was really a front. The boss was a Chinese man who had access to a stream of diamonds taken from the Lundas, said Cardoso. He could guarantee me a good price.

Diamonds are not solely to blame for Angola's misery. Any understanding of the nation's current predicament must also account for the personality of Jonas Savimbi, who embodied a dangerous mix: a lust for power, the charisma to achieve it, the right historical moment to seize, and the ability to conceal his own nihilism in the guise of a grand ideology.

He was born into a comfortable level of the Ovimbundu tribe on August 6, 1934, the son of a stationmaster on the Benguela Railroad. The young Savimbi was sent to Protestant missionary schools, where he displayed a quick tongue and a knack for foreign languages. His teachers arranged for him to study political philosophy and medicine at universities in Portugal and Switzerland. Then came a crucial period—one he would spend the rest of his life either glorifying or trying to explain away, depending on who was listening. The Maoist government in China saw him as a potential revolutionary and recruited him to attend a nine-month guerrilla training course in the Asian mountains. Savimbi learned military tactics and embraced the doctrine of triggering violent overthrow through raising the consciousness of peasants to their plight.

This message had particular resonance in the Portuguese colonial Africa of the 1960s, where the old system of government was refusing to die. Most European governments had already lowered their flags over Africa, but the government in Lisbon was determined to hang on. It had first set up its base in Angola with slavers' galleons in the fifteenth century, a decade before Christopher Columbus first sailed. The rationale was more than sentimental: Angola was one of the last reliable cashboxes left over from the old empire. Diamonds were discovered in the Lunda provinces in 1912 and the government set up a monopoly company called Diamang to divert rivers, operate mills, and build towns for the miners. Along with cotton and coffee, diamonds helped to prop up the near-bankrupt regime of Dr. Antonio de Oliveira Salazar, a European dictator of the old quasi-fascist school. Salazar declared it to be an "integral part" of Portugal, replaced local currency with the Portuguese *escudo*, and erected trade barriers designed to discourage foreigners from investing in the country.

There was also a cultural element in this policy. For years, Portugal had been encouraging its poor whites, many of them illiterate and some with criminal records, to migrate to Angola, where they could have jobs, highrise apartments, and servants—opportunities far beyond anything they could have at home. Angola became known as an expatriate paradise, a place of relentless sunny weather, lobster dinners at outdoor cafés, and motorcycles puttering along beach roads. And there was the sex. One important aspect of the Portuguese colonial experience—almost unique among the European powers—was the relative lack of personalized racism toward their subjects, an attitude that has been described by scholars with the word "tenderness." For the men, this had a special translation. "There is no sin south of the Equator," was a popular saying in Portugal. African wives and mistresses were commonplace and an entire class of mixed-race *mestiços* were accepted into their fathers' families and became something of an elite layer. This social division would come to have wide-ranging consequences.

By the late 1960s, it was becoming clear to Savimbi and others that Portugal's grip was weakening. Revolutionary movements formed and divided and began to fight each other almost as bitterly as if they were the colonists. Savimbi split with the Frente Nacional de Libertação de Angola (FNLA) and formed the National Union for the Total Independence of Angola (UNITA), composed mainly of Ovimbundi peasants in the highlands, in opposition to the Popular Movement for the Liberation of Angola (MPLA), a Marxist group which had its greatest support among the Mbundu tribe and the *mestiço* elites in the capital, with outside help from Cuba and the Soviet Union.

These factions enjoyed an unlikely common ally: Portugal's own military, which saw the beginnings of a quagmire. A group of generals overthrew the government in a 1974 coup and announced Angola would become an independent nation the following year. A committee was formed to broker a peace between the warring independence groups, but the real exit plan was to simply hand over the reins to whichever side controlled the streets of the capital at that time.

What followed was a colossal disgrace. As the transition date approached, white Portuguese citizens left in droves "with their middle fingers extended," as one Angolan put it to me. For five centuries, they had taken cotton, coffee, slaves, and diamonds out of their colony and they now seemed determined to leave it in the worst possible condition—one final looting. Sports cars that could not be shipped back to Europe were crashed in daredevil games and abandoned on the street. Copper wiring was pried from the cores of buildings and there were reports of concrete poured down elevator shafts to make them unusable. *Los Angeles Times* correspondent David Lamb described the scene vividly: "Telephones were ripped from the walls, typewriters were packed, plantations abandoned, mansions shuttered. Doctors walked out of the hospitals and professors emptied their desks at the university. In the course of a single week, 95 percent of the employees of the Bank of Angola departed, leaving junior clerks and janitors to run it." It was as if the colonists had *wanted* their former charge to drown in confusion and violence.

Jonas Savimbi saw a historical moment and seized it. The story of the civil war that followed can be told in a few paragraphs, although there was unimaginable suffering between the machinations: brutal acts and useless pain that went unrecorded by history except in the memories of those who loved the dead.

UNITA established a bush camp in the southern part of the country and started launching commando raids. More than 10 million land mines were laid, claiming an estimated 300,000 lives and an unknown number of limbs. Rebel troops also attacked schools and hospitals. Savimbi began selling his cause to anybody who could help him, always tailoring his message to fit the audience. To the Ovimbundu tribesmen, he preached revenge against the *mestiços* in the capital. To Prime Minister P. W. Botha of South Africa, he promised a friendly buffer state on the north of the occupied territory of Namibia. To Zaire's corrupt Mobutu Sese Seko, he promised diamonds. To the United States, he promised a fight against the Marxists.

Angola became a battlefield of the Cold War. The CIA began recruiting mercenaries to help UNITA fight. Savimbi also made regular fund-raising trips to Washington, D.C., where his charisma helped accentuate his anti-Communist message. Ronald Reagan called him a "freedom fighter" and likened him to Abraham Lincoln. To those conservatives who questioned his training in China and his former embrace of Maoist principles, he invoked the historical example of Franklin D. Roosevelt making a pragmatic alliance with Joseph Stalin to fight Hitler. To African listeners, he used the same analogy to defend his friendship with the racist regime in South Africa. It is sometimes acceptable, he said, to partner with the devil in order to achieve a just end. And he left no doubt that those ends would be achieved from the barrel of a gun.

"I believe you know what we need," Savimbi told a 1986 dinner audience at the Capitol Hilton in downtown Washington, D.C., with Senator Orrin Hatch (R-Utah) in attendance. "If you give us aspirin, we will take them, but they will not solve our problem. If you give us books, we will take them but they will not solve our problem. If you give us anti-tank weapons and anti-aircraft weapons—*that* will make a difference that the MPLA and the Russians will understand."

The American interest in toppling the MPLA helped obscure a fundamental question about Savimbi. It was impossible to know what he really believed, if anything. He claimed to be a supporter of free markets, but observers noted the lack of any functioning businesses in UNITA territory and the leadership's control of all money. He touted his commitment to education and health care for all Angolans, but ordered shelling attacks on schools and hospitals. Most troubling to his conservative backers, he continued to wear Mao-style headgear in the bush and made his lieutenants carry a book of dialectical materialist sayings called *Practical Guide for the Cadre*. Years after the Portuguese exit, classified documents revealed that Savimbi had been an informer to Salazar's secret police. What was he? A spy? A free market champion? An autocrat? A Communist? A neocolonialist? A little of everything?

All of these contradictions helped fuel the impression that Savimbi actually believed in nothing at all except for the acquisition of power. His supernatural charisma, however, could work magic on anyone prone to doubt him. In this sense, he was a little bit like a diamond—a total creation of its own image, but one whose *nothingness* carries immense powers. "He would take command of any room he would walk into," said former UNITA general Armindo Paulo "Gato" Lukamba. "It was as if all the rest of us had sunk into the floor."

The vacancy at the heart of the rebel movement was complemented by a spectacle that only heightened the sense that the entire nation of Angola was a hall of mirrors. When the Portuguese left in 1975, Gulf Oil Company had refused to abandon its offshore platforms in the Cabinda region. A contract with the MPLA government was arranged. Gulf would pay royalties on the oil—a sum that amounted to $5 million a day—in exchange for continued drilling rights and protection against bombing attacks from Savimbi's rebel army. President Jose Eduardo dos Santos assigned squads of Cuban soldiers to guarantee the safety of Gulf and the other Western oil giants based in Luanda, including Chevron's new office tower.* And thus, Angola became the only place in the world where Cuban troops, supposedly sworn to the destruction of capitalism, were protecting U.S. multinational oil companies against attacks from U.S.-backed guerrillas.

Devoid of any real ideological clarity, the war had even less reason to continue after the Soviet Union ceased to exist. A peace treaty was

---

*Located on Avenida Lenin.

signed in Bicesse, elections were called, and Savimbi pledged to disarm and abide by the results. The turnout in the 1992 election was surprisingly large—91 percent of the eligible population cast a vote—and Savimbi wound up losing to dos Santos in an election observers proclaimed (more or less) clean. Savimbi nonetheless accused the government of committing voter fraud. He quickly reconstituted his army and launched attacks on several cities and diamond mines, plunging the war into its most bloody phase yet. Caught unguarded, the MPLA handed out handguns and rifles to ordinary civilians. The violence caused nearly all of Savimbi's international clients to desert him. The United States, in particular, grew closer to dos Santos after he distanced himself from Cuba and began to voice support for free markets. After the inauguration of Bill Clinton in 1993, the stream of American aid to Savimbi was cut off completely.

Another way to buy guns would have to be found.

At the height of the blood diamond trade in the late 1990s, anywhere from 4 to 14 percent of the diamonds that found their way to America had been smuggled out of war zones or bartered to buy bombs and guns. That ratio has shrunk today, but those stones with tainted histories are still circulating around the jewelry stores. My own diamond—the one I had given to Anne when I proposed to her in 2000—could have easily been responsible for planting a few hundred cheap land mines on a road somewhere in Africa. The odds of this were one in twenty-five on the low side, and one in six on the high side.

The diamond needed a personal mythology to give it power in our engagement. It was insignia to the outside world that Anne belonged to me, and I to her. It was the first thing we ever owned together. The stone crystallized our promise to love each other as hard as we could. We told a new story around it, never knowing its history and not really wanting to.

"You cannot tell me that diamonds caused this war," said General Lukamba. "A diamond is a beautiful thing. It brings life, not wars."

We were sitting in padded chairs in his living room. A stereo tucked underneath the television set played soft American pop songs. On the far wall was a Cubist painting of a couple having sex. There was an armed guard standing outside on the patio.

Lukamba is better known as "General Gato." He was the guerrilla fighter who took control of the rebel group after Savimbi's death and made peace overtures to dos Santos, the final step toward ending the war. Gato had since been forced out of the chairmanship as UNITA made the awkward transition from rebel army to opposition political party. He was wearing a wine-colored shirt bearing an abstract pattern of waves and fish; the cloth looked stiff and scratchy.

I had been given Gato's cell phone number by a friend of his in London and he had agreed to see me without knowing what I wanted to talk about. When I brought up diamonds, he grew quiet for a long minute. I thought Gato might end the conversation before it began, but as he talked, he began to warm to his subject.

"I don't believe people who say the war went on because of diamonds," he told me. "There is no link, no cause and effect, it needs to be out of the calculation. We started fighting against the Portuguese without them. We were using bows and arrows back then."

As Gato continued talking, his position began to shift. He eventually told me that, yes, diamond sales had indeed fueled the conflict, especially after the United States withdrew its support. But he characterized this commerce as a necessity to continue the fight for UNITA's end goal of "a multiparty system and a market economy" for Angola.

"We needed diamonds only to improve our capacity," he told me. "Look, we had no normal state relations. We could not buy armaments through conventional channels. Our whole process was more taxing. We had to pay three times as much as anyone else for a tank."

These high prices were charged by international arms smugglers. UNITA had to rely on the black market when it became a global pariah after the disputed election of 1992. The UN Security Council decided the best way to end Savimbi's war was to choke off the illicit diamond trade. UNITA was placed under trade sanctions in 1993 and criminal penalties were threatened for anyone who tried to buy illegal diamonds from Angola. There were multiple ways around this, however.

Seven years after the Security Council first took action, a UN investigation found that Bulgarian suppliers were using an "engineering company" registered in Gibraltar to trade armaments for Angola diamonds. The African nation of Togo was frequently used as a phantom "country of origin." The list of military hardware that likely passed between Bulgaria and the African battlefield was impressive: 20,000 mortar bombs, 12 million rifle rounds, 6,300 antitank rockets, and 20 antiaircraft guns, just in the space of two years.

Matthew Hart, a former editor at the trade journal *Rapaport Diamond Report*, describes the preparations for a typical exchange of diamonds for a tank. In this case the military equipment is being flown in from Bulgaria.

> The flight plan lists Lusaka, Zambia, as the final destination. The crew flies to Uganda, refuels, then resumes the flight in the direction of Zambia. They reach Zambian airspace at nightfall, where, under cover of darkness, they abruptly change course to the west and fly to Angola. At night, the plane is invisible to American satellites, which could otherwise track its course and report it to the Angolan military. Once inside Angola, the Russian pilots head for a landing strip specified in advance by UNITA. Or it might be a new strip—a straight stretch of road bulldozed flat and watered. . . . UNITA never widens such a strip because a widened road is visible from space and will be detected by a computer tasked to scan satellite images for just such a change. Because the roads are narrow, and the bush on either side would tear the wings off a plane, UNITA prunes the vegetation beside the road to a height of two feet. . . .

These airstrip deals were helped significantly by the unique qualities of a diamond—small, easy to transport, impossible to trace. It was the ultimate tool of money laundering. This explained why the mines were such important military targets and raised the question of whether the war could have gone on if this ready source of wealth were not available. Savimbi himself had said in 1996: "UNITA keeps control of diamond areas in northeastern Angola for the sake of its own survival." The diamonds were also useful as tools for subterranean diplomacy. According to Belgian intelligence agents, Savimbi had sealed a lasting friendship with the president of the impoverished nation of Burkina Faso by making a gift of diamonds to him in 1995. Shortly thereafter, UNITA began using Burkina Faso as a smuggling platform.

Unlike other regional strongmen in Africa, Savimbi apparently did not sock away revenue for himself through overseas bank accounts or investments. He was known, however, to keep large amounts of cash and some of the most valuable diamonds in his field tent or on his person. Savimbi

was supposed to have been carrying up to $3 million in both cash and di-
amonds with him on the day he was killed. This personal reserve has
never been found, leading to speculation that people within UNITA had
been bribed to reveal their leader's position.

Financial ties were already known to exist between the rebels and the
government, who also saw a profitable nexus between war and diamonds.
Many of the people in the upper ranks of the MPLA—a group known as
"the diamond generals"—reportedly had mining interests of their own
and were trading diamonds, weapons, and fuel with the same army that
they were allegedly trying to crush. Planes belonging to the government
oil company Sonagol were spotted making numerous landings at airfields
known to be controlled by UNITA. Apparently, some MPLA generals
were also in the business of capturing diamond fields and then selling the
diamonds back to UNITA in exchange for gasoline or cash. According to
a 2001 classified report from the Belgian government's Intelligence and
Security Services, these generals used the state-run marketing company
Endiama as a shield for their activities. War was good business for the
leadership, and the troops under their command were not so much soldiers fighting for a political cause as they were grabbers of diamonds.

"It is in their interest for the conflict *not* to be ended quickly, as this
would interrupt their lucrative trade, including that with the enemy,
UNITA," stated the report. "They use military equipment and government army soldiers to conduct their trade." This scam would have been
equivalent to Ulysses Grant sending his divisions to capture the cotton
warehouses of Mississippi and then selling the cotton back to Robert E.
Lee for resale overseas. It was Angola's house of mirrors all over again.

The smuggling capital was—and still is—a town of concrete blocks and
rutted streets called Cafunfo, which sprang up almost overnight near the
deposits of the Cuango River in the midst of the war. The population
soared eight times over between 1990 and 1992. Most of the new migrants
were young men coming over from the Congo, at Savimbi's encouragement, to mine the astonishingly colorless alluvial diamonds that fetched
such a high price in Antwerp. The Congolese miners brought all sorts of
things with them: guns, radios, matches, whiskey, AIDS, and condoms
used more for smuggling hundred-dollar bills than they were for safe sex.
Buyers from Belgium also moved in with satellite phones and Range
Rovers and figured out how to get small planes in and out of the dirt
airstrips around Cafunfo without being shot down by shoulder-launched

missiles. Pilots learned how to fly corkscrewing patterns that made it difficult for a soldier on the ground to draw a clear bead on the fuselage.

Savimbi had ordered a strike on Cafunfo in 1992 in a bid to control
more diamonds. His troops slaughtered the workers they found at the
mine sites and held the town itself for several months before the MPLA
launched a ground assault and a bombing campaign. They had purchased
the help of a private security company called Executive Outcomes, composed in part of retired white South African soldiers who had learned the
art of counterinsurgency while putting down antiapartheid uprisings in
the townships around Johannesburg.*

How can you say the war wasn't about diamonds, I asked Gato, when
the mines were considered profit centers by both UNITA and the MPLA?

The diamond was only a means to an end, he told me again. And that
end was the creation of a more effective fighting force.

"They influenced the way the war was fought," he said. "It will be a
more sophisticated war with diamonds. In Palestine, it started with rocks.
What if they had diamonds to use? The MPLA used its oil for the same
purpose—to buy weapons. I don't understand why you are drawing this
distinction between diamonds and oil."

"Some would say it's a lot easier to smuggle a diamond than a super-
tanker full of oil," I said, trying to keep my voice casual.

"I totally remove myself from that idea," he said. "Diamonds will
change the quality of a war, but they are not the cause. Dr. Savimbi never
saw it as an ostentatious thing to display, but as an instrument of combat.
He always said, 'Money gives us liberty.'"

While he was saying this, Gato's eyes flicked toward a painting on the
wall behind me that I hadn't noticed when I came in. It was a large portrait of Savimbi, posing in heroic style. He was dressed in a high-collared
blue coat with a paisley pocket-square on the breast. The UNITA flag
was floating in the air to his left.

Gato's wife served us a pungent tea made of caxinda leaves and the
conversation moved on to other directions. But before I was escorted out,
I asked Gato what he thought of a sentiment I had heard voiced several
times since I had been in Angola: that the nation's awesome wealth in diamonds had actually proved to be a curse.

---

*That any self-respecting African government would hire such people was a loud testament to
the true nature of the war.

"I totally reject that!" he said angrily. "It's a very pretty thing, very hard to produce. You have to move mountains in order to find it. So much labor to find this little rock that winds up on the neck of some lady in America. It's a very pretty thing, but it can't be connected to violence. It gives life. If we all had diamonds, we wouldn't be fighting. Peace is not where doves are flying all around."

Gato then pulled a slim leather wallet out of his pants and tapped it on top. "Peace is money," he said.

If you were a smuggler trying to unload the spoils of Angolan war, this is what you would have done. You would have concealed the diamonds on yourself, either with an envelope taped to the chest, or inside a thermos that you carried inside a briefcase. You would have dressed casually in a button-down shirt and slacks, looking relaxed but not rich. You would have then booked a flight from Kinshasa or Johannesburg into Zurich. There, you would have declared your diamonds and received certification of their import into Switzerland. From this point forward, their true point of origin is effectively concealed behind the Swiss paperwork. You would have then caught a short flight to Brussels International Airport and boarded a train to Antwerp. The trip takes less than an hour, and you would have seen snug half-timbered farmhouses and children on bicycles and fields fat with beets and barley. You would have disembarked at Antwerp's Central Station, where the platforms are covered with a vault of glass and iron and the station itself is a gray cathedral made of twenty kinds of marble. You would walk down the grand staircase and out the north entrance of the station, from which it is a three-minute walk to the street called Hovenierstraat, the heart of the diamond district. More than a hundred brokers have their offices here in mid-sized office buildings. Quite a few once displayed the UNITA symbol—a black rooster—in their window. It was a way of communicating that that particular buyer was friendly toward Angolan stones, the very kind you would have had tucked inside your shirt or your briefcase.

You would have shown your passport to the guard behind the glass booth, taken the elevator upstairs, and met your contact. He would have peered at your diamonds with a loupe. There would have been some poker-faced negotiations before the handshake. You would have been handed American dollars and then you would have left immediately.

There would have been no contract. Nothing would have been written down. The only remaining evidence of the transaction was the diamonds themselves, which would have been quickly polished, resold, sold again, and eventually ended up in an engagement setting under the glass at Zales, Macy's, Wal-Mart, or a hundred other jewelry outlets in America and elsewhere.

The black roosters are gone from the windows now. The Antwerp street was badly stung by the conclusions of the 2001 United Nations Inspector's report, which concluded that the ancient diamond market of Northern Europe had acted as an open bazaar for war goods from Africa. Suddenly, the whole world knew Antwerp's dirty secret. Canada's ambassador to the UN, Robert Fowler, went so far as to call diamonds "one of the most corrosive substances known to man."

Even before the Kimberley Process got off the ground, the industry tried to police itself. A powerful industry collective called the High Diamond Council created a "watchlist" for sensitive African countries whose imports might contain diamonds from Sierra Leone or Angola. Those packages were given special scrutiny by customs officials. But there were still two easy ways around the barriers. One was simply to put a fictitious label on the parcel, which was rarely checked at the customs office. The other way was to "mix" a parcel by filling it halfway with UNITA stones and half from a blameless country like Namibia and then labeling the entire parcel as Namibian. The difference in color and quality between the two kinds of stones would have been obvious to any trained broker, but the Old World culture of Antwerp's diamond district was not geared toward asking many questions about the source of a delivery.

The port city on the Scheldt River has been receiving diamonds ever since the first importations from India in the sixteenth century. With direct access to the Atlantic, a well-fed middle class, a tolerant attitude toward religious minorities, and a soaring Roman Catholic cathedral spire that could be seen for miles in every direction, Antwerp was already one of Europe's most prominent trading centers. Its merchant grandees employed halls full of artisans, who cut stones imported from India and Brazil into sparkling jewels for the necks of the aristocracy.

Antwerp's role as the world capital of diamonds was sealed in the late 1880s after the arrival of several families of Lithuanian Jews fleeing the czar's pogroms. The new emigrants placed a high value on diamonds as a source of wealth for common people that could be easily transported in times of political or religious persecution. They also brought a business ethic based on trust and a certain amount of secrecy. Written contracts were shunned and disputes were settled by a committee of impartial observers. Deals were customarily sealed by a handshake and a Hebrew phrase: *mazel und brocha*, which means "luck and blessing." That phrase—and the conviviality that it represents—is widespread today in diamond centers from New York to Bombay.

The layout of Antwerp's diamond district also recalls the diamond's power as portable wealth. Nearly all of the city's gem dealers have offices in the tightly packed blocks just north of Central Station and radiating from Hovenierstraat. Most diamond transactions used to be conducted inside brightly lit cafés near the train station so traveling brokers and overseas customers could do business quickly and leave town without having to stay the night. The sales tables have since migrated behind turnstiles and guard booths, but the geography remains the same.

I went there on a cold drizzly day just before Christmas in 2004 to see Mark H. G. Van Bockstael, the director of international affairs and trade for the High Diamond Council. He wore a blue turtleneck underneath his blazer and has a wide and open face. During our conversation, he made intricate doodles on a piece of typing paper that lay before him. Some of his sentences were leavened with the phrase "my good friend," as in, "Well, my good friend, that is a very important question. . . ." This flourish could have sounded hostile in another mouth, but Van Bockstael carries with him the air of courtly liberalism that helped make Antwerp the place that it is.

When the Kimberley Process needs a human face, the face usually belongs to Van Bockstael. He was one of its major architects and continues to serve as the chairman of a subcommittee that works on technical issues. There is hardly a trade magazine serving the jewelry business that has not carried his photograph at one time or another.

We talked for a while about African politics and he reminded me of a recent Kimberley Process victory: the July 2004 decision to evict the Republic of the Congo from the system for blatant irregularities in its diamond export process. The nation had been claiming a production level of 5.2 million carats a year, but Von Bockstael and a team of geologists had done aerial surveys of the nation's alluvial mines and concluded the land was capable of yielding only about 55,000 carats a year. The smuggled extras had been coming mainly from the similarly named (but much more politically turbulent) Democratic Republic of the Congo. It was a gap so obvious as to be laughable, and the wonder was that the nation had ever been admitted to the international scheme with such a slipshod record. Kimberley's cheerleaders nevertheless held it up as proof that the system was not—as sometimes alleged—a toothless tiger.

When I asked him about potential loopholes in the system, Van Bockstael readily admitted that the current state of affairs was not perfect. One of the flaws was the built-in assumption that a tranquil African nation was always going to remain at peace. It was true that the three worst diamond wars of the 1990s—in Sierra Leone, Angola, and the Democratic Republic of the Congo—had recently come to an end. But any student of African politics knows that debt-riddled regimes are often built on a foundation of sand, particularly when methods of raising cash to buy guns are nearby and the people are beaten down enough to listen to a demagogue. On the world's richest diamond continent, anything can happen.

"Let's be honest," said Van Bockstael. "An arena that looks completely stable can go sour. The Ivory Coast was once the showcase of French West Africa and now look at it! It's endangering the stability of the entire region."

He was referring to the entirely unexpected meltdown the month before of what was once a functional, if impoverished, Francophone port colony and the world's largest producer of cocoa. The government of President Laurent Gbagbo had broken a peace agreement on November 4, 2004, by launching small bombing attacks on rebel bases in the north, which also happened to kill nine French peacekeeping troops and an American agricultural researcher. The French military responded by destroying the entire Ivory Coast air force, which consisted of two planes and four helicopters. Angry crowds burned cars, broke into stores, and demonstrated in the streets against their former colonial masters, and more than ninety thousand foreigners were forced to evacuate. The nation produces a tiny share of the world's annual diamond harvest, only about 200,000 carats a year, but functioned as a Laundromat nation for stones from Sierra Leone during that nation's brutal civil war. The near war with the French also provides an example of how the paper reality of international pacts can sometimes provide cover to the reality of an internal security disaster.

Nowhere is this more vivid than in Angola—a nation officially clean by the narrow definitions of the diamond industry, but one where the stones are still mined under some of the most miserable conditions imaginable, and where the diamond that goes on to sparkle on the left hand of a bride on a country club dance floor in Minnesota may once have been pulled from the lower intestine of a slain Congolese miner like a pearl out of an oyster.

"In terms of the social atmosphere where diamonds are produced—the Kimberley Process is not at all concerned with that," Van Bockstael admitted in a later conversation with me. "It is only concerned with a formal definition of war."

Two weeks after I left Antwerp, I met a researcher named Justin Pearce who had traveled through the diamond regions of Angola on behalf of a respected South Africa think tank called the Institute for Security Studies. He found clinics which had been turned into police stations and schools that provided no education beyond the fourth grade. Numerous Lunda-Chokwe villagers told him conditions were so bad they didn't feel like they were a part of Angola anymore. The isolation from the capital and the smuggling that lived on after the death of Savimbi had created an especially violent *confusão* at the source of some of the best diamonds in the world. But on paper—the only place it mattered—everything was just fine. That was all it took to make an Angolan diamond as clean as a fresh snowflake.

"The Kimberley Process whitewashes all kinds of things in Angola," Pearce told me. "The government has effectively won the war, but they have no intention of changing the system."

His report concluded: "Perhaps it is time to rethink the idea of what constitutes a 'blood diamond.'"

The diamond miners I met in Angola were, in most essential ways, just like their counterparts all over the world. They were tough and canny and had a dark sense of humor. They worked long hours with bad equipment. They saw friends die in wall collapses. They worked on faith for no wages whatsoever and got paid only if diamonds were found. Many of them entered the business because they had no other choice: either their fathers had introduced them to it and they knew nothing else, or they had started having children themselves and needed to feed the babies. They spent their lives in pursuit of the big stone that would bring them new cars and easy women. Those few that did get a windfall never managed to keep it.

I sat with one *garimpeiro* named Jorge against a mud wall outside his relative's house in a slum neighborhood of Luanda. He was forty-two, but looked much older. He was taking bootleg painkillers to quench the flames in his back.

"It is not good work," he told me. "You may not find anything. You may die." Jorge showed me the hidden seam in his pants that he used to smuggle a large-carat stone to Luanda. He had bought a red Yamaha motorcycle with the fence money. Where was the bike now? I asked Jorge, and he didn't answer. He didn't want to admit that it was gone.

The miners were partial to *kizomba*, a uniquely Angolan style of music that sounds like a more languid form of a samba. It can be alternatively sensual and moody and often both at once. A dance to *kizomba* under the lights of a beach bar looks like the flow of mercury. One of the popular singers is named Rey Webba and he became a favorite of the nation's miners when he recorded a song called *"Camanga,"* or "Diamond." If it weren't for the Portuguese lyrics, it would be well-understood in any of the diamond-bearing nations of the world where men chase their dreams in the form of a little white rock and sometimes get lucky.

The song tells the story of a nameless miner in the backcountry who finds a brilliant stone and finds himself instantly rich. He uses the money to buy a luxury car and expensive brand-name clothes, and nights out dancing with girls. But he blows through his fortune in the blink of an eye and finds himself just as poor as when he began. "Diamond" closes this way:

> My money was gone
> My friends were gone
> I had to go work at the construction buildings
> My life is hard now

The song, of course, was about "miner's disease"—that universal affliction which causes the lucky ones to throw away their money almost immediately. That tendency was just as strong in Angola as anywhere, but what the song didn't say was that miner's disease was often a fatal disease here. That was what made Angola unique. Finding too large a diamond marked one for death if the army found out about it. But the dreams of escaping poverty kept driving more men out into fields to take their chances.

Cassanga Coimbra, the man who showed me how to swallow the hundred-dollar bills, was not one of them. He said he was done with diamond mining forever. The end of the war, oddly enough, had made it too dangerous to continue.

"There is more chance of you dying than ever finding a stone," he said.

Eight

THE STONE MILLS

India

There is nothing particularly attractive about a rough diamond. Its surface is almost always cloudy and its shape is warped. Seen fresh from the earth, it might easily be mistaken for a small chip of quartz or even a blob of tree sap. Nobody would think to fasten it to the ear or hang it around the neck. Whatever beauty there is to a diamond comes—like the power of a local god—from what is offered to it.

What India offers is sweat.

It was at least 90 degrees at midday inside the Sanghavi Diamond Company plant in the northern India city of Surat, where hundreds of men were grinding stones on spinning metal wheels. There were four men assigned to each wheel and they hunched around it like poker players around a pot. I watched a young man named Manesh Amvalin putting facets into a tiny stone. His hands were covered with sweat. He had already done twenty-five diamonds that day, and he would be paid the equivalent of a dime for each. "If you have patience, this is easy," Amvalin told me. "My eyes sometimes hurt at the end of the day, but that's my only complaint."

There are more than four thousand workers in this particular factory, which is the largest one in Surat and claims to be the largest diamond-polishing facility in the world. There are three levels here, connected by a clanking elevator with lattice gates. It is about the shape and size of an airplane hangar. Two bored security men dressed in olive uniforms and holding bolt-action rifles stand at the front door, but they are mostly for ceremony. Anybody who would steal stones from this place would do it from the inside.

The owner, Chandrakant Sanghavi, has rich tufts of coffee-colored hair sprouting from the tops of his ears. He stands six feet tall and has a voice like a truck horn. He greeted me in his office, and after the customary offer of water and Pepsi, told me that he moves more than 10 million diamonds out of his plant every year.

Diamonds were the revolution that India needed, he said. They were bringing jobs and housing to people who had nothing before. In just under a decade of wild growth, these stones had impacted the household economies of 10 million people in the state of Gujarat—meaning that either that person, or somebody in their family, had a job polishing diamonds, twelve hours a day, ten cents per stone. This was a mass of people equivalent to the population of Los Angeles.

"We are doing something big here," said Sanghavi. "This will change India."

Not far away from the factory is a place called Mancharpura Road, where finished diamonds are sold by the bagful. Open-air rooms, their walls plated with butcher-white tiles, are set into the storefronts like caves. The merchants sit cross-legged on mattresses and sort through their stones with little pincers. I went up to one of them, an older man in a golf shirt, who offered me a cup of tea before he pulled a small leather case out of his pocket that looked like a pouch for business cards. It was full of paper packets. He unwrapped one to show me what was inside: a galaxy of poorly colored diamonds, literally thousands of them, each no bigger than a granule of salt.

"Where did they come from?" I ask. He shrugged, handed me a jeweler's loupe, and I peered closer at the incredibly small stone.

This was the genius of India. It takes in the garbage of the diamond world, slaps fifty-eight facets on it, sets it into gold, and sends it onward. These tiny specks are now the fifth most valuable export product of a nation that hasn't mined diamonds from its own soil for more than a century. The factories of India are now processing an astonishing 92 percent of the world's diamonds and have stolen the majority of business away from the old master craftsmen of New York, Israel, and Belgium.

This open-air market on Mancharpura Road is where many of today's diamonds are traded on their twisting journey to the display cases of an American discount store, with no remaining sign that they may well have been carved by a teenage boy who was paid wages of no more than a dollar a day, for dirty, dangerous work that leaves its laborers at risk for permanent lung damage.

This is one emerging legacy of the stone mills of India—an overnight industry that has forever changed the diamond trade and brought both hope and misery to its host country.

"India is the cradle of the human race," wrote Mark Twain, "the birthplace of human speech, the mother of history, the grandmother of legend and the great-grandmother of tradition." It is also the first place on the globe where people decided that diamonds were something valuable, and worthy to kill and die for.

Diamonds were dug out of shallow pits near the Krishna River in the region of Golconda 2,400 years ago. Local strongmen and rajahs collected them as marks of royalty, and the belief emerged that each stone was connected to a star in the heavens and would influence the fortunes of whoever wore it. A history of social customs written in the ninth century, the *Garuda-Puranam*, contains a passage explaining the exacting quality standards of the time: "Gods are supposed to dwell in a particle of diamond, wherever found, which is possessed of a clear, light shade and the usual commendable features, is smooth and even at the sides, and is divested of all threatening traits such as scratches, dot-like impressions, marks of crow's feet, or clouding impurities in its interior."

An ardent trade developed for these god-homes, and it wasn't long before the diamond fields of Golconda became a military target. A magnificent stone fortress was erected on a hilltop to protect the bazaar, and both were besieged many times over. While Europe went through its Dark Ages and fought off the Black Death, the Vijayanagar and Bahamani empires of India were wrestling over control of the diamond fields. Marco Polo visited the region on his way to China in 1292 and reported amazing—and highly embroidered—tales of palace flunkies dispatching eagles to retrieve the precious stones from a valley in the mountains. The reality was more dismal. Children as young as twelve were being made to dig trenches and sort through the earth for the rocks that sparkled. Nothing was known of kimberlite pipes or ancient volcanoes at that time; contemporary scientific thinkers concluded that the diamonds had once been pieces of quartz, and had naturally "ripened" into gemstones.

Indian diamonds were first brought to Europe by the French merchant Jean-Baptiste Tavernier, who made six trips to Golconda between 1631 and 1668 and won the trust of the local princes. The new stones immediately sparked a fad among European nobles. The infancy of the diamond trade happened to coincide with an important development in Western architecture: the increasing use of light. Whale oil was becoming cheaper and more plentiful as fishing vessels penetrated deeper into the North Atlantic. Rooms could be lit with more than just hearths. Moreover, as the art of masonry grew more sophisticated, the architects of royal palaces were able to incorporate larger windows into their designs, allowing for more natural sunlight to penetrate inside. It was also now fashionable for the upper classes to decorate the walls of their dwellings with mirrors, which bounced the light around a room. Europe was becoming less and less of a dark place, and diamonds looked exquisite in the Rembrandt light of a whale-oil candle.

Nearly all the famous diamonds that would come to fire the imagination of the Western world were dug from Krishna River sand. They were generally the size of apricots. The Regent Diamond was stolen from a slave by an English sea captain, and later wound up in a shoulder ornament worn by Louis XV, and then in the hilt of Napoleon's ceremonial sword. The Hope Diamond was acquired by Tavernier himself and given to the French court. It passed through a chain of unlucky owners before falling into the hands of the twentieth-century celebrity New York jeweler Harry Winston, who hyped the gem's supposedly cursed history (as well as his own reputation) in the media before donating it to the Smithsonian. The massive Koh-i-noor, or "mountain of light," was said to be worth half the daily expense of the entire world in the sixteenth century. The British had swindled it from a boy-prince of Punjab in 1849 during the negotiation of a treaty, and it was set into a tiara for Queen Victoria.

European hunger for the exotic stones grew as titled nobles and some of the wealthier merchants began to imitate the royals. The demand fed a massive expansion of the Indian mines, which could not support the exploitation. By the 1830s, they were completely empty. Prospectors made new discoveries in Brazil and South Africa. The stone fortress at Golconda was sacked and dismantled. Indians made gold their talisman of choice and forgot about the transparent god-homes, except as just another part of their national wealth that had been trundled off by the colonists.

It was not the end of the story. Diamonds would eventually come back to India, but in a way that nobody could have guessed.

It started in the classic way of economic revolutions: with a migration from the farm to the city. In this case, it was the movement of a handful of families from the scrubby village of Palanpur to the port of Bombay in 1909. They were Jains, one of the oldest religions in a nation of old religions. They believed in no particular gods, but embraced the core Hindu belief that the universe has no beginning or end, and consists of an endless cycle of birth, copulation, death, and rebirth. Jains revere life above all else and refuse to eat any meat because of the suffering it would bring to the slaughtered animal. Their abhorrence of killing is almost Talmudic in its expression: devout Jains even shun potatoes, radishes, and any other vegetable with a root because pulling such plants from the soil might kill insects living around the roots. To smash a bug in the presence of a Jain is a serious social faux pas. Although they make up less than 0.5 percent of India's population, their cultural influence has spread far beyond their numbers. Their insistence on never doing harm to a living creature made a deep impression on Mahatma Gandhi when he was developing his philosophy of nonviolence. He and countless other Indians embraced Jainist ideas about vegetarianism and abstinence from alcohol. And although Jain doctrine emphasizes detachment from the world and all of its sensual charms, it is because of the Jains that India has become the procurer of one of the world's premier tokens of luxury. At the beginning of the twentieth century, the Jain families from Palanpur were looking for a new business to adopt when they moved to Bombay, and they found diamonds.

The De Beers cartel was trying to develop new markets for the huge amounts of stone being pulled out of South Africa. India was a natural, given its long history of personal ornamentation and the cultural memory of Mughal kings dripping with baubles, and the Jains, with their famous rectitude, were a natural to take up the trade. Their ancestors had been the official jewelers to the nawab of Palanpur and they knew how to handle treasure, even if they mostly renounced it for themselves. Before long, the ships bearing tea and jute around South Asia began to carry pouches of Jain diamonds in the officers' cabins. New customers were found and seduced in the wealthy dinner party circles of Rangoon, Bangkok, Shanghai, and Singapore.

The business might have died in the chaos of World War I, but the Jains were helped by a remarkable collision of cultures—a transoceanic friendship that would, over time, help to reinvent India as a diamond powerhouse.

The world diamond capital in the 1910s was Amsterdam, where many of the brokers were Hasidic immigrants from Eastern Europe. The Jains traveled frequently to Amsterdam on buying trips. And as they did more and more business together, the Jews of Holland looked closely at the Jains of India and saw people who could be trusted with large-volume deals. Who could export diamonds to obscure corners of the globe, and do it with efficiency. Who dressed conservatively, treasured family, preferred verbal promises to written contracts, stuck to their own circles, and observed exacting dietary laws prescribed by the heavens.

In short, people very much like themselves.

"This was a relationship to last the century," Mahendra Mehta told me over tea in a Bombay hotel. A member of a prominent Jain family, he was in the diamond business for fifty years and now runs a charitable foundation. "The Jews found us very reliable," he said. "We were on the same cultural wavelength. The trust level was very high."

After India gained its independence from Great Britain in 1947, the Jains hit upon an idea: why not take the cheapest rough for sale in Belgium—the trash of the diamond world—and have it polished back home instead of sending it to the craftsmen? A small cottage industry in India began to grow, and the first full-scale polishing plant opened in the Colaba neighborhood of Bombay. A cutter was hired to teach faceting. But India's government at the time had socialist leanings, and discouraged the business by issuing only a limited number of permission licenses. The diamond men figured out how to get around the regulations—by smuggling rough into the country, and smuggling the polished products out—with the help of moles within Air India and other carriers. "Let's just say we made a lot of friends in the aviation industry," one executive told me with a slight smile. "It was a parallel industry—a window for a lot of people who made a quick buck."

India might have stayed this way: a slightly disreputable low-cost alternative to the artisans of Belgium and Israel, where most of the grinding was done inside dim and sweltering shacks, by young mothers with a

baby balanced on one knee. But then came the discovery of the Argyle
Mine in Australia, an event that changed the diamond world—and part of
the history of India—forever. The brownish stones were perfect for the
Indian market: cheap, plentiful, and good for the manufacture of discount
jewelry. The rift between Argyle and the De Beers cartel only made
things better. In 1996, De Beers flooded the market with a stockpile of
low-quality stones in an attempt to undercut prices. It only served to raise
the demand. The Indians discovered they had the ability to erect factories and hire teenagers on a grand scale to take on the sudden cascade of
stones from Australia.

"It was an amazing bit of good fortune," one Australian mining executive told an industry newsletter. "Our thanks to the Indians, who made so
much of our product and without whom there would have been no point
in digging it out at all."

There was another powerful global trend at work. The expansion of
Wal-Mart and the rest of the American discount store market in the 1970s
and 1980s meant there was a reliable overseas buyer with a seemingly
bottomless appetite for the small and dingy stones. Diamonds were becoming increasingly democratic—no longer the exclusive province of
movie starlets or middle-class brides, but for everybody with a checking
account or a job. In the space of three decades, Indian exports grew from
$13 million to $12 *billion*, with the majority going straight to the United
States.

What had happened with diamonds was a pioneering version of the
high-tech outsourcing practices pioneered by American technology firms
in the late 1990s. With its endless pool of hungry workers, India was well
on its way to mastering the portable end of business operations: cheap
tech support, cheap call centers, and cheap movie animation. Cheap diamonds had already been locked down. They were catering to American
tastes for a song, giving America what it wanted at the right price point.

"If it wasn't for you guys, we wouldn't be here," said Thomas Anthony,
the spokesman for the India Gem & Jewellery Export Promotion Council
in Bombay. Anthony studied to work in the chemical industry, but his
eyes watered in the refineries. He now has an office with a window and
reads American history for leisure. He told me in the conference room
about his fascination with Henry Ford's idea of the division of labor.

"That's what we have with Indian diamonds—an assembly-line system," he said. "One room does the pavilions, the next does the facets, the

next does the girdling. It's mass production that makes luxury affordable. But it's different from the automobile, because we have developed a market for a product that people do not need."

The biggest challenge to India is not a fear that people will stop wanting diamonds but the probability that other nations with oceans of cheap labor could steal their contracts: China, for example, whose Communist government recently lowered tariffs on the import of rough diamonds. About two dozen Indian companies have already set up shop in China, hoping to cash in on a market where even the rock-bottom wages of India look extravagant by comparison.

"Wherever you get a competitive cost advantage, globalization takes you there," said S. Ramswamy, the genial executive director of the Promotion Council. "If Zales or Wal-Mart wanted to buy somewhere else at a more advantageous price point, they will." He went on to tell me about distressing reports out of Tanzania and Sri Lanka, where businessmen had asked experts to train their own impoverished countrymen in the art of putting facets on a speck.

The sybaritic dreams of America are ground out in one of the more tragic places in South Asia. The city of Surat was once known as the filthiest city in India, which is saying quite a lot in a nation of widespread poverty. Silk used to be the big manufactured product here, and is still strong. The clatterslap of power looms resounds through the streets at every hour of the day and the smokestacks of the textile plants chug out endless rivers of gray-yellow grit. A particularly deadly strain of bubonic plague broke out here in 1994 and caused a mass panic. Many of the darkened slums now have running water and garbage no longer piles up in the streets, but Surat still groans under the weight of nearly 3 million people chasing industrial jobs.

Shortly after I arrived, I climbed to the top of a twelve-story building near the railroad station and looked out over a white carpet of settlement and haze. Surat was a vista of shantytowns and blank-eyed tenement buildings. It was what Chicago or Pittsburgh would have looked like a hundred years ago: a single vast organism humming with production. Except that what was being produced here was not windmill motors, or iron plows, or pork bellies, but small bits of carbon.

I took a walk through one of the slums, a place called Ambawadi Pitichawl on the east side of the Indian Railways tracks. A man mixing detergent in a plastic barrel told me that a set of faucets had been installed shortly after the bubonic plague outbreak. A few of the paths through the maze of ricket-shacks were now paved with flagstones, but most were still dirt and reeking of urine, with a stream of evil-colored water trickling down the middle. Behind the blue tarp doors of the shacks, I could see neat lines of cooking pots and rugs on the floor. Televisions flickered in a few. Pregnant dogs wandered about a sloped field, looking for something to eat. Naked children nearby played an inscrutable game with rocks. In a clearing littered with broken glass, some older children played a game of whiffle cricket.

More than three hundred of these slums fester in the spaghetti of the city's road system, which is mostly dirt. The diamond boom had only made things worse, as factories expanded at a rapid clip in the 1990s, and more and more workers came in to take the jobs. Surat was considered an ideal place for diamonds. It was close to the financial center in Bombay, but free of the city's labor unions, high taxes, and protection rackets. Wage standards were much lower here. Best of all, it was located in the state of Gujarat—the most business-friendly state in India—where the government was sensitive to the needs of large industrial concerns and usually turned a blind eye to dangerous workplace conditions.

But the city could not hold all the laborers. Garbage stacked up and raw sewage dried in the sun. When the plague hit in 1994, it drove nearly 1 million people out of the city on a highway that came to be known as the "Road to Hell." Conditions in Surat have improved noticeably since the Plague Year, thanks to the hard-driving municipal commissioner, S. A. Rao, who organized better garbage pickups and health inspections. He also authorized a report that laid part of the blame for the squalor on the diamond mills and the culture of "remittance" that encourages single male workers to send all their wages to their home villages.

On my first day in Surat, I met a clerk named Sunil Desai who agreed to translate some conversations for me in his native language of Gujarati. He put me onto the back of his Honda Hero motorcycle and we headed to the diamond plants. We scooted past rattling silk mills and traffic snarls before merging onto a four-lane elevated expressway called Varracha Road. It cut through a long corridor of five-story factories like a knitting needle. Through the windows, we could see hundreds of men dressed in blue workshirts and bent over their wheels. It was 8 P.M.

"The work culture is amazing here," said Sunil, as we stood on the edge of the road. "These men are all from dry villages where nothing grows."

Diamonds brought them here because there were few other places to earn a wage, he said. Most men started as teenagers and never stopped. The only things required were youth, able hands, and a friend inside who could vouch for your honesty. Sunil and I stopped to talk to several of them.

Jidendra Ghetian, a man with teeth indelibly stained with tobacco, spoke like a fighter pilot as he talked about his proficiency at cutting stone. He had started in the mills at eighteen, and his bosses eventually allowed him to carve diamonds over 1 carat in size. This advanced income allowed him to take a second wife.

"There's a system here—you gain trust and they'll let you start polishing the big diamonds," he told me, as the three of us stood at a cigarette stand outside the Diamond Nagar plant. Ghetian was wearing a thick wristwatch with stones marking each hour. He identified them as cubic zirconium.

Was he happy with his work? I wanted to know, and he nodded vigorously.

"You don't have to study, you get in easy, there's no investment to make. Easy money," he said. "And when you're at work, you don't think about anything but the money."

A more frequently repeated thought, especially among the workers who had children, was that nobody should get into the business unless it was absolutely necessary. In many parts of India, of course, "absolutely necessary" was a good description of the situation. For many, it came down to diamonds or begging.

Rajen Radhou, a man with a sad, moon-shaped face, told me he had once wanted to be a policeman. "I was good at cricket, too, and all other kinds of sports," he said. "But I couldn't find a job and had to go into diamonds." He had been faceting for more than twenty years, and now his options were gone. "I wouldn't advise any other man to get into this business," he said. "This new generation should not go into diamonds. It is very hard work and very unsteady. We get paid only when the boss wants us to get paid."

We were standing behind a mango stand on Varracha Road. A cow was tethered nearby to a withered little tree. It was the time when most diamond plants closed for the night. There was a tremendous river of taxis, auto-rickshaws, scooters, and Honda motorcycles pouring out of the side roads and onto the rutted expressway. I asked Radhou about his family and had to stand close to hear the answer over the engines. He told me he had four boys, and two of them were already working as full-time diamond polishers. The two others were apprenticing.

"They didn't study hard enough to get better jobs," he said, sadly. "It is so easy in Surat to go into diamonds and make decent money fast. That was the only way for them to go. I am not happy with how it turned out."

He added: "Or how I turned out."

Polishing a diamond is a surprisingly simple task to learn, requiring only good eyes and a strong sense of patience. Each worker holds a short metal rod called a dop. The diamond is clamped into one end at a precise angle. The worker then draws the dop across the spinning metal wheel like a hip-hop DJ scratching a needle across a vinyl record. Since the only thing that can cut a diamond is another diamond, the wheel is coated with sharp diamond shavings that reliably devour the bumps and rises on the surface of a rough stone.

There is no particular skill to moving a dop across a wheel. It is like stirring soup, or painting a wall. The only real expertise lies in clicking the diamond into the right position within the dop, and making sure each facet is put in the right place. This requires intense concentration and steady vision, because most of the diamonds being polished are no bigger than gnats. An estimated 1 million people in India make their living this way.

Child labor had been a feature of the diamond business as recently as six years ago, acknowledged Chandrakant Sanghavi, the owner of the largest diamond plant in Surat. But he stressed the industry had made a successful effort to get rid of it.

"Day by day, year by year, it has been receding," he said. "It maybe still happens in small villages where diamond polishing is a family business."

As if to prove his blamelessness, he asked the general manager, a quiet, intense man named Suresh Patel, to show me around his factory. We went through several different levels, from the rooms where the misshapen stones are planned and shaped with computers, to the polishing rooms with their spinning wheels, to a room where men squatted on the concrete floor before tubs of water. True to Sanghavi's word, all his employees appeared to be in their twenties and early thirties.

It happened to be the day when the monthly awards for the top polishers were announced. "This makes our workers feel recognized," Patel told me. Then he handed me an electric hand-mixer, the first of a large stack on a nearby table.

"What's this for?" I asked.

"You are our guest today from another country. We would be honored if you would present these awards to our workers."

Fifteen men had been called from their wheels and were lining up in front of me. A photographer appeared at my side.

"This will be in the newsletter," said Patel. "It is a very big competition in this facility."

I hesitated. There was probably an ethical problem in here somewhere, but if I refused, I would be insulting them. It seemed safest to just be a graceful guest. So somewhere in an Indian corporate newsletter, there exist photographs of me shaking the hands of the top diamond polishers for the month of May, with the solemnity of a college president, and handing over prizes of electric hand-mixers and plastic lunch pails.

Before I left, Patel took me into the sorting room. This was the last step of the process, the place where the finished diamonds of like size and cut were poured into paper envelopes for the jewelry manufacturers, street merchants, and whoever else wants to buy them. Indian diamonds typically don't come any bigger than a carat, and so the stones are measured by a lesser gradient called "points." There are 100 points to every carat. Most of the 10 million diamonds that Sanghavi cuts every year are smaller than 10 points.

Patel took two envelopes that were no bigger than sugar packets in a diner. He dumped out their contents onto a velvet blotter for me to see. These diamonds were all 3 points big, and the pile looked like a few pinches of salt. How many in the pile, I wanted to know. Patel conferred with the sorters and came back with the answer: a little more than six thousand diamonds.

I pushed at the pile with my finger and a few of the tiny stones clung to my finger like beach sand. They were all "ideal cut," which is the classic solitaire shape: a wide, round edge tapering down to a point with an eight-side table on top.

Patel handed me a loupe and bid me look closer. "This is Indian crafts-manship," he said.

I cannot exactly describe the surprise I experienced looking into that pile of six thousand diamonds. It was like being at the center of a giant snowflake, or seeing water molecules tumbling inside a cloud. The piles of diamonds formed a landscape of brilliant light and folds of shadow, mountains and canyons of perfect crystalline boulders. They were unbe-lievably delicate, each one a little world of light and color, and each a tiny mimic of the stone in Anne's engagement ring. All the swelter and pa-tience in the factory above us came down to these chiaroscuro dots. I felt a confusing urge to possess them—to slip them into my pocket and take them home—even though they would have been entirely useless.

As I was led outside the front door past the men with the impotent ri-fles, I realized what it was, exactly, that I had been feeling. It was a kind of happiness.

The idea of diamonds as a personal ornament was born on the Deccan plateau more than twenty-four centuries ago, but the 1 billion citizens of modern India have been slow to re-embrace the stone as something to possess for themselves. Domestic sales are growing, but they have hardly caught fire.

I went to see De Beers' advertising representative in Bombay, a smart and tidy man from the J. Walter Thompson advertising agency named Prasad Kapre. He received me in the firm's outer lobby after an hour's wait, and apologized for his tardiness in a clipped upper-class accent. A conference call to London had tied him up, he explained. Kapre was still in the midst of a massive campaign to sell India its own diamonds, a mar-keting push that had begun in 1995 with a survey that showed some dis-couraging attitudes.

The most important precious material in India, by far, was gold. Women draped it around their necks, farmers buried it in their fields, fam-ilies stockpiled it behind their cooking pots as a bulwark against hard times. Diamonds had fallen out of the picture centuries ago. "We discov-ered that consumers really didn't know anything about diamonds," Kapre told me. "It was presumed that our sales difficulties were because of the price issue, but that wasn't really it. There was also this perception that they were only for the rich and famous."

De Beers immediately employed those same rich and famous to tout diamonds. As it had with Hollywood in the 1950s, it reached out to court Bollywood—the nickname for the Bombay-based film industry that churns out thousands of genre-bending movies each year. Well-paid actresses were encouraged to talk up diamonds in press interviews and off-the-cuff remarks. Diamonds were donated as props to be worn, stolen, and fought over in various potboiler flicks. Off the screen, the celebrity press delighted in the 21-carat ring worn by Sushmita Sen, the beautiful star of *Main Hoon Na* (*I Will Be There*) and a former Miss Universe. Her comments were in line with De Beers' goal of encouraging women to buy diamonds for themselves. "The actress with the enigmatic smile says she doesn't need any man to gift her diamonds," said one Bollywood fan publication. Another brand aimed at professional women was given the brand name *Asmi*, which means "I am me" in Sanskrit. That the posh class would be sent out to dispel fears about diamonds being *too* posh was a deft move of counterintuition—an assumption that celebrities are like a surrogate family to the nation, to be envied and emulated, and that the vague unhappiness of the rising middle class would compel them to do something about it. Namely, buy diamonds.

De Beers helped fuel this unease with several well-displayed stories in the Indian media. Kapre himself was the subject of a pre–Valentine's Day Q&A interview in the nation's most respected newspaper, *The Times of India*. His comments were topical, even if historically dubious.

"So you know that no other gift can thrill and delight her quite as much as a diamond," he told *The Times* when asked about the ideal Valentine's Day gift. "Look at it another way, buy her diamonds and you'll be in brilliant company. . . . For thousands of years, diamonds have been the number one gift of choice for men who have wanted to melt a heart. Since the dawn of history, diamonds have been fought over and prized by kings and princes."

One magazine advertisement played on the Indian obsession with caste and birth station. The ad featured Gayatri Devi, a figure beloved by Indians as a symbol of the lost Hindi royalty that once ruled the subcontinent before the arrival of the British. Devi's role in the collective imagination of India might be compared that of Princess Diana or Jacqueline Kennedy in the West. She was born in 1919, the daughter of a socialite and a Bengalese maharaja. *Vogue* magazine once called her "one of the world's most beautiful women." De Beers found her useful. She was photographed gliding into a room wearing only a simple sari and large diamond earrings. When shown an early version of this ad, a woman in a focus group marveled: "It shouts with a whisper."

The Devi ad was a brilliant manipulation. It tweaked a sensitive subject for millions of Indians. The ancient caste system lives on in the Indian psyche, though not necessarily in terms of material comfort. Caste has largely decoupled from income in the last several years and it is not uncommon, for example, to see a *brahmin* living in squalor, just as it is now possible for a *dalit* (the new polite word for "untouchable," those whose ancestors picked through garbage) to make a fortune as an entrepreneur. But nobody's caste label ever disappears from their minds. The only way out is to live a virtuous life and hope to be reborn higher in the next life. The Devi ad shows another kind of escape, a materialistic kind of *moktar,* or release from the cycle. *Diamonds are your ticket upward,* whispered the ad. Or as Kapre put it to me: "This one is for the elites who have everything but the blue blood."

Even with nudges from the media, many Indians are reluctant to buy diamonds out of superstition. Ancient Indian lore says that every gemstone is invisibly linked to a star in the sky. Wear the wrong one, and you could get cancer or be hit by a truck. A nationally respected heart surgeon is said to make his patients wear rubies on their chests after bypass surgery in the belief that healing is channeled through the red stone. This is why most jewelry stores in India have a unique return policy. Customers are allowed to take away gemstones for a trial period lasting up to thirty days. If they hit a sudden run of bad luck, or even feel squeamish about the stone, they can bring it back for a full refund. Despite this, there is no consensus on what a diamond is supposed to represent in the cosmology. During one week in Bombay, I heard a variety of theories, ranging from lust to strength to moral clarity to the planet Venus. One factory foreman insisted that it was connected to the sun, and then added that he was of the priestly *brahmin* caste and so he ought to know.

A man behind the counter of one jewelry store took the safe approach. "It is totally independent of the horoscope," he told me, smiling widely. "It will not affect you at all."

This particular store was one of the few in Bombay that sold real diamonds. The majority either did not stock them or sold what were slyly termed "American diamonds"—that is, cubic zirconium. Even in India's financial center, nobody seemed to be buying them except the polishing plants. And those stones were destined for overseas markets.

It only seemed to reaffirm the conclusions of the 1995 De Beers survey. Diamonds may have been India's fifth largest export product, but the people who live there still had no good idea what they were supposed to be for.

"This is only one of the illusory practices I can show you," said Rajendra Chouse.

He held up a pendant with a large diamond in the middle. The stone threw off spears of light that deflected close inspection. It hurt my eyes to look at it directly, and it took a long squint to see it was actually not one diamond but an arrangement of smaller stones—one in the center connected with tiny silver spokes to a nimbus of six.

Within a month, this pendant would be inside either a JCPenney or a Kmart, the two large American retailers supplied by this particular factory. It would be marked up at least four times the wholesale price.

"Everything not painted with lacquer in there is specially coated with rhodium," said Chouse, a balding man with huge earlobes and a strand of pink yarn tied around his left wrist. He is one of the chief officers of Gemplus, a company on the edge of Bombay where more than a half-billion individual diamonds a year are artfully wrapped into gold, silver, and platinum to become finished jewelry. The factory resembles something you might find in a ratty industrial park in some forlorn suburb of Miami. It is the final stop for Indian diamonds before they arrive in America.

"Those seven stones must be lined up exactly on the same geometric plane or it won't sparkle correctly," Chouse continued. "Even a millimeter would make a difference. So now anybody looking at this from any distance is going to think it's just one diamond. It sparkles like a solitaire, doesn't it?"

I agreed that it did.

"This is art," he concluded. "It is *me* that makes that piece look beautiful."

Visual alchemy is the name of the game at Gemplus, where the tiny dots from Surat are arranged in thousands of different ways to make them look bigger than they really are. Chouse takes a gleeful pride in squeezing as much sparkle from the cent as physics can manage. He showed me a bracelet that winked ferociously and looked like an inheritance from a Beverly Hills dowager. It was made with a rhodium-treated backing and more than five hundred diamonds. But each stone in it was no bigger than a strawberry seed. He handed me yet another piece, this one a hideous necklace. It looked like a Celtic cross, but it had curves and bulges like a sea monster's tentacle. It was flecked with small diamonds. I asked him who the likely buyer would be.

"This one is going to the United States, too," he said, laughing. "And I can tell you, this model sells *well*."

His cell phone rang and he excused himself to snap a few orders to somebody in Hindi. The telephone's customized ring was a 1970s disco riff that sounded familiar, and while he spoke, I tried to recall the song. Eventually I did, and then it banged around inside my head while he took me on a tour of his plant. *You'd better knock, knock, knock on wood. You'd better knock, knock, knock on wood . . .*

We went up to the top floor, the best-lit part of the factory, where the designers had their desks. The windows looked out upon a pond of opaque gray water with a pile of garbage on the shore. A girl no older than nineteen sat at one of the desks, her high-heeled sandals kicked off, a blueprint of a diamond necklace in front of her. There were 345 diamonds of varying size in her design, but the piece was going to hold a total of just 7 carats.

These designers live on a heavy diet of American magazines and television. Watching the Oscar broadcasts was mandatory. Reading fashion periodicals also is part of the job. The factory may be in India, but the mind-set was geared completely to what might strike a customer's fancy in Topeka or Sarasota.

"We have to be U.S.-centric," said Chouse. "We have to respect our markets. All my people are conditioned to think like the culture they are working for." Gemplus does a small business with Japan, but 90 percent of the contracts are in America.

Youth is a prized commodity here, as it is in the mills of Surat. Nobody in the design department, for example, appeared to be older than twenty-five. Age discrimination is widespread and blatant in India, a nation of endless human capital and weak labor laws. Classified ads in the newspapers coolly make note of the maximum age an employer will tolerate, and the ceiling is often set in the early twenties. Out on the patio overlooking the darkwater pond, I asked Chouse why he didn't employ anybody older than college age to dream up the shapes of his rings and bracelets.

"Creativity comes when you're young," he explained. "The old get rigid."

He went on to show me the rest of the plant, which was arranged room-to-room like an industrial flow chart. The designers' shapes are turned into metal models with the help of drills similar to those used by dentists. The model is pressed between sheets of hot rubber to form a mold. Blue wax is injected into the mold to form a pliable simulacrum of the metal model. ("This is an art," Chouse reminded me at every step.) Tiny polished diamonds are carefully pressed into the wax, which is then covered in plaster and set into a chamber where molten gold is poured at a temperature of 1,076 Celsius. Polishing, lacquering, and rhodium-plating down the line helps ensure that the mini-sparkle of the diamond chips is amplified several times over for size-conscious American consumers. The factory is inside a "special export zone," which spares it from the usual Indian layers of local bureaucracy and corruption. Customs clearance takes only four hours. A load of jewelry can be manufactured on a Monday, shipped to the airport that evening, flown to Zurich or London at 10 P.M., arrive in New Jersey at around 1 P.M. Tuesday, and be hanging on a Kmart customer's neck by Thursday afternoon. Chouse told me he has more than 35,000 different models in his catalogue, with his team of designers turning out an average of twenty new variations *each day*, and the retailers keep thirsting for more.

Gemplus goes to extraordinary lengths to make sure that not even a fragment of diamond or grain of gold is lost. The sanding tables are equipped with powerful vacuums that suck away dust particles for later retrieval. At the end of each shift, all employees turn in their coats to be washed in an on-site laundry. Lint from the driers is then burned and the ashes probed for anything that sparkles. Floor sweepings get the same treatment. All employees are made to wash their hands in special sinks that channel the water to four holding tanks where the sediment is carefully sifted for gold and diamond at the end of each month. The diligence* extends even to the air.

---

*This is one of the only places in India where what the workers happen to be taking into their lungs is of any concern to the ownership.

"This is the most expensive air anyone could breathe," said Chouse, as he proudly showed me the filters in the central air-conditioning units, which are regularly burned to recapture the atomized gold and diamond suspended in the factory atmosphere. All this recovered wealth is balanced against total loss in Chouse's monthly "broken stone report," in which he explains to his bosses what happened to the approximately 1 percent of diamonds that did not leave the factory in the form of some kind of jewelry. This amounts to a value of about $140,000 a year—or to be put in Indian terms, the annual wages of 112 polishers. "Broken stone" is a calculated euphemism. "We don't like the word 'loss,'" said Chouse. "It's a psychological perception. Workers would think we could afford to lose them."

Such reminders would seem to be unnecessary, as everyone who works here is watched constantly by security cameras and must line up for an electronic wand search at the end of each shift. The wand can detect precious metals, but not diamonds, so some laborers are subject to spot checks. Unlike some other diamond concerns, the relatively liberal Gemplus allows employees to come to work wearing clothes with pockets. Theft seems to be rare in any case. Each tiny diamond is scrupulously inventoried every time it passes from one department to another; disappearances are investigated on the spot. "We have millions of stones passing through here each month, and you'd be amazed—almost none get lost," said Chouse. "We have such tight margins that we can't afford any pilferage."

We settled back in a corner office, where a servant brought us tea and bottled water. The name of the factory was stitched over the servant's breast pocket in gold thread. I asked Chouse why he wasn't wearing any diamonds himself. The only ornamentation on his entire body seemed to be a simple wedding ring and the pink yarn around his wrist.

I was somehow not surprised to hear his answer.

"I really don't know what people find so fascinating about a piece of stone," he told me. "I mean, what's so great about it? If you hadn't been told it was a diamond, you wouldn't give it a second look. Approaching a need so inessential and then getting paid for it is a pretty neat trick, I think."

The most accurate registry of power in the diamond world is the De Beers Sightholder Diary, the list of the *diamantiers*, masters of the diamond universe, who are invited to London ten times a year to be presented with boxes full of rough. At last count, nearly three quarters of the men on this elite list were from India.

There is also some serious talk of creating an exchange in India to usurp the historic role of Belgium as the world's gem-trading center. The Gem & Jewellery Export Promotion Council (GJEPC) has said it wants to persuade De Beers and other diamond producers to cut out the European middlemen and route all their stones directly to Bombay. "Antwerp had better watch out," intoned India's *Business Today* magazine as it reported this news.

The famous relationship between the Jews and the Jains has begun to fray, as Israeli craftsmen are slowly pushed out of the business. Quite a few are now employed by their former tutees. "Israel and Belgium are out of the race," one Indian dealer told me with a laugh. "They're all here working for us now, in quality control. What else are they going to do?"

Jains are in control of more than 95 percent of Indian diamond companies, and their low-key way of doing business permeates the field. No employee of the GJEPC is allowed to submit a restaurant bill that includes meat or alcohol. Hospitality is the rule, and visitors are unfailingly served chai or coffee. Written contracts are shunned. Almost nobody breaks verbal agreements or attempts to shave a shipment, because to be marked as dishonest means never to work in the business again.

The epicenter of the Indian diamond trade is a shabby yellow skyscraper called Prasad Chambers, which sits down a moped-choked alleyway in Bombay's Opera House neighborhood. There is no more opera. Traders cluster in the dirt yard outside the skyscraper, loupes around their necks, haggling with each other over volume deals. The inside hallways of Prasad Chambers are hot and dingy, and unless a visitor is willing to wait half an hour for a crowded elevator, it is quicker to go up the stairs. On the sixteenth floor are the offices of Rosy Blue, the largest diamond retailer in the world, with offices in nine countries. The chief operating officer, Russell Mehta, talked to me as he sorted through a pile of tiny polished diamonds on his desk.

"Trust is the strength of the industry," he said. "There is little security here. If I know and trust a broker, he might come in here with a million dollars' worth of stones in his pocket and we can do a deal right then. I don't need to put anything on paper. This is the basic nature of Indians. We're hospitable."

Mehta told me that Indian companies were now targeting luxury buyers and the kind of high-fashion markets that used to be the exclusive province of Israeli master cutters. The factories of Surat were designed to process motes and dust—"all the rubbish, frankly," said Mehta. But these same factories are now handling bigger and bigger stones, with 1- and 2-carat rocks receiving the same kind of assembly-line treatment as the gem trash.

"We like to move volumes, so if there's a mistake, it's not that big of a deal," he told me. "We make it affordable to the American middle classes."

I asked if diamond work was hazardous, and he smiled.

"This trade was made for Jains," he said. "We couldn't be in construction because we'd kill too many insects when we dug into the ground. We really take care of our factories. The conditions are nice. The workers are typically happy."

This was a thought echoed by nearly everyone I spoke with who had a stake in the business. Wages were fair. The work was as safe as software. There are no children here.

Child labor is a delicate subject in India in general, and an especially incendiary topic within the diamond industry. India's traditional economy was built on artisan labor, and it is considered normal in many quarters for children to go to work in a family business as soon as they are able. The line between household chores and hard industrial labor is either blurred or nonexistent. This is all to the good for large corporations that seek India's cheap labor. For an industry like diamond polishing, which puts a premium on small hands and sharp young eyes, the temptation was overwhelming. In 1997, the International Confederation of Free Trade Unions estimated that at least 10 percent of India's diamond polishers were children. Mill owners responded by making a public effort to self-police, and emphasized that they would certainly face penalties—a $500 fine—if state inspectors found any children in their workrooms.

The practice is now all but eradicated. I was told this over and over.

"Child labor? Why would we do that? There is no reason for it," K. K. Sharma told me over a lunch of curried chicken. He was the executive director of the Indian Diamond Institute, the nation's largest trade school of its kind. The institute admits new students at the age of sixteen and offers diplomas in all the skills associated with India's newest export dynamo. Sharma himself is a tightly compacted man in a golf shirt, with a laugh that sounds like a porch swing creaking.

"It is not even half a percent now. There is no need for it," he said. "There is no labor shortage in this industry. In India, what is the population? We have so many people here wandering around and doing nothing. Children would only spoil diamonds."

I met a boy named Haresh Basubhai Koladia one Sunday night on the streets of Surat. He was wearing purple sandals and held a shopping bag containing a new pair of pants and was standing outside the front door of the mill where he had been put to work at the age of twelve.

Haresh had the misfortune to be born the first boy in a family with three older sisters, in the dried-out village of Amreli in southwest Gujarat state. His family owned no land and his father was unable to find any real work. But the family believed strongly in Hindu tradition. They were obligated to provide weddings and dowry for the daughters. Haresh was told he was going "on a vacation" to visit an uncle in Surat and was put on the bus. His cousin quickly found him a job polishing tiny stones—twelve hours every day, six days every week—with all of his wages promptly sent home. That amounted to eleven cents an hour.

"I was afraid of the machines and scared of screwing up the diamond, but they got a guru to help me," Haresh said. He learned that the punishment for mistakes is harsh. It never happened to him, but he witnessed boys and men being beaten for losing the minuscule diamonds, which are so lightweight that even breathing on them the wrong way can send them flying. The only hope for a polisher in this case is to enlist a friend outside to buy a tiny stone on Mancharpura Road and hope the overseer doesn't notice the difference. The polishers show enormous loyalty to one another when this happens.

"If a diamond gets lost, the kids pool their money," Haresh told me. "But it's risky. If you're caught, you'll be punished and beaten. People in the industry will refuse to hire you again."

After two years at work, Haresh had missed a substantial portion of his education, and it was becoming clear to him that the rest of his life would be spent carving facets if he did not take some kind of action. Child polishers are usually able to see their parents only once every year: during the festival of Diwali in late October. Diwali is a kind of national Christmastime in

India in which Hindu families light up their homes with colorful decorations and celebrate the triumph of knowledge over ignorance. Diamond plants slow their work schedule for two weeks and hundreds of buses line up along Surat's narrow streets to take the mill workers back to their home villages. Haresh traveled back to Amreli and got his father alone in a room.

"Why did you do this to me?" he asked.

"I did not do anything," was the reply. "It was perhaps your cousins or your uncles that did this to you. This was not by us. But now we need to depend on your income."

It was during this festival of Diwali, when he was only fourteen years old, that Haresh made the decision that would change his life. It was an act of astonishing maturity, even though it would cost him dearly in the end.

"I said to myself, 'All right, then. I won't study. I will do this. I will make money.'" And he stayed on at the plant.

Haresh is certainly not the only child forced to lay down his future for the sake of diamonds, and his experience is more typical than any top industry representative will admit publicly. Estimates of the number of child polishers in Surat run anywhere from 2,500 to 100,000, depending on who is doing the counting. The act of going to work in the city is regarded as a heroic journey in many of the rural villages, and boys who do it are often held up as role models. The heroes envied by many young boys in outer Gujarat are not NBA forwards or rock stars but adolescent diamond polishers supporting the weight of a family on their backs and becoming men ahead of their time. Unlike sports or music fame, however, this dream is all too attainable in Surat—even though it amounts to a version of slavery.

Another man I met, Bhiru Kalathila, had a dirty callus on his thumb and an empty look in his eyes. He was cradling his son in his arms. The boy wore a tank top decorated with colored balloons and the legend: CHOOSE YOUR COLOUR! Kalathila told me he had started in the diamond factories when he was thirteen years old, at a wage of one cent per hour.

"I didn't know what was going on in the shop, I did what they told me," he said. "The work was so hard, it made my eyes blur. But my boss never punished me. At the end of the day, I got money." Kalathila said he had been drafted into the business after completing the sixth grade in school. He and his brother moved to Surat during a drought to make money for the family. "I would never want my son to do this," he said. "And I'd never want a diamond. It's very costly. I just polish it, move it along, and forget it. Only the bosses wear them. We don't even think about it."

A manager for one of Surat's diamond factories told me how plant owners get away with packing their workforce with children. The manager's name is Manubahi Patel and he wore a look of pinched disgust under gold-rimmed glasses.

"There is still a flood of boys coming in at about fourteen years of age," he said. "What the bosses do is hide the children whenever an inspection is coming through. They will keep doing this forever. The only thing that will stop it is if the village families stop sending their children to the cities. If you're running short of money, you'll send your boy to live with relatives and work in the plant and have him send money home. You'll live off that. That's how it works in Gujarat. That's the deal."

Patel admitted that children were employed in his own factory. He said that he had been in several arguments with his bosses about it, but had been overruled each time. He would quit, but couldn't afford to. He estimated that 20 percent of the workforce in Surat was underage, a number that lines up with the 1997 estimate of the International Confederation of Free Trade Unions. This would amount to an entire city of children—100,000 of them—squinting at the polishing wheels.

"This is very sad," Patel told me. "When families are settled here, they try to put their kids in school but the teachers don't care if they study or not. Many parents have large families and they can't even afford to send the children to school. So the fourteen-year-old kid is expected to be the breadwinner."

Large factories aren't the only place where boys labor over diamonds. There are hundreds of smaller polishing shops scattered all over Gujarat, down alleyways and inside slum quarters—anywhere that enough electricity can be commandeered to spin the metal wheel. Conditions in these family-owned shops vary from the adequate to the deplorable. There is a near-complete lack of oversight. The finished diamonds are sold to the traders on Mancharpura Road, who then sell them to large diamond companies in Bombay for use in jewelry for the American market.

Haresh is skilled enough now that he can process up to eighty diamonds a day. He is well liked by his bosses. He is now eighteen years old, with the first wispy traces of a beard coming into his chin. At night, he reads old copies of business magazines, hoping to learn something from them.

"I really want to study, even today," he told me. "My family cheated me—I know this—but I also understand why this may have happened. It was very hard for my father. It all comes from the family and the responsibility to support the family. My parents weren't able to care for all of us. I knew that when I joined I would never get another chance anywhere else, so I make the best of it. I made my own decision—stay in the factory, work hard, send money home, and make it work. But I dream. There is a scratch in my heart. I compare my life to what I see in the movies and I feel unsatisfied. But I have to live with it and bear my responsibilities."

At this point, my translator, Sunil, turned and said to me in English: "I feel right now that he is comparing his life to mine. Look, you can see it in his eyes. His eyes are going through me like a bullet."

Haresh looked up at me without blinking, clutching his store-bought pants in front of him with both hands. He couldn't have weighed more than 100 pounds. And I thought of myself when I was about his age, working at a Carl's Jr. fast-food restaurant in Tucson, Arizona. I hated my officious bosses and the nerdy uniform, but I loved the paycheck. I felt quite wealthy for my age and rejoiced in the responsibility, even though my grades suffered and I quit the track team for the sake of making more money. I was oblivious to whatever kind of long-term damage I was doing to myself. But I was always free to go, nobody was beating me, and the work that seemed so intense at the time was a vacation compared to grinding diamonds in a warehouse for twelve hours a day. Haresh valued his education infinitely more than I did, even though his was stolen from him. He wants to try passing the Secondary School Certification exam, India's version of the high school GED, but he isn't sure that he can afford to take time off to study properly. There is a vocational school in Surat that teaches soapmaking and it offers a section on business management that he would like to join, but that, too, requires time he cannot afford. In a nation where education makes the difference between comfort and squalor, and where youth is a commodity prized over all other, his options are almost all gone. At age eighteen, he has courage that I never knew, but he is already a spent old man.

Haresh is not sure where to turn, but he knows that he is thoroughly sick of diamonds. He does not believe that they contain a god, or are connected to a star.

"I have no wish to wear one," he said. "People say that gemstones will change your destiny. I don't believe that. It has no effect on life."

Diamond grinders, like coal miners, often leave work with blackened faces. The polishing wheels throw up an aerosol mixture of diamond dust and tiny shards of cobalt and other hard metals. The polishers are supposed to wear masks, but almost nobody does and many factories don't make them available. "We know we should wear them, but we don't," one polisher told me. Coughing and headaches are frequent complaints. "The powder affects a lot of people," said a polisher I spoke with named Mukesh Pipalava. "They get respiratory problems and headaches."

The long-term effects of breathing the mixture of diamond dust and metal shavings are unpredictable, although there is abundant evidence that it can lead to asthma and lung fibrosis. The risks of "cobalt lung" have been known ever since the end of World War II. Diamond grinders who work without adequate facial protection—such as those in India—are an especially susceptible occupational group. A group of doctors documented "significant impairment" of the lungs in a group of teenage Indian diamond polishers in a study published in 1992. More recently, the medical journal *Environmental Health Perspectives* noted the case of an American polisher who went on to develop severe heart arrhythmia as a result of the dust he had been inhaling in his Manhattan workshop. The condition has been known to be fatal in some instances.

Health experts in the United States told me that the factories and home workshops of India—many of them poorly ventilated—are ideal breeding grounds for the kind of lung disorders noted in the studies. The work can leave polishers vulnerable to serious health problems later in life, particularly if they started young.

"They're going to be inhaling a lot of particulate," said Dr. Joseph Garcia, a professor of medicine and head of pulmonary and critical care medicine at Johns Hopkins University School of Medicine in Baltimore. "There would certainly be a higher risk of developing asthma or lung fibrosis."

Lung damage among diamond polishers is a subject that receives scant attention in India, and is completely ignored by officials in Surat, where the industry is based.

"We don't collect any data on that," I. C. Patel, Surat's deputy commissioner of health, told me when I visited him in his office. "It's nothing we're monitoring. The only danger to the men is from tuberculosis when they work close together."

The state of Gujarat is known as the Chicago of India—the silk weaver, fish packer, chemical refiner, salt maker, ship breaker, and diamond grinder to the world—and the pro-business outlook of the government does not leave much room for oversight of any of those industries, or even the compilation of meaningful statistics. I was warned about this ahead of time by Bharat Desai, an editor in the Ahmadabad bureau of *The Times of India*, and an astute observer of the local scene.

"This has a long history in Gujarat," he said. "They do not want to meddle with the diamond industry. It's 'hands off.' I'd be surprised if they give you what you're looking for."

I wanted to try anyway, and took a bus to the capital of Gujarat. It is a strange Brasilia of government office towers on a sunbaked plain in the middle of nowhere. The Gandhinagar complex, as it is known, is a half-hour drive from the nearest city and looks like the evacuated remains of a 1960s-era community college. The buildings are surrounded on all sides by hardpan desert, and separated from one another by large expanses of dry grass. The Department of Industry—where all diamond companies must officially register—occupies a yellow ten-story building with large signs hanging from its sides. One appeared to be an advertisement for an exporter of rugs.

I was shown to an office piled high with typewritten pages and old ledgers turning yellow. Nine ceiling fans pushed around stale air while I waited to see O. H. Shah, the deputy industries commissioner. Eventually he appeared, and immediately shut down my questions.

"There is no doubt about safety," he snapped. "The diamond industry is a very good one. Very safe. All processes are automatic."

Automatic? That certainly wasn't what I had witnessed in the plants. I mentioned this, and asked him to elaborate.

"There is no danger whatsoever," he said again. "They do not breathe the dust."

Um, they don't breathe the dust?

He added vaguely: "Maybe we get a few cases of this or that."

I decided to leave this line of conversation behind for the moment and ask him about enforcement of child labor standards. Shah's office was responsible for making sure some of the smaller outfits were properly registered, so enforcement could—theoretically—take place.

He pushed a button behind his desk as he talked.

"Children are not working in the plants," he said emphatically. "Only eighteen and over."

A flunkie appeared at Shah's office door, and Shah made a motion toward me. I was promptly escorted out. The interview was over. In my career as a newspaper reporter, I talked to probably more than a thousand representatives of various governments, and nearly all of them spun to some degree. Some were more gymnastic than others. Quite a few looked me in the eye and told me what I knew to be bald-faced lies. Others did not seem to know what they were talking about at all. But of all the technocrats and politicians I have talked to in my life, I have met very few who appeared to be more disconnected from reality than Mr. O. H. Shah.

I got a more candid appraisal from Vinod Babbar, the recently appointed head of Gujarat's Labor and Employment Department. He freely admitted that child labor is rampant in the informal sectors of the diamond industry—the small-scale businesses that are supposed to register with Shah's department, but never do. He also told me flat out that child labor in the diamond mills was on the bottom of his list of priorities.

It was easy to understand why. Babbar has the unenviable task of enforcing workplace safety in one of the most rapidly industrializing regions in the world—a sloppy steel-and-asbestos hive of textile mills, rubber factories, chemical refineries, food-processing plants, and assorted other workhouses—a state with the population of Michigan times five, where wages are rock-bottom, jobs are prized, and the walls are crumbling. An earthquake in 2001 near the town of Bhuj killed 19,727 and highlighted the fact that many buildings in Gujarat are of flimsy construction and dangerous to those inside. Babbar's department also has to get some kind of grip on the massive ship-breaking yard at Alang on the coast of the Arabian Sea, where giant cargo vessels from all over the world are methodically taken apart by barefoot workers wielding sledgehammers and blowtorches. As for the chemical plants, at least three people are killed there every week in various accidents. With such a massive job description, Babbar barely had any time left to go rooting through the diamond plants, where at least nobody dies violently. Petty corruption makes effective regulation even harder, because bosses have a way of getting tipped off to the infrequent "surprise inspections."

"The message spreads fast," Babbar said. "When we go through these factories, word leaks out and the children disappear. When we do find them, they refuse to speak. Even if we can get enough evidence to issue a penalty, it takes three to four years to make its way through the courts."

Babbar has largely given up on police tactics and tried to take a soft approach. His office of six inspectors in Surat has partnered with a women's advocacy group to encourage those caught making children polish diamonds to send their young employees to school instead. Violators are offered this choice in lieu of the $500 fine. But Babbar was unable to tell me how many children his inspectors had contacted, or how many fines he had issued in the last year. I suspected it was not very much. But it was still an acknowledgment of the scope of the problem—and an admission that the practice will probably continue as long as India wants jobs and America wants jewelry.

Therein lay the dilemma of India, as old as the day when the first sails of the European colonists twinkled off the coast of the Arabian Sea nearly five hundred years ago.

"We have to change our whole mind-set," said Babbar. "People didn't use to care about this. They thought, 'Well, the family is poor and the child is making good money and supporting them.' But they are depriving the child of the best years of his life."

India has 1 billion people, and most of them are very poor. This simple fact made the polishing revolution possible, and explains nearly everything about the Indian diamond business today. The stone mills will never lack for teenage carvers to pick up when the old ones tire or grow sick with asthma.

I found myself thinking of sex a great deal when I was in India, though not in the usual way. I thought of it instead as an omnipresent reality that fueled nearly everything in the world.

Anne and I had planned to start having children soon after we were married. I had always wanted to be a father for reasons I couldn't quite explain. But she channeled my thoughts brilliantly one day as we were driving up from San Diego after visiting her parents. "I think it's the most important thing a person can ever do while they're alive," she told me.

I had to admit that the argument was bulletproof, from a biological point of view. At the root of romance is the pink fog of making babies and the pushing forward of the species. It was odd to think of myself, and her, reduced to a pair of seeds and all of the love between us as a rationale for the production of new seeds, but that was the mystical imperative that drove us both into each other. We were engaged at that point and she was wearing the diamond, a stone seal on the partnership. It never occurred to me that it might have been ground by somebody else's kid.

An estimated seventy thousand babies are born in India every single day. Coupling and babymaking is at the center of the national faith; the god Shiva is often depicted in temples as a giant penis set within a ring, suggesting that divinity lies at the very heart of sex. It turns the wheel of life in the ceaseless passage through death and rebirth. Hindus and Muslims are both quite modest about public affection—kissing is never seen in Bollywood movies—but sex is everywhere: in the tenements, in the slum shacks, under the blue tarpaulins in the railyards; little explosions of delight, like gasoline sparks in a piston chamber ("a bliss as dense as an ingot of gold," John Updike once called orgasm), that keep the species alive and the world moving. To commemorate and sanctify the act, Western couples wanted diamonds—a kind of frozen burst of joy in themselves. They are the talismans of procreation, the marks of sexual union, little crystal-white seeds loaded with instant meaning. And India, with its oceans of ready flesh, was there to make sure we got them.

I met a gem dealer with a wooden statue of Ganesh perched over his desk. He spoke to me in the brief intervals between calls on his phones; at one point, he had one clasped to each ear like a 1950s cartoon of a New York industrialist. He told me he never worried about a drop in demand, even if the American sales numbers should plateau. There was a very simple reason for this. As nations around the world grow incrementally richer, and advertising keeps promulgating the myth, there will never be a lack of markets to conquer. For the visionaries of the diamond industry, a rising Third World—all that joyful sex, all that new life everywhere—only means new customers for diamonds.

"This is going to get big," said the dealer. "God willing, if everything goes smoothly, I can see a time when we won't have to depend on America."

Nine

ALCHEMY

Russia

In early December 1995, a retired U.S. Army general named Carter Clarke went to Moscow for the first time in his life. He was there to buy invisible ink.

Clarke was the chief executive officer of a Florida company called Security Tag Systems, which had helped to invent the clunky plastic devices that attach to pieces of clothing in shopping mall stores. "Electronic article surveillance" was the formal name of his product line, but to the layperson, it was antitheft detection. At sixty-five, Clarke was having the time of his life. He loved being an entrepreneur; in some ways, he loved it even more than he had loved being an army general. It involved creativity and the taking of calculated risk, two areas in which he excelled.

There was a problem he was trying to crack that allowed him to flex both traits. Some of the retail store managers, particularly those who sold high-end women's dresses, had told him customers thought the tags ruined silk and delicate fabrics because they dragged the material out of shape. They had a point. The electronic clips were quite heavy. Paper triggers wouldn't work in this case because the super-sticky adhesive would have destroyed the fabric. An ideal solution, thought Clarke, would be a kind of chemical painted on the dress that could electronically trigger an alarm, but remain hidden to the naked eye. But nobody in America knew how to make that kind of thing.

Clarke had talked over his idea with a Greek friend from Athens, who suggested a possible solution. Why not look for this ink in the former Soviet Union? It was four years after the collapse of communism and all kinds of previously secret technologies were leaking out, through channels both legal and illegal. Disgruntled scientists who had gone without paychecks were bartering off the classified treasures of the Cold War to Western businesses. This ink—if it existed—sounded like it probably had an espionage use, and was therefore unpatented.

Why not? thought Clarke. It would be a satisfying piece of personal symmetry, in any case. He had spent his entire military career fighting communism, having joined up at the beginning of the Korean War. After three tours of duty in Vietnam, he had served on a base in West Germany whose tactical purpose was to have parried the advance of Soviet tank divisions into Europe. Now, if garage-sale Russian goods could help him stop people from stealing dresses from Talbots, he was all for it.

The friend in Athens made a call to a Russian he knew, a man named Yuri Semanov who worked for a quasi-government agency called the High Tech Bureau. Semanov was in charge of finding Western buyers for Soviet-era technology and he knew of just such a chemical that had been produced at a university in Moscow. He'd be happy to introduce the general to the scientists. Clarke flew to Russia and was given a presentation on December 4, 1995. It looked like the kind of ink he had been searching for, and the scientists seemed willing to make a deal. Clarke was saying good-bye to them in a chilly parking lot, when Semanov—flush with his apparent sales victory—leaned in to ask a question.

"Would you also be interested in diamonds?" he said.

"Pardon?" said Clarke.

"How would you like to grow diamonds?"

The next day, Clarke was loaded into a car and driven outside Moscow. The buildings and the clothes grew shabbier the farther they traveled from the city center. "My God, they're so poor out here," he thought, and it reminded him of everything he had read about the Soviet regime: a facade of strength that concealed a weak core. On a later trip, he would notice the lack of animals in the farm country north of the capital. "Where are the cows?" Clarke asked. His Russian traveling companion laughed and said, "We ate them all."

After an hour and a half of traveling, the car turned into a compound ringed with coils of barbed wire and guarded by soldiers with machine guns. Semanov explained they were going inside a factory where rocket propellant and other explosives were manufactured. Inside one of the buildings, a scientist shook their hands and then rolled out blueprints of a strange-looking device about the size of a Maytag washing machine. This was a high-pressure chamber, designed by a team of mineralogists in Siberia, he explained. It could essentially mimic the conditions inside the earth's mantle in which temperatures reached 2,700 Fahrenheit and bits of carbon were slowly turned into diamonds. The Russian machine itself would theoretically be able to make chemically perfect diamonds at a very low cost. Was the American interested in buying a machine? The asking price was $57,000.

Clarke thought about it on the way back to his room at the Metropol Hotel and decided he wasn't interested. His business was shoplifting prevention and he wasn't about to go throwing away money on an untested process. Besides, the only diamond he'd ever thought about was the one on his wife's finger. He also knew the world's diamond supply was supposed to have been completely controlled by De Beers. Who would want to compete with that?

On the flight back, he tried to sleep but couldn't. The process might have all been some elaborate con, but what if the machine really could make diamonds? It would shake up De Beers—that was for sure. "It was a long flight and it whittled away at me," he said later. "I thought this could be the beginning of a whole new industry." By the time the plane touched down in New York, Clarke decided to gamble the $57,000 and hope he wasn't being played for a sucker.

He collected the front money, wired most of it to an offshore account the Russians kept on the island of Cyprus, and brought the balance of $20,000 with him to Moscow in a briefcase the following April. This time, he was taken to a warehouse where one of the scientists from the original team in Siberia—Nikolai Polushin—presented him with a dull yellow diamond he pulled from the high-pressure chamber. Clarke was impressed enough to buy two more of the machines and have them shipped via ocean vessel from St. Petersburg to America. If he was going to make diamonds, Clarke figured he'd be better off doing it in his home state of Florida where he wouldn't have to worry about mafia shakedowns.

Ten years later, Clarke's company—the Gemesis Corporation—is now creating approximately five hundred tangerine-colored diamonds every month in its warehouse in Sarasota, Florida. They are completely indistinguishable from a natural diamond with the naked eye, and can fool experienced gemologists who fail to put them under an ultraviolet lamp.

The retail price for a 1-carat gem is approximately $5,000, which is a quarter of what the same diamond might cost if it had come from underneath the ground in Botswana or Brazil. Gemesis yellow diamonds are also guaranteed to be free of the taint of warfare that has dogged the industry in recent years, and the company isn't shy about pointing that out. "The only thing *clear* should be your conscious," said one recent ad in *Harper's Bazaar.*

Gemesis isn't the only one now making diamonds out of black carbon powder, either. Other factories using the Russian method—some of them clandestine—are known to be operating in various places around Eastern Europe, and possibly China. A Massachusetts firm called Apollo is using a different method called chemical vapor deposition whereby molecules of carbon cling to superheated hydrogen and then deposit themselves onto a tiny seed of a diamond at the bottom of a vacuum chamber. Dozens of plants all over the world are using the Russian high-pressure machines to improve the color of natural stones. A company called LifeGem in Elk Grove Village, Illinois, will even cook a real diamond out of the cremated remains of a human being (your body is, after all, only carbon). The hardest substance on earth turns out not to be so hard to make, or to remake.

The Siberian breakthrough represents a serious challenge to the De Beers stranglehold on most of the world's diamond supply. The cartel has responded by giving away ultraviolet equipment to gemologists so that any diamond made above ground can be detected. But the bigger battle is over image. A diamond is nothing if not a story in distillation, and the diamond industry understands the power of *story* better than few others on the globe.

A fight is currently underway at several world trade courts, including the U.S. Federal Trade Commission, over what to call the new stones. Companies like Gemesis prefer "created diamond" or "cultured diamond," while the old guard argues for the term "synthetic diamond"—assuming the thing must be admitted to be a diamond at all. Atom-for-atom, the Siberian diamonds are chemically indistinguishable from the pressurized carbon that comes from the earth. But De Beers and its buyers claim that it is missing something magical; the same way that a bioethicist might argue that a cloned human lacks a soul.

"Diamonds are created by nature over millions of years of volcanic activity," chairman Nicky Oppenheimer told *The Times* of London in 2004. "They come from the bowels of the earth—not a laboratory."

Clarke and his colleagues have said they pose no serious threat to the stability of the diamond industry because earth-mined diamonds are still abundant and easy to find. It still takes three whole days to cook a 3-carat diamond in a very expensive high-pressure machine. While it might be done profitably for the first time in history, it still can't be done at a rate that will make natural diamonds obsolete.

"Tell me the difference between this and opening up a new mine," Gemesis president David Hellier asked me as we sat in a conference room at the company Florida headquarters. "Ninety percent of the diamond industry doesn't understand what we're doing and is afraid of us. But we're not going to endanger the market because the people who can afford it are still going to buy natural diamonds." Danny Goeman of the British mining giant Rio Tinto concurred. "Counterfeit handbags did not destroy Louis Vuitton," he told me.

But this argument makes a false assumption about technology: that it ever stands still. An analogy might be drawn with electronics. The most advanced computer of 1968, named UNIVAC 1107, took up two large rooms. The sum of its brainpower is today surpassed thousands of times over by even the slowest laptop on the market. The first machines to make diamonds in 1955 were the size of two-story buildings and they produced gray industrial specks. Today's diamond incubators are the size of kitchen oven ranges and they yield stunningly perfect yellow gems in three days. The cost and the ease are only destined to fall further.

Russia didn't invent the synthetic diamond process. But it unleashed a technology on the world that has the potential to destroy the most valuable aspect of a diamond: its cherished myth of scarcity.

Any map that shows the accurate whole of Russia must, by necessity, show the curvature of the earth. The nation's lines are those of a prehistoric fish, its curved spine hackled with icy fjords and wrapped around the great twilight arc of the North Pole as if caught in a trawler's net. Siberia is one seventh of the world's total landmass, but remains unknown to most Russians except in rumor: a vast freezing slate of empty steppe and forest yawning from the Ural Mountains to the Pacific Ocean—"an immense tablecloth," in the words of onetime gulag resident Fyodor Dostoyevsky—composing the entire northern half of the Asian continent. There are ten time zones in Siberia, almost half of a day happening all at once. The world's largest lake by volume is here, as is the longest railroad. The land itself looks like the cleared prairies of northern Minnesota, gray-and-white fields dull under weak winter sunlight.

The sheer vertiginous capacity of emptiness in Siberia is difficult to overstate. In 1908, a meteor slammed into a forest near the Tunguska River and exploded with the force of a thousand Hiroshima bombs, completely defoliating an area the size of greater London. Total reported casualties: one. Nobody made it out to the scene to investigate for another eighteen years.

I arrived in the town of Novosibirsk—"New Siberia"—in the darkness on a morning in mid-January. The temperature was 30 degrees below zero, cold enough to freeze the hair in my nostrils into splinters on the second breath. In the luggage shed of the airport, I met an enthusiastic capitalist named Sergey who had founded the region's very first fast-food restaurant ("New York Pizza") several years ago. He was returning from a ski vacation in France. "Don't bother with these taxi drivers," he told me. "I'll take you into town." He was full of laughter and plans. "This is a good town for business—all kinds of things going on. Not a lot of money, though," he said. When he wanted to know what brought an American to Novosibirsk, I began to tell him about the artificial diamonds being grown out at the Institute of Mineralogy, and he nodded enthusiastically from the wheel of his Toyota SUV. "I've heard of that," he said. "Good stuff. Just like the real thing." He dropped me off with an invitation to go have caviar and vodka later in the week.

The next day, I caught a taxi to the institute. We went through the center of town with its town houses and wide Soviet-era boulevards and public buildings, and then found a two-lane highway that paralleled the Ob River. On the other side was a line of smokestacks and power lines and grimy skies. Little clusters of log cabins hugged the shore and I could see thin curves of smoke coming from some of the chimneys. The only rivers in the world any longer than this one are the Amazon, the Nile, and the Yangtze. It is reportedly so full of spilled oil and other waste that it does not freeze in places.

We went twenty miles south, past more cabin clusters and through birch forests until we reached a turnoff for the Russian Academy of Sciences. My driver squinted at the address I had given him while he drove us past row after row of blocky institutional buildings. It looked as if a set of California junior colleges had been airlifted to the middle of the forest and tossed down into the trees.

This was Akademgorodok, or "Academic City." The entire complex might be said to represent a utopia that failed, a belief in pure rationalism gone sour. In 1957, Soviet premier Nikita Khrushchev had decreed the construction of a great research facility in Siberia to help split atoms, prevent crop failure, find petroleum, build computers, cure diseases, reverse the flow of rivers, and launch cosmonauts into space, all to the glory of the workers. Nearly forty thousand of the best scientists in the USSR were induced to resettle here. A huge undergraduate university was built next door. There were markets, theaters, clubs, an artificial "sea" created from the Ob River so there could be a beach for the scientists to lie upon in brief summer months. A network of heated tunnels was built beneath the labs so that nobody wasted precious research time bundling up against the cold. It became known as a place where a thinker did not need to watch his mouth so much, because the eavesdroppers were not as thick as they were in Moscow. That was on purpose. But Akademgorodok foundered over the years, thanks to increasing micromanagement by local Communist Party officials, as well as dwindling interest from the Kremlin. Equipment rusted, textbooks grew dated, and some of the best scientists left. By the time of the Soviet Union's collapse, some of the Ph.D.s who remained had been reduced to selling potatoes or cooking illicit drugs in their labs to make ends meet.

It was in this decaying era of Akademgorodok that a small group of scientists in the Institute of Mineralogy discovered and perfected a method to make diamonds cheaper and better than anybody else in the world.

The head of the research team, Yuri Palyanov, greeted me at the door of his office with a handshake and a nervous laugh. He is an avuncular man of well-creased middle age who smokes a constant stream of L & M cigarettes. He wore a gray sweater dusted with ash and he keeps the diamonds his team has grown in a cardboard box that looks like a chocolate sampler.

"We did not set out to create diamonds," Palyanov told me in thickly accented English after we sat down. "The main goal was to study the effect of pressure on various minerals. We wanted to recreate the conditions in the middle of the earth. This was for research purposes only."

Carbon, of course, was a substance that everyone on the team wanted to subject to pressure, but authorities in Moscow—seeing no end use—took almost no interest in the project and gave the team only minimal support. Diamonds were simply not a priority in the Soviet Union. The government already had a reliable supply of industrial diamonds from a mine at Yakutia in northeastern Siberia, and the gem-quality stones were being sold through the De Beers cartel.

Making diamonds in machines was old news, anyway. Scientists, visionaries, and not a small number of con men had been trying to do it since the mid-nineteenth century, with usually dismal results. They used electric currents, iron furnaces, and massive vise-presses. The Scottish chemist James Ballantyne Hannay nearly killed himself in a series of explosions while trying to crystallize carbon at high temperatures. A researcher from General Electric named Tracy Hall finally solved the puzzle in 1954 with a huge device called a belt press that pressed and heated carbon between a set of anvils powered by pistons. GE began making diamonds by the millions for use as tool sharpeners, drill bits, and grinding wheels, surviving a lengthy patent lawsuit from De Beers. In 1970, GE even announced it had made gem-quality diamonds at its facility in Worthington, Ohio. But these stones took more than a week to grow and never proved economical as a commercial venture. Natural diamonds were too plentiful.

Palyanov wasn't interested in becoming a gem baron, but he was interested in what happens to minerals when they are heated and squeezed. The Russians set out to build a high-pressure chamber similar to the model pioneered by the Harvard physicist Percy Bridgman, who had built a hydraulic vise with tapered anvils to simulate the conditions inside the earth. The Russians' key divergence from this model was "multi-anvil equipment." Instead of putting the center under pressure from two points, the Russians would employ six. Palyanov drew me a diagram on a sheet of paper showing flattened points aimed at the pressure cell where the carbon was stored. These were the "anvils," which actually functioned more like plates of a vise-grip.

They were supposed to be made of tungsten carbide, which was tough enough to conduct the necessary heat and pressure. But this presented a problem. Even though Palyanov needed metal anvils no bigger than draft beer glasses, metallurgy wasn't advanced enough at the time to make them that big without cracking. The solution was simply to build the high-pressure sphere with smaller blocks arranged in concentric layers. ("Like *matrioska*," Palyanov told me with a chuckle, referring to the famous Russian dolls-within-dolls.) Some of the pressure would leak away because of the blocks grinding against one another. But there was no other way.

"It was a kind of compromise," said researcher Igor Kupriyanov. "If we could have produced high-quality tungsten blocks, this could have gone another way." This "split sphere" design turned out to be one of the key breakthroughs that made the Russian method of gem growth so successful.

The sphere was coated with a thin layer of oil and wrapped inside a chamber of rubber and steel that resembled a clamshell. The entire apparatus was armored with a coat of conventional steel four inches thick in case of explosion. Everybody remembered Percy Bridgman had a consistent problem with stressing his equipment past the breaking point. His laboratory walls were studded with holes from all the shrapnel that had blown into them over the years. And in 1922, two Harvard researchers had been killed by a high-pressure accident, though not with one of Bridgman's presses.

By 1980, the Russian engineering team had built a machine weighing 55 tons that filled up an entire room. It was ready for a test.

"Nobody wanted to be in the same room with it when we turned it on," recalled Yuri. "We all stood at the windows." That turned out to be a good decision. When the pressure reached the level of 1,000 atmospheres—a level comparable to the weight of three pickup trucks concentrated on a poker chip—the machine blew apart, sending steel particles flying and drenching the walls with hot oil. It wasn't hard to diagnose the problem. The casing had cracked wide open.

The project head, Yuri Malinovski, got on the phone with Moscow and raised as much hell as he thought he could afford. How can you expect us to do any useful research with this poor-quality steel you give us? he demanded. The Soviet authorities were not sympathetic. The kind of reinforced metal that was necessary to contain the pressure was in limited supply, he was told. The steel he was asking for was military-grade only, for use in artillery-barrel forging. And his was not a state-prioritized program. In any case, the research offered no prospects for beneficial use that anybody in Moscow could understand.

This was the opening the scientists were looking for. According to Yuri, the high-pressure team got around the funding problem by hinting at a future military use for the technology. With its high conductivity and resistance to melting, diamond could be used as a material for semiconductors. This was not the real point of the research, but it helped unleash some more rubles, which was really all that was necessary. Better steel was delivered, but the scientists still had to jerry-rig certain parts of their unit. They used analog pressure dials that looked like timers from a high school basketball game. A truck's engine block was used to make part of the casing for one machine. In another case, a piston from a helicopter was clamped into place. Meanwhile, Palyanov decided to change the shape of the high-pressure cell from an octahedron to a cube.

The results got better and better. By 1985, when Ronald Reagan called the Soviet Union an "evil empire," the team was growing tiny gray diamonds that measured 300 microns in diameter, about the size of an invisible speck of dust. By 1988, when the Soviet Union retreated from Afghanistan, the impurities had been filtered enough to make tiny yellow diamonds. By 1989, as the Warsaw Pact disintegrated, Palyanov's yellow diamonds had grown to a half-carat. By 1991, when the Soviet Union itself collapsed and the Commonwealth of Independent States took its place, Palyanov reached his dream of growing a full-formed 1-carat diamond. And by 1997, when Boris Yeltsin was making futile pledges to end corruption in government, a diamond as big as 4 carats, the size of a garbanzo bean, was grown in a processor in a Novosibirsk warehouse.

After we shared a late lunch of whitefish and vodka, Palyanov offered to let me look at the machines. He sent Igor Kupriyanov to take me to the place they were stored. We trudged in the subzero cold down a road that led to a building with a bare white front. Inside were five steel units lined up like coffins. Each had a hinged metal lid that opened from the top into a space about the size of a basketball. This was the compression chamber, Kupriyanov explained. It was where a small piece of graphite was subject to the same intense heat and pressure at the center of the mantle.

The machine works like this: A tiny piece of diamond is surrounded with graphite and a metal catalyst within a small ceramic cube. This is called the high-pressure cell. It is sealed into the compression chamber with a clamp, the power is turned on, and oil is circulated around the chamber. The tungsten anvils—the same ones that Palyanov worked so hard to get right—press inward with more and more force. Heat is applied. The carbon atoms in the graphite begin to shake loose and then start to cling to the closest available relative: the tiny seed of diamond at the bottom of the cell. But this time, they crystallize in the unique atomic matrix of a diamond. It forms layer-over-layer until all the graphite is spent. A diamond of any size might theoretically be grown this way. Palyanov named this process the "Pressless Split-Sphere Apparatus." The Russian acronym is BARS.

De Beers had known all about what was going on in the Siberian warehouse. In 1994, a group of managers from the Central Selling Office in England asked Yuri to meet with them in Moscow. They had read of his work in the journal of the Russian Academy of Sciences and were quite interested. Did he know they were already growing industrial diamonds as big as 25 carats at their facility outside London?

Then they got to the point. The Siberian project could do great damage to the price of diamonds if it ever went commercial. The gem-quality stones produced by the new Russian technique were far superior to those coming from other foundries, which worked from the General Electric model. "They were concerned for their business," recalled Yuri. "We told them it was never our goal to create a factory. We didn't want to make jewelry. From the very beginning, we were only trying to improve high-pressure techniques." The two parties agreed to exchange information.

But it was not Palyanov that De Beers needed to worry about. The game was already up. During the confusing period following Gorbachev's resignation and the dissolving of the Politburo, when a large number of Russian academics went without paychecks and nobody was quite sure where the lines of authority ran, it is almost certain that some previously secret specifications of the BARS diamond machines were stolen and bartered off to outside parties.

"It was a very bad time and maybe people used their positions in an improper way," said V. S. Sobolev, the head of the Mineralogy and Petrography Institute, when I asked him about this. He looked like a shorter version of Cary Grant, except gray at the temples and with a square jaw going soft.

I asked him what he meant by improper use, and he coughed and shook his head.

"Maybe some drawings escaped the building," he said. "I have no idea if they sold them or just showed them or what happened."

When I pressed him for more details, he cut me off.

"It's old history," he said. "We would not like to emphasize this period."

Having failed to stop the Russian technology from being loosed on the world, De Beers attempted to persuade General Clarke to abandon his start-up. They invited him to their own diamond-making facility outside London, and, over a lunch of chicken and white wine, told him in exactingly polite language that his enterprise was doomed to fail and that they, De Beers, were not concerned about it at all.

"They lectured me that the general public would never accept my product," Clarke recalled. "They kept saying that people will want something that comes from nature."

At one point, a De Beers director chimed in and said: "It's a very nice product, but women will never accept it." Clarke responded good naturedly: "Why don't you go home and ask your wife?"

The only crack in the facade showed near the end of the meeting when Clarke was saying good-bye to Matthew Cooper, the head of the facility. Clarke mentioned that he had just hired Dr. Reza Abbaschian, the head of the materials science department at the University of Florida, to help him get the machines operational. Cooper reportedly turned white and started to stammer.

"I think at that point, they realized we were serious," said Clarke. "I really thought they thought we were just going to go away."

The world headquarters of the Gemesis Corporation is now located on a brand-new street called Professional Park Road on the north side of Sarasota. On the empty lots nearby are patches of southern slash pine and dwarf palmettos, much of which will soon be bulldozed to make way for new light-industrial. The neighborhood, known arbitrarily as "Lakewood Ranch," is barely five years old and is considered hot by Sarasota's commercial real estate brokers. Down the road is a strip mall called Towne Center that contains a Chili's restaurant, a Walgreens drugstore, a Wachovia bank, a Publix supermarket, an American Family Dental office, a Hallmark store, and a Fairfield Suites hotel that serves mini-bagels and mixed fruit jelly in the mornings. The landscape is both casual and confident. It is the New Sunbelt rezoned commercial, easing into work at 8 A.M. in Dockers and a golf shirt.

I came down on a sunny winter day to see the warehouse-sized facility and was shown around by the director of research, an amiable man in his thirties named Rob Chodelka. "The industry hates us, but the consumers love us," he told me. "I can't keep up with demand."

Gemesis was by then on the verge of its first profitable year and preparing to open a sales office in New York City. It was a happy accident of chemistry for Gemesis that yellow diamonds—a comparatively rare and expensive form of diamond—were actually the easiest to make in a machine. The yellow was caused by tiny amounts of ambient nitrogen in the high-pressure chamber. Making pure white diamonds was possible, but it took more time to expel the nitrogen and was therefore more expensive.

Chodelka took me into a two-room laboratory where a researcher named Chad Cassidy was cutting open a ceramic cube that had just come from one of the diamond-making machines. Inside was a metal cylinder that looked like a round of ammunition sliced open, and inside that sat a dull brown octahedral stone. Three days ago, it had been a scoop of graphite that had cost less than a cent. Cassidy gave the stone to a colleague named Lydia Patria, who put the stone inside a beaker of acid solution and swirled it around to remove the graphite powder on the surface. Then she boiled it in water, dried it, and examined it with a microscope, noting the flaws.

"It's like an orchid—you will never get a perfect one," Chodelka told me. "Whether it comes from a jungle or a greenhouse, there are still going to be slight imperfections. Mother Nature is still at work here."

Patria had skin the color of bronze but spoke with a thick Russian accent. She was one of the researchers from Novosibirsk whom Clarke had been able to entice to work with his new company in America. "When I first got here, every building was too cold, but when I went outside it was like being in a sauna," she told me. "Our kids were sick all the time." She and her husband got used to the Florida heat, however, and now spend most weekends at Lido Beach.

She showed me the diamond. It looked like any other piece of rough I had seen from Brazil or Africa, except it was slightly squat, as if it had been mashed down with a giant hand. Its sides also bore the surface imprint of the high-pressure cell. They looked like the thick lines of silicon pathways on a computer chip. "Those will be polished off," Chodelka assured me.

We went back into the rear of the facility where the BARS machines are kept. There were thirty-two of them arranged in neat rows, each slightly larger than a conventional electric oven. They looked similar to the machines in Novosibirsk, except newer and with LED electronic displays. "We can power these with less electricity than it takes to run a hairdryer," said Chodelka. "Touch one if you want."

I lay my hand on top of one and felt only cool metal. But deep inside the apparatus, aimed at the center of the high-pressure cell, was a temperature hot enough to melt steel and more pressure than the weight of 315 automobiles piled on top of a silver dollar. It was completely silent.

There are at least five factories in the world known to produce diamonds using the Russian BARS method. The first is Gemesis. The others are located in Moscow, the Ukraine, Minsk, and St. Petersburg. The one in Moscow—innocuously named Advanced Optic Technology—is located behind a guarded gate near the old printing presses of the Communist newspaper *Pravda*. It is also down the block from one of the hundreds of casinos that have sprung up in Moscow since the collapse of the Soviet Union. This one is called the Golden Palace Casino and it features a pair of gilded elephants standing upon pedestals outside.

The company in Minsk is called Adamas, which is the Greek word for diamond. It has almost four times the number of BARS machines at Gemesis. There is said to be yet another in China, and there may be still others located in nations with even less oversight of their industries, and who would not require the manufacturer to disclose that their stones were created in a machine.

What is certain, however, is that diamonds with suspect inclusion patterns are turning up with increasing frequency at gemological laboratories in the United States. These are machine-made diamonds that somebody is trying to pass off as natural. The largest lab, the Gemological Institute of America, sees one at least every two weeks, to say nothing of the ones that they don't happen to catch. The ersatz stones are likely being smuggled into the mainstream through traditionally loose source points, probably Antwerp. The factories in Russia, for example, do not dope their stones with nickel, which gives them a telltale fluorescence under an ultraviolet lamp. The new underground stream of machine-created stones is of special worry to the diamond industry, because sloppy reviews are known to occur at even the best gemological laboratories. If a synthetic diamond can acquire a certificate, its value will sky-rocket.

"Right now, most jewelers and even many gemologists cannot tell the difference between a synthetic diamond and a natural stone," warned a story in the trade journal *Jewelers Circular Keystone*. "A TV reporter armed with this information could cause a lot of trouble." Indeed, the occasional unreliability of the labs was highlighted in 2005 after the Gemological Institute of America fired four employees who were accused of taking bribes to proclaim certain diamonds being more costly than they really were.

I conducted an experiment of my own. A publicity official at Gemesis let me borrow a 1-carat canary-yellow diamond for a week and I took it down to the block-long gem bazaar on Forty-seventh Street in New York City. This is one of the busiest markets in the world for used diamonds, and a legendary rip-off haven. I showed the canary to six experienced buyers without explanation. Half of them proclaimed it genuine. "Yep, it's a diamond, the real thing," said one, after peering at it through a high-powered loupe and giving it a heat test. "How much do you want for it?"

This isn't the only technological threat to the diamond empire. The same kind of BARS device that cooks a diamond in three days can also be used to vastly increase the value of a poorly colored stone. The high pressures and high temperatures are used to straighten out the molecular structure of cheap brownish gems and render them pure white or some exotic color of the rainbow. There are several overseas facilities now in the business of doing this, and nearly all are publicity-shy.

I was able to get inside one of them in Russia. Its main processing plant is in the basement of a nondescript building near the center of Akademgorodok. A policeman of the Russian Federation stands near a heavy metal door. On the door is a sign: DON'T ENTER! HIGH PRESSURE! Inside is a small laboratory where three young men are at work at a bench. One is using a pair of pliers to adjust a white ceramic capsule that, by this point, I recognize as a high-pressure cell containing a diamond seed. Lurking behind them are two square chunks of metal the size of washing machines. They are high-pressure devices exactly like the ones invented by Yuri Palyanov's team, and this is where inferior brown rough stones from Siberian mines are slowly remade into gorgeous red stones whose natural equivalent can sell for up to $1 million a carat.

Red diamonds are among the rarest kind of diamond found in nature. Fewer than twenty of them have ever been certified by the Gemological Institute of America. In this basement in Siberia, they can be turned out in about two months.

"De Beers needs to understand they can't stop technology," says Victor Vins, the research and development manager for the company known as New Siberian Diamonds. His company used to be in the business of growing canary-yellow diamonds from graphite. Then Vins and his partners decided there was more profit in using Palyanov's machines to improve the color and the clarity of natural diamonds.

"Treating" a diamond is a quicker process than creating one, though the mechanics remain poorly understood by most mineralogists. It seems clear, however, that subjecting an existing diamond to intense heat and pressure once again causes the bond between the cube-shaped molecules to briefly uncouple, shift, and then reattach. The resulting lattice tends to be cleaner and tighter.

It helps to think of the chemical structure of a diamond like a stack of typing paper. The carbon atoms are linked together in a lateral structure that is incredibly tough, but they grow atop one another in layers, much like that stack of paper. The bonds between these sheets can be quite weak.* When the sheets are slightly misaligned, that rough spot is unable to absorb part of the visual spectrum and the diamond appears brownish or yellowish in color. The more disharmony between sheets, the more dingy a diamond appears. Putting one in a BARS machine has the effect of straightening the molecular lines, leading to a more vibrant appearance.

A second step in the process involves "irradiating" the cheap diamonds, whose brownish color comes from an overabundance of nitrogen (known by chemists as "Type I" diamonds). A stream of electrons is aimed at the stone. These subatomic particles are intended to knock away one out of every ten thousand or so carbon atoms and create vacancies within the latticelike molecular structure. If done correctly, these vacancies within the subatomic skeleton will trap and hold the end of the

---

*This is why the fabled "hardest rock on earth" can be shattered with a carefully aimed hammer—the fracture occurs between the sheets, not through them.

light spectrum that includes the color red, making the diamond shine like a ruby.

Vins is a short man, wearing a bright red cable sweater over a comfortable belly. In his first-floor office is a flag of the Russian Federation and a conference table sprouting out of the desk. He takes out a pair of pincers and shows me an "ideal-cut" diamond as deep red as pomegranate juice. "Imperial Red," Vins calls it. Such a stone would probably sell for a quarter million dollars if it came from underground. This one he plans to sell retail in America through a partner in Boulder, Colorado, for about $10,000.

Aren't you worried you'll flood the market with red diamonds and make them not so rare? I ask him. Won't that drive down your prices?

"That's nothing to worry about," he says. "It's very hard to create them. It's a multistep process that takes nearly two months. We have to produce a hundred stones just to get five good red ones."

What happens, I ask Vins, if one of the customers should try to pass off a treated diamond as the genuine article?

"We have no responsibility for that," he tells me. "We can't take a gun and protect these diamonds until they get to the market."

Ask anyone in the conventional diamond industry about synthetic stones, and you're likely to get a response laden with poetry. The exquisite *mystery* and *purity* of natural diamonds will be extolled to the heavens. You'll hear phrases like "the depths of the earth," "the hammerstroke of nature," or "millions of years." After hearing this speech dozens of times, quite often as a rebuttal to lab diamonds, I came to think of it as "The Diamond Song." It was only a slightly more anxious version of the same myth that De Beers and the rest of the industry have been spinning around their product for more than a hundred years. This is, after all, *no ordinary rock*. Otherwise there would be no money in it.

I heard a very good version of "The Diamond Song" from Andy Bone, the head of external relations for the De Beers Group in London. When I asked him about the potential threat from Gemesis and unknown others in China or Russia, he gave me this response: "We don't really see that synthetics and diamonds are the same product. You've got this whole mysterious creation process—nature created a diamond. Except for the polishing, nothing has been done to it by man. We don't smelt them. All we do is recover them. It is as old as time itself. They are made of the same thing we are—carbon. And when you give one to a woman, it's a symbolic exchange of a commitment. You have to remember, a diamond is much more than the physical thing. The physical intercourse between men and women is something without words, and that's what a diamond conveys—something without words. Now take a diamond created by this mysterious process of nature and put that next to one created in a lab in Florida six months ago. Which of these are you going to choose to carry your message? That diamond created in the laboratory has lost the mystery."

He went on to tell me that De Beers had discussed launching an ad campaign with the tagline "Real Men with Real Emotions use Real Diamonds," the upshot being that any kind of love expressed with a lab diamond was equally as sterile. Or in other words, diamonds needed the wild and turbulent fires of the mantle to express the wild and turbulent urges of our subconscious. Never mind, of course, that almost every metamorphic rock on the surface of the planet was created by the hammerstroke-of-nature-in-the-bowels-of-the-earth-millions-of-years-ago, etc., etc. That the "mysterious process" involved in the production of natural diamonds might also involve civil wars, murder, starvation wages, child labor, and price-fixing was also left unmentioned. Yet, when faced with the threat of infinite supply, this is where the De Beers cartel and the rest of the industry are choosing to make their symbolic stand: on top of a mineshaft.

Created diamonds scored a huge victory of legitimacy in 2003 when the European Gemological Laboratory (EGL) agreed to certify diamonds which did not necessarily come from a mine. "Ignoring them won't make them go away," one of the staff told me. "By certifying and inscribing these stones, we're making sure the true origin of the gem is disclosed to the consumer." The world's other giant labs—the Gemological Institute of America, the High Diamond Council of Belgium, and the American Gemological Society—listened to the outcry from the rest of the industry and declined to inspect synthetic gems. But at the EGL, a diamond grown in a machine can be graded by the standards of color, clarity, carat, and cut just like any other diamond. This is viewed as a sacrilege in some quarters.

"It's a fundamental mistake to certify synthetic stones," complained Peter Meeus of the High Diamond Council to the trade magazine *IDEX*. "Diamonds are unique, with an intrinsic value. A lab cannot give the 4Cs to something found in a bucket that is twenty minutes old."

The other big fight is over the name. De Beers and the rest of the old guard prefer the term "synthetic diamonds," invoking as it does something vaguely plastic and smelling of chemicals. The U.S. Federal Trade Commission weighed in with an inconclusive ruling in April 2001 which said it would be deceptive to call a lab-created diamond simply a "diamond." But it offered no opinion as to the legality of the dueling terms "synthetic diamond," "man-made diamond," or—Gemesis's current favorite—"cultured diamond," which carries the pleasing whiff of warm leather and sherry.

The analogy that Clarke likes to invoke is that of Mikimoto, the once-reviled Japanese company that invented the "cultured pearl," or a pearl grown inside of an oyster as the result of human inducement rather than an accident involving a grain of sand. The modern process was invented in 1893 by Kokichi Mikimoto, a Tokyo noodle salesman who figured out how to inject mollusks with bits of shell and other irritants. After years of trial and error, Mikimoto had a field of mollusks producing semispherical pearls beautiful enough to be threaded onto a necklace. His "cultured pearls" sold well in Japan at the beginning of the century, but caused a kerfuffle when they were introduced to Europe. Said the *London Star* on May 4, 1921: "As a result of the appearance of this counterfeit gem, the pearl market is completely in a panic and jewel merchants of London fear chaos and confusion." Under pressure from jewelers, the local chamber of commerce passed a resolution branding the Japanese imports "counterfeits." Mikimoto had an even harder time in France, where gem dealers took the extraordinary step of asking the Customs Court *not* to charge import duties on Mikimoto, reasoning that to do so would be akin to legal recognition of the white spheroids as actual pearls. Mikimoto sued for the right to pay French import duties, and three years later, the court ruled in his favor. The trial and the surrounding controversy afforded the new pearls a huge amount of publicity, giving many Parisian jewelers no choice but to stock them. The old guard had made a critical public relations error by suing Mikimoto. Cultured pearls eventually became a lucrative sector of the gem trade and their dubious parentage was accepted. You can find them today at almost every jewelry store.

The word "cultured" has a way to go, however, when it comes to diamonds. A German court ruled in 2004 that the disputed term—known to some De Beers officials only as "the c-word"—could not be used to advertise man-made diamonds and threatened a fine of $400,000 for any importer who disobeyed. Cecelia Gardner, the lead attorney for the Jewelers' Vigilance Committee, hailed the German ruling as a victory for the reign of natural stones. "It is the view of the JVC that the use of the term 'cultured' as applied to diamonds is insufficient disclosure to describe the true nature of a synthetic or a laboratory grown diamond," she told *Professional Jeweler* magazine.

The dispute over a single word highlights an essential question, the one that has been at the heart of the industry since the local princes of India decided that the mysterious rocks from the river were precious and worthy of hoarding. The question is not where the diamond came from (this has always been a tertiary concern in the diamond business) but who will control its narrative once it is out of the forge. A diamond is lost without its mythology; it becomes nothing but a chunk of clear carbon polished to a high sheen, no better than a piece of common quartz picked from a streambed during a summer picnic. We thirst for diamonds because we believe them to be rare and because they are perceived by others to have a certain power—power from wealth, power from love, power from crackling sexuality, power from kinship with all of the above. The belief in a diamond's power *is* its power. It is the only one it really has, outside of a factory or a sawmill where it would be nothing more than a tool point.

If the majority of the world's consumers can be persuaded to believe that a structurally flawless diamond from a machine is just as desirable as one dug out of a pit in Africa—in short, if "The Diamond Song" can be hijacked—then the $6 billion business of mining diamonds will be rocked to its core, and could quite possibly fade into irrelevance as the technology gets better and better, in the same way that developing countries around the world aren't even bothering laying telephone cables in the ground anymore because cell phones have become so efficient.

It all comes down to control of "The Diamond Song," and how well the new chemical lords can weave a convincing mystique around their stones.

"I have a mine," Carter Clarke told me. "It only happens to be above the ground."

Ten

THE BIG NOTHING

United States of America

When I was twelve years old, I began to toss my unused pocket change into a jar on my dresser. I kept filling it, handful by handful, through high school. The collection overflowed from one jar, then another, and finally into a giant plastic bottle, which eventually weighed about 70 pounds.

"Why don't you get rid of that?" my father would ask from time to time.

"I'm saving it for something special," I would tell him, having no idea what.

When I got engaged to Anne, I went home to Arizona and rolled all those pennies, nickels, dimes, and quarters up into paper tubes supplied by the bank. The pocket change of twenty years totaled just over $338, but it was still going to go toward the engagement ring. There at last was the meaning of all those uncirculated coins. The child and the man were linked in that diamond; it became the long symbol.

Now it was time to let it go.

It was in a safety deposit box, tucked among some family silverware and photographs. Getting rid of it was always on my list of things to do whenever I went home to see my parents, but I could never quite bring myself to actually remove it from its hiding place, let alone say good-bye to it.

Anne was gone forever. According to mutual friends, she had married a commercial airline pilot and was very happy. We hadn't talked for years. I wrote her a few letters, but she didn't answer and I didn't really blame her. It was time for us both to move on. Nothing was left for me but a palsied sadness whenever I thought of her. That, and the diamond.

In April 2005, I finally asked my father to take me to the bank branch where the ring was stored. In the privacy of a booth, I took out the little blue jewelry box and opened it up.

I don't think I was prepared for how it would make me feel. It made me remember things I thought were dead. I could remember exactly how it had looked on Anne's fourth finger. The way she tucked her long blond hair behind her ear. Her laughter over the phone. Her flashing green eyes. The smell of her shampoo. Looking at that hoop made me know again what it was like to be fastened to her, and how rich and strange and thrilling that was.

The next day, I took the ring to a strip mall jeweler to have it appraised. He was an older man, a bit hard of hearing. He turned it over in his hands.

"I could probably give you twenty percent below wholesale," he told me. "But since you don't have the certification, I'll have to measure the caratage."

When he shuffled off with it to the back end of the store, I felt a brief tug of panic. I wanted my ring back.

The United States is the end of the road for about half of the world's production of diamonds. Of that, about 19 percent of the total value is devoted to engagement rings. The act of buying diamonds to seal a marriage proposal is a $4.5 billion business in the United States—about as much as the entire gross domestic product of the Central African Republic. Engagement rings are the inner stitching of the diamond empire, a leading product category and one that constantly replenishes the mythology of love the stone needs for its survival.

The price markup on engagement rings, and on all kind of diamond jewelry sold in the United States, is nothing short of outrageous. This fact is widely accepted within the industry, but rarely discussed out in the open. Jewelers are so loath to discuss their margins that a euphemism was developed several years ago. "Keystone" is a word that implies a conservative base price, but it actually means a gross profit margin of 50 percent. "You buy a diamond for a dollar and sell it for two," said the industry consultant Ken Gassman. "That's the keystone—the doubling of what the retailer paid for the diamond."

This price differential exists for few other consumer products. For an independent jeweler operating in the suburbs, gross margins can approach a stratospheric 60 percent. Mall jewelers have the power to foist some of the worst deals onto the customer, thanks to their mammoth volumes. The largest specialty retailer jeweler in America, Zale Corporation of Irving, Texas, runs more than two thousand outlets in various shopping malls across the nation. According to documents filed to the Securities and Exchange Commission, its gross margin on jewelry is 51.3 percent. Rare breeds of yellows, pinks, and blues are typically sold for three or four times the wholesale price. Compare this with average gross margins in other large retail sectors—electronic goods at 31 percent, for example, and groceries at just 26 percent—and you get an idea of the enormous profit guarantees built into the retail diamond market.

Why is this? When challenged, jewelers will point to the slow turnover of the merchandise in the store. An average supermarket, with lots of perishable refrigerated goods, can expect to sell out its entire stock about eighteen times a year. For a department store, the inventory rotates about four times per year. Jewelry stores, by contrast, are lucky if they get their store cleaned out once a year. The high prices, they claim, are used to compensate for the slow pace. There are also overhead costs for high-quality burglar alarms, secure transportation, and well-trained sales staff that go beyond those of a usual store.

The other reason for the large markups is the staggering number of middlemen involved in bringing the typical diamond to market. Between the jungle and the velvet pad of the jewelry store, the diamond changes hands an average of seven times, with each layer taking its own nick. It must go from the mine to a broker to a polishing factory to a wholesaler to a manufacturer to another broker and, at last, to the retailer. This journey can take anywhere from six months to two years. In Africa, I had seen beautiful stones dug fresh out of the river sands. Their finders were paid about $100 a carat for their troubles. Those same rocks would be worth about $20,000 under the glass at Zales.

"This is absurd," said Gassman. "Far too many people touch that diamond on the way from the mine to the market."

Prices are only going to get higher. De Beers' Supplier of Choice business strategy seems designed to create a rigid monopolistic channel for stones over 1 carat. De Beers is also enjoying success with its campaign to entice unmarried American women to buy diamond rings for themselves. The "Right Hand Ring" concept has convinced most high-end jewelers to expand their inventory to accommodate single women seeking a bit of *Sex and the City* glamour. An existing social trend was already in place: the average age for a woman's first marriage rose two years, to twenty-five, during the 1990s, and nearly 40 percent of college-educated women were still unmarried by the age of twenty-eight. The implicit message of the Right Hand Ring is that women don't necessarily need a man to buy them diamonds, and that female empowerment is only one purchase away. Said one splashy ad in *Vanity Fair:* "Your left hand celebrates the day you were married. Your right hand celebrates the day you were born." Or put more simply in another ad: "Your left hand says 'We.' Your right hand says 'Me.'"

De Beers spokeswoman Sally Morrison said the ultimate goal for the Right Hand Ring was to create a "cultural imperative." That is the magic phrase for the diamond industry—the creation of a desire where none existed before. The creation of an urgent mythology was what fueled the runaway market for diamonds in 1960s Japan. It was also what launched the engagement ring market in the United States in 1938. In other words, if De Beers had its way, women who left the house without a ring on their right hand would feel inadequate, like they were missing something vital; a need only a diamond could satisfy. The market for this product was estimated to be $5.2 billion.

The drive to "brand" stones with the name of a luxury retailer—Tiffany, Harry Winston, De Beers, Kwiat—will only add to the basic upward trend in prices. A gradual decline of the production of rough diamonds worldwide, combined with rising demand from China and the rest of Southeast Asia, means that everyone on the supply chain can afford to push their margins upward. For the consumer, this is not good news.

There is one counterweight, however, and that is the rise of the Internet jeweler. In the summer of 1998, a young graduate of the Stanford Business School named Mark Vadon went shopping for an engagement ring and was treated rudely by the sales clerks at the Tiffany store in San Francisco. It was a snub that would help change the industry. After a long and frustrating search for his fiancée's ring, Vadon discovered a threadbare Web site called Internet Diamonds operating out of a jewelry store near the Seattle-Tacoma International Airport. He raised venture capital to buy the site, renamed it "Blue Nile," gave it a sharp new design, and launched a publicity blitz. It took off on the same late-1990s wave of e-commerce that boosted companies like Amazon and Fresh Direct and other online retailers into the minds of the public and the upper tiers of American corporate respectability. Customers can choose from among fifty thousand diamonds offered online by anonymous wholesalers. The ring arrives via Federal Express the next day. The gross margins at Blue Nile are quite substantial—about 23 percent—but still less insane than the "keystone" reapings of most independent jewelers. The everyday buyer can now print out the Internet price and use it as a bargaining chip at the local jewelry store. This kind of transparency has always been like kryptonite to the diamond business.

Vadon is still the CEO of Blue Nile. His marriage fell apart, but the company hasn't. Analysts from Bear Stearns believe the Web site will enjoy strong growth in diamond sales for at least the next five years, regardless of what happens in the economy as a whole. The company's spokesman, John Baird, told me there was a simple reason for this.

"If you think about it," he said, "it's the only luxury product that everybody *has* to buy."

They looked like the all-American couple as they walked into the jewelry store, and, in almost every respect, they were. Stacey Babyak is twenty-three years old and works as an assistant account executive with an advertising and public relations firm. She has lush dark hair and olive skin and is wearing jeans, high-heeled boots, and a mock football jersey with the number "01." Erick Pabis is twenty-four, making good money at his first real job out of college. He is a loan officer for a mortgage broker and is having no problem making his quarterly numbers thus far. They work nearby each other, in glass office buildings in downtown Pittsburgh, and have been dating for three years. They both speak in the shot-and-beer accent of western Pennsylvania, pronouncing "on" as *oan* and "walk" as *wulk*. There is a gentle physical energy between them. She touches him frequently when they talk, smoothing his short hair, pinching the bulge under his chin, rubbing his wide shoulders. This year, they will be only one of 1.7 million American couples to go through the ritual of buying an engagement ring.

"I don't want that flaky guy to be here again," Erick murmurs to her as they look around the store. "He was a jerk to us." The salesman, Erick felt, had marked them as dream shoppers on their first visit. But despite their youth, they were serious. Erick had already asked permission of her parents to marry their daughter. He would surprise her with the exact timing of his proposal, but virtually everything else was a foregone conclusion. Stacey knows pretty much what she wants: a square princess-cut diamond with two smaller stones on the side and several tiny diamonds set into a white-gold band. She has seen a picture of it in a department store advertisement in a Sunday circular in the *Pittsburgh Post-Gazette*. The picture rides around in her purse so she can show the jewelers what she has in mind. She has a hard time controlling the giddiness when she talks about the color and clarity of the ring she wants on her finger. Erick, too, can throw around terms like "inclusions" and "pavilion" like an expert. In them, I see a bit of myself when I was shopping for Anne's ring.

They settle themselves on a padded bench in front of one of the cases and wait to be noticed. To their relief, the salesman who had rubbed them the wrong way does not approach. Instead, they draw a petite blonde named Meg, who quickly recognizes what Stacey is looking for. She disappears into the back to find some 2 carat diamonds—a bit larger than the size Stacey and Erick had agreed on.

Erick looks uncomfortable and works a stick of Stacey's pink Carefree sugarless gum between his teeth. He will not tell the jewelers, but his absolute ceiling is $7,000. It is an amount equal to the faux Victorian custom of about two months of his salary. Erick has seen how dramatically the price ascends when the main stone gets any larger than 1.25 carats. He is doing well enough to afford the 2-carat, although people got fired from First Franklin all the time for not meeting quotas. Erick will be taking a gamble that that won't happen to him. He wants this to be a special purchase, and one that Stacey will treasure.

"I want it to be a symbol of where I was at this point in my life, and what I did for her," he had told me earlier. "If it's a piece-of-shit ring, I'll have to look at it forever. I want it to be the best I can manage. And this is the one thing she really, really wants."

They had met in college. She had been slightly afraid of Erick at first. He was big: a defensive lineman on the football team, with girder arms. And he was a member of Sigma Nu, the fraternity with a rowdy reputation. Her friends thought it was troublesome that he kept sending her instant messages. They called him "that scary guy." One night, Stacey was working on a spreadsheet in the computer lab when his America Online screen name—threat91—popped up in a box on her screen. They began to type friendly banalities to each other. When he teased her about the shape of her headphones, she had to ask how he knew she was wearing them. *Just turn around* was the reply from threat91. There he was smiling at her, a few terminals away.

Stacey saw him again in a beery hip-hop haze at a Sigma Nu party a few weeks later. In the middle of the night, he walked her home to her dorm room and didn't even try to kiss her. That was impressive. But her opinion of him really began to change when he learned she didn't know how to drive a stick shift. Erick sat her behind the wheel of his black 1999 Mercury Cougar and explained how to find the sweet zone between the clutch and the gas. She stuttered it down the road all that afternoon but finally found the trick. He told her all about his family and his Great Dane named Cici, and she began to think there was more to him than lineman. A week later, in the Cougar, they kissed for the first time. A shy confession of mutual attraction followed. She asked him why he didn't try to make out with her on that drunken night after the Sigma Nu party.

"Was I supposed to?" he said.

"He was nervous," Stacey told me. "He had just gotten out of a six-year relationship with this girl he had been dating since high school."

It was a slow courtship by the standards of Westminster College, but by Christmas of that year, they were seeing each other exclusively. Erick got his job at the mortgage broker and Stacey moved in with her parents to save money. He stopped smoking at her request, a huge sacrifice on his part, he thought. After a while, it only seemed natural to start looking for a ring together. For Erick, buying the diamond was more than just a show of his commitment to a life with Stacey. Wrapped up in it, too, he told me, was his sense of wanting to show his mother that "she raised a good son." He had grown up in a single-parent family and had worked menial side jobs ever since he was fifteen years old. The ring would be the biggest purchase of his life so far, and one he felt could prove that he would be a good husband and father.

Erick and Stacey talk quietly while they wait for the diamonds to come out from the back room.

"We can just boot off the side stones," Stacey says, touching his knee and smiling. "We'll just go with the solitaire in a channel setting."

He takes a breath, blows a Carefree bubble, and says, "We'll have to see how it looks. If we can get the other store to custom-make the band, maybe they can just sell us the loose diamond."

I had been watching them go back and forth like this all day long, as they slowly felt out a point of compromise that both could live with, and it occurred to me that this would be, in the best of circumstances, a fore-taste of everything they would have to negotiate together in the years to come: house, jobs, sex, children, money, in-laws, vacations, everything.

I had asked Stacey and Erick if they ever thought about where the stone would be coming from. There would be no way to tell if their dia-mond had been polished by a child, or killed for in Africa. They both told me they had never heard of such things. Stacey told me she was surprised she hadn't, because she tried to be a socially conscientious shopper. She refused to shop at large discount stores, she said, because she suspected their clothes were made in overseas sweatshops.

"This is probably going to sound pretty bad," Erick told me, "but that stuff doesn't really bother me. It doesn't mean anything to me."

"No one would think you were getting married if you were wearing a ruby," volunteered Stacey.

"You wouldn't take it seriously," nodded Erick.

"This is what we're supposed to do," said Stacey. "I've never heard of somebody getting married without a diamond."

Meg comes out bearing a tray full of princess-cut stones. She lays the first one—the 2-carat—into the open prongs of a setting and slides it onto Stacey's fourth finger. Stacey holds it at arm's length and regards it with an embarrassed smile.

"This is so classy and sparkly," she says. "The way it looks now in the light, it's so beautiful."

"Gorgeous," murmurs Meg.

How do you get rid of something like this? A friend suggested I post it on eBay. But this didn't feel right. The ring deserved better.

I could make a dramatic gesture and hurl it into the Atlantic Ocean. But this seemed inexcusably wasteful.

I could give it to my grandmother, or my mother, or my sister. But this seemed too weird, too incestuous.

I could sell it back to a jeweler. But then I would be contributing, in a tiny way, to a trade that brings misery to millions of people across the world. On the other hand, I would be increasing the world's supply by a single stone. One less diamond that had to be mined.

I could have it reset into a tie clip or a pinky ring or something else I would never wear.

I could frame it on my wall, a permanent exhibit to my idiocy.

I could do nothing. Hide it back in the safety deposit box. Wait for my feelings to fade.

There was, of course, one thing I couldn't do.

I asked a number of my female friends this hypothetical question: "Let's say you met a guy and fell madly in love with him. He is your soul mate in every way and you can't believe someone could be so perfect for you. He asks you to marry him, but he wants to give you a diamond from a previous engagement or marriage. He says his feelings for the first woman are gone, and he now wants you to take the diamond and make it your own. What would you say?"

The universal answer was *no*.

"That diamond is tainted," said one friend. "It would say to me he doesn't care about me very much," said another. "He's showing me that he's cheap enough to give me used goods," said a third. "I don't want the memory of the other person in my marriage—bad karma," was yet another answer. And: "It's dehumanizing."

But *why*? I always pressed this point. What is tainted or cursed about the diamond when you compare it to the man? He's been affected much more by the other woman than the stone ever was. He gave her his commitment, his heart, his sexuality. His mind is indelibly imprinted with memories of her. *He* is the truly used goods. The diamond is a blank slate. It has no feelings or memories. So can't you reclaim it for your own?

"No way. It wouldn't feel right," one friend concluded, and I had to admit that I agreed with her. Because the truth is, you *can't* really write a new history onto a stone. I had been raised on American notions of romance and a lifetime of television ads and there was no traveling backwards. I still believed—despite all my skepticism—that an engagement ring did carry some kind of mystical charge, even though logic said otherwise. It had a memory inside of it that could not be erased, at least not as long as it remained attached to the owner. It was a living reliquary.

Handing down a family heirloom is one thing. But to take a ring worn by a previous woman and bring it into another relationship was out of the question.

I have a theory as to why this inspires such distaste. It threatens the story we tell ourselves, the myth of our own uniqueness. Near the heart of love is a dread that rarely finds words: the fear that when the candles burn away and the conversation gets old, we, too, could be like an object: replaceable.

Martin Rapaport stood up before a room full of microscopes, loosened his bow tie, and launched at motormouth speed into his favorite topic, the high price of diamonds in America—a subject in which he is regarded as either a crusading hero to the consumer or a gleeful destroyer of fortunes, depending on who is making the assessment. To many, he is a lot of both.

"So you think that if you know about the four Cs—clarity, color, cut, and carat—you know everything there is to know about diamonds?" he asked. "No, you'll take Daddy's business and run it into the ground. . . . So who here can tell me, what is the difference between diamonds and bananas?" He was wearing a business shirt made of cotton so thin you could see the crescent of his undershirt smiling through it, even from the back of the room.

The students blinked back at him. It was just past nine in the morning and none of them seemed fully awake. They were all young, in their early twenties, and taking courses in jewelry making at the Gemological Institute of America in a blank-faced office building on New York City's Madison Avenue. We were all sitting in a laboratory classroom in which each desk was fitted with a microscope.

"Diamonds and bananas?" asked Rapaport again. "How are they different?"

A student in the front row finally ventured a guess. "Diamonds are rare and bananas are not?" she said.

"That's cute," said Rapaport, and everybody laughed nervously.

He then turned to the board behind him and started drawing a diagram with a Magic Marker. Diamonds are different from bananas, he explained, because of the concept of size. A banana large enough to be double the size of an average banana is probably going to be worth two times as much. But a 2-carat diamond is not merely twice the price of a 1-carat. It is going to be more costly by an exponential factor, and there is no easy benchmark for what that scaling might be. This is just one of the elements that make the art of diamond valuation such a Byzantine calculus for anyone outside the business.

"If you leave this room confused," he said, "I'm going to be happy about it."

Martin Rapaport is famous—or notorious, depending on your perspective—for publishing the *Rapaport Diamond Report,* which is a rudimentary table that lists "high cash asking price" for various types of rough and polished diamonds. The *Rapaport Report,* known as "The Rap Sheet," is unscientific and sometimes inaccurate. But it is the closest thing that diamonds have ever had to a Dow Jones stock ticker and this is why Rapaport is one of the pivotal figures of the trade in the last one hundred years. Any customer buying diamonds can now learn the approximate price paid for the stone in the wholesale market, and can negotiate accordingly. The blatant rip-offs that used to be a hallmark of the diamond business are today much harder to achieve. Ask dealers about Rapaport, and the response might be laced with profanity. "The guy ruined everything," one told me. "Things were great until he came along." But Rapaport has also been credited with bringing a necessary dose of transparency to one of the least transparent industries on the globe.

It started in 1978, when he was a newcomer to New York, an Orthodox Jew with a taste for rock music and a seemingly compulsive need to make people irritated with him. He had already had a few false starts in the business world. A career as a sugar dealer in Tel Aviv had left him broke. He had a degree in computer engineering from a university in Israel, but he also knew a little bit about diamonds, having studied the art of cleaving from one of the old masters in Antwerp. He even had a burn mark on his thumb to show for the experience. Rapaport paid $25 weekly rent for a table in a closet-sized office on Forty-seventh Street, then, as now, the heart of the diamond district in New York.

The character of this short stretch of asphalt between Fifth and Sixth avenues is derivative more of a Moroccan *souk* than midtown Manhattan. Neon signs flash in windows: WE BUY JEWELRY. CHEAP DIAMONDS. FAST CASH. Armored cars make deliveries with a contingent of guards packing guns. Hasidic men in black coats, curly forelocks, and broad-brimmed hats line up to catch commuter buses at the end of the day. More than 80 percent of diamonds sold in America pass through this block, and the transactions amount to tens of millions of dollars on a daily basis. But there are almost never any written contracts. Deals are sealed with a handshake and the

Yiddish words *mazel und brocha*. Businesses here typically pass down from fathers to their sons and nephews. The atmosphere is intensely clubby; a man is nothing here without a long reputation for honesty, and part of the ethical code of the business was not to reveal insider prices. Until Rapaport came along.

His arrival on Forty-seventh Street happened to coincide with the last wild fluctuation in diamond prices. During the oil crisis and the economic slump of Jimmy Carter's presidency, worried investors were looking for safe places to put their liquid funds. Precious metals were popular for a while, and then the investment community found diamonds. Diamond prices tripled in the space of three years, and De Beers seemed powerless to stop it. Rapaport noticed there was frequently a large gap in what people were paying for the stones versus the actual consensus price in New York. Buyers were in the dark, and the old guard preferred it that way. Rapaport bought a manual typewriter, pecked out a chart showing the price-per-carat of the major kinds of diamonds, mimeographed several hundred copies, and sold them for 25 cents apiece.

The first issues of the *Rapaport Diamond Report* went unnoticed. The older Yiddish-speaking dealers considered the twenty-eight-year-old Rapaport a *pisher*—a young person of no consequence. Even the man who rented Rapaport his polishing table, an old master named Carl Miles who lunched on a baseball-sized onion each day, thought his young tenant was crazy and shook his head. But then the worldwide diamond market began to slump in the late 1970s and the suspicions over dishonest pricing grew as the margins got tighter. The newsletter was suddenly indispensable; it was no longer possible to make a large diamond deal without consulting it. Rapaport's price effectively became the ceiling price, and family-run shops stood to lose millions. They had always argued that no standardized price could be fixed to diamonds, because no two were exactly alike, and also because they carried with them an intangible factor of emotion. Rapaport's newsletter claimed otherwise. It treated diamonds as an ordinary commodity like pork bellies or copper. This was heresy.

The powerful Diamond Dealers Club attempted to throw the *pisher* out of the trading hall. It would have meant the end of the newsletter, because Rapaport would have no longer had access to the daily flow of trading information. He sued the club for damages and was reinstated. The Union of Orthodox Rabbis passed a resolution barring anyone from publishing diamond prices. They called Rapaport directly and ordered him to quit.

Then the threats started. "Killing you would be a *mitzvah* [charitable act]," said one anonymous caller. Several other ominous calls were eventually traced to a matzoh factory in Brooklyn. In one week alone, forty bomb threats were called in to Rapaport's apartment on Central Park West. He started wearing a bulletproof vest to work. When he went into the Diamond Dealers Club, he faced a rain of invective; one hulking man called him "Hitler" and began to chase him around the trading tables, threatening to strangle him.

This dispute over diamond pricing had complex religious undertones. Since the end of World War II, the wholesale diamond trade in the United States has been heavily influenced by Hasidic Jews who live in one of three distinct Brooklyn neighborhoods. They wear long black coats and black stockings and the men often walk with their hands clasped behind their backs to avoid inadvertently touching a woman. They are one of America's most fascinating and misunderstood religious minorities.

The Hasidic movement was founded along the border between Ukraine and Poland in 1736 by a charismatic teacher named Israel Ba'al Shem Tov, who shook up the stern Judaism of his day by preaching that God must be worshiped in a state of constant joyfulness. Their Amish-like clothing is reminiscent of the fashions of the Eastern European steppes of two centuries ago. They also take certain commands from the Bible literally, most famously, Leviticus 19:27, which says: "Do not cut the hair at the sides of your head or clip off the edges of your beard." This is the origin of the curled forelocks, known as *peyos*, which most Hasidic men grow to emphasize their obedience to even the most minor admonitions of Scripture. But while their distinctive clothing creates an image of religious zealotry, they defy easy categorization. There is a strong mystical element to the faith, for example. Outsiders are surprised to learn that many believe in such New Age–style things as reincarnation, angels, and spiritual healings. These beliefs have a fluid nature and believers are taught to ponder constantly the various emanations of God and what God might mean in each individual moment.

Centuries of persecution and murder at the hands of various European dictators have caused the Hasidim to have a deep mistrust of those outside their own circles. There is no accurate count of the number of Hasidim in America, for example, because they refuse to participate in any kind of census. In Europe, counting the Jews was often a precursor to rounding them up and killing them en masse. Many of the rebbes taught that Holocaust was God's punishment for the assimilation of the Jewish people into the mainstream of European life—a mistake many were determined not to repeat in their new home of America. The detachment from society gives them an unapproachable air, and so the intense spiritual joyfulness preached by the Ba'al Shem Tov is most often expressed behind closed doors.

Rapaport shared an uneasy coexistence with the Hasidic mainstays of the diamond trade—made all the more complicated because of his family's own history in Eastern Europe. His father was born in the town of Satu-Mare in Hungary, which happened to be the center of one of the strictest and most inward-looking sects of Hasidism. But the elder Rapaport was not one of them. He was a hard-driving wheat dealer, who observed a more conventional form of Orthodox Judaism that emphasized obedience to the law of the Talmud over the emotional displays of worship practiced by the followers of the Ba'al Shem Tov. For the Nazis, though, they were all the same and Rapaport's father was taken to Auschwitz along with his Hasidic neighbors. He emerged from the camp weighing only 60 pounds, migrated to America without a penny, and settled in Miami Beach, where Martin Rapaport was born in 1952. Martin grew up observing Saturday *Shabbes,* keeping kosher, and wearing a yarmulke. It was partly because of this long-shared history of strife and faith that the Hasidim, and the rest of the diamond gentry, felt like the *pisher* should have seen things their way. He didn't.

"There was a guild mentality going on," he told me. "We stood up for free and fair trade. This has always been a very moral industry in how people deal with one another. I challenged the industry to apply the same standards externally as they did internally."

There was another reason for the scorn heaped on Rapaport in the early 1980s. He was hitting at a sensitive spot—the stability of the diamond business itself, which was the underpinning of thousands of careers and family nest eggs in the Jewish community, and not just among the Hasidim. The question is often asked: Why is there such a heavy Jewish influence in the diamond business? The answer is multifaceted, and goes back to events more than two thousand years in the past.

During the Middle Ages, trade guilds barred the Jews from taking part in almost every conventional occupation—except gem polishing. The residents of Israel who fled Palestine after the sacking of Herod's Second Temple in A.D. 70 had taken with them a reputation as expert metallur-

gists and craftsmen of gold and other precious metals. The artisanal skills
of the Jews that were shunned in other areas were welcomed in the delicate science of cutting diamonds and minting coins. Prejudice in the me-
dieval era extended to another realm: most feudal rulers did not permit
the Jews to own any real estate, and so diamonds became a convenient lo-
cale for the storage of family wealth. They were a stand-in for land, a farm
poured into an octahedron. They also served as excellent tools of collateral for making loans across national borders where no sophisticated currency exchanges were in place.

Yet another reason had to do with the unique qualities of a diamond.
There is simply no better way to cram an immense amount of wealth into
a small package. The successive waves of Crusades and pogroms that
swept across Europe during the last millennium had taught the Jews bitter lessons about the need to stay flexible and mobile. Diamonds could be
sewn into the seams of coats, tucked into the spaces between toes. They
were an indispensable tool in the face of persecution. During the Inquisi-
tion of the sixteenth century, when the king of Portugal made conditions
intolerable, the Jews simply moved their gem-cutting operations from
Lisbon to the more tolerant city of Amsterdam, which then became the
diamond capital of the world until it was supplanted by Antwerp. Diamonds had a high and nearly mystical place in the consciousness of the
Jews and this *pisher* had challenged their stability.

Rapaport survived the bomb threats and kept his membership in the
Diamond Dealers Club. The club tried publishing its own sheet to
counter Rapaport, but it quickly folded. Diamond prices began to climb
out of the crater in the early 1980s, and as the margins grew back to their
previous levels, the bitterness gave way to low muttering and even a reluctant respect for the *pisher.*

The *Rapaport Diamond Report* is now regarded as the bible of the trade,
even among those who don't like him personally. Jewelers everywhere in
America keep copies of the Rap Sheet inside their stores to convince customers they are not being taken to the cleaners. Rapaport has begun to
publish detailed listings on the Internet, as well as an expanded version of
the *Report,* which looks and feels like a sophisticated business magazine,
with staff-written dispatches from Japan, Belgium, India, Russia, and
other key locations in the diamond world. An annual subscription for the
weekly costs $250. Rapaport was also a major instigator behind the forma-
tion of the Kimberley Process and has been outspoken about what he

sees as some of the social evils in the Third World brought about by the trade. Because of the *Report*, and because of his own diamond brokerage on the side, he became quite wealthy, and shuttles every two weeks between New York and Jerusalem, where he maintains a house with his wife and ten children.

He is not an easy man to see. I had made three separate appointments with him over the course of a week, and he canceled all three of them. After hearing about the last broken appointment, I was told he was leaving for Israel in twenty minutes. It was unclear if he was trying to avoid me, or just scattered, but when I asked if I could ride with him to the airport, I was told: yes, but get here *now*. I raced uptown in a cab and caught him outside his office near Forty-seventh Street as he was climbing into a Lincoln Continental from a car service.

While we were stuck in traffic on the Van Wyck Expressway, I asked him about a common criticism aimed at him: that he typically inflates the prices of diamonds. Almost everybody in the trade adjusts their prices accordingly—it is common, for example, to hear the phrase "twenty below Rap," which means the diamond will be sold for 20 percent below what Rapaport says. This markdown is closely tied with a general complaint about the Rap Sheet: that the numbers do not truly reflect the vicissitudes of the market.

"Look, we move carefully," he told me, thumping his leather bag for emphasis. "Our goal is not to be responsive to every little tick in the markets. Our goal is not to move ahead of the market. Our job is to stabilize."

As for the high valuations, Rapaport acknowledged it was true. The "cash asking price" was a way for conversations to get started, he told me, much the same way that a sticker price on an automobile is very rarely the final price. But he was vague on exactly where he gets his trading information. This has been a guarded secret at *Rapaport Diamond Report* for years; some suspicious dealers have even accused him of pulling the numbers out of thin air. All he would tell me is that he takes information from "well over a thousand dealers all over the world" and collates it via computers into the final published grid.

After we arrived at JFK, we shared a late lunch of tuna fish and pasta salad in the El Al Airlines departure lounge. Diamonds had been good to him, Rapaport told me, but his real passion lay in bringing an even stronger sense of morality to the business. He is an enthusiastic supporter of efforts to end the trade in blood diamonds and help impoverished nations make lasting investments with profits from the gem trade. He has used the *Report* as a platform to crusade for better working conditions in Sierra Leone and other African sources of diamonds.

"What happens in Africa really is a problem, not because it hurts demand, but because treating people the right way is the right thing to do—it's a *mitzvah*," he said, before we shook hands outside the security checkpoint. He wanted to add a new set of values to the stone which stood for love. It was, after all, nothing but America's most highly priced household symbol. And symbolism was the very foundation of the business. Rapaport had made this point in a slightly different way when I first heard him talking in the classroom on Madison Avenue.

"Think of a woman working in an office," he had told the gemology students. "Her boyfriend gives her a fur coat, she shows it to her girlfriends, and they say, 'Oh, that's nice.' Her boyfriend gives her a Mercedes, they say, 'Oh, that's nice.' But her boyfriend gives her a diamond, they say, 'Oh, he's *serious*.' It's not just the gift of love—it's the gift of commitment. She's not jumping up and down because she got a diamond ring but because she got a *guy*! There are those who say you don't *need* diamonds. I say they're right. Just like you don't *need* sex."

Rapaport paced back and forth in front of the microscopes, building to his point.

"People die for flags, right? That's because it's a symbol for something bigger. Symbols have unbelievable value in society. It's all about symbols. We communicate with icons!"

The personal diamond collection of Sean "Sean Gemini" Coles now exceeds fifty carats. There's a stone-spangled pendant in the shape of Michael Jordan going up for a dunk, a ring with a huge princess-cut stone, a medallion the size of a tea saucer with forty small diamonds, and yet another twinkling pendant in the shape of the Statue of Liberty in which the torch is a giant diamond.

"Now this is 'iced out,'" he tells me. "The idea behind everything is, I can get any girl I want, I get the attention in the club, I am treated a certain way, I get the respect. The bling-bling is a status thing. That's the way it is in corporate America. You walk in there shining all over the place."

Sean Gemini is a full-time hip-hop musician with his own record label,

Parthenie Entertainment. He named it after his late mother. We are sitting together in Parthenie's old bedroom on the seventh floor of a tenement building in the Crown Heights section of Brooklyn. Sean Gemini tapes all his music in here as a memorial to her. He ripped the shelves out of her closet and turned it into a sound booth, installed an MPC60 drum machine where her bed used to be, and lined all the walls with two inches of upholstered foam. When he speaks, his words drop like feathers on velvet in the soundproofed air.

He is on the verge of professional breakthrough. His first album, *Inner Me,* sold more than 114,000 downloads and led to a distribution deal with Warner Brothers. The centerpiece song, "Cocain," is a lengthy comparison of a delicious one-night stand to a drug. Sean Gemini grew up without a lot of money, but he now has quite a lot of it. And he estimates that he has spent at least a quarter million dollars thus far on diamond jewelry of all styles. He admitted to me that he feels two ways about this buying habit. As he speaks, he gesticulates with his forearms; the right one bears a tattoo that says: OUTLAW JEWELS.

"There's both positive and negative to it, plus and minus," he said. "It can get you robbed. It can bring harm to you. It can bring harm to your friends. Cops will pull you over for some bullshit, not wearing seat belts, whatever, when they see you wearing it. They can see it even if you have tinted windows. Diamonds tell the world that you *have* to have this to be a man of substance—that's the evil part of it. It sets up a false god. It doesn't make you who you are—you get that from the work you put into your life. But the good part is, you're going to look attractive. The air will be all shining around you. Will you get the women, will you smack somebody across the face, bust a gun? You're going to feel just like a king on a throne, back to the days when they sat up on Roman chairs with all the crowns and the rubies, and people will say, there is the man, I have to respect him."

Diamonds have been a potent fashion symbol in the hip-hop world since the early 1990s. Their sales among musicians and fans makes up less than 5 percent of the U.S. consumer market, totaling at most an annual half-billion dollars. But their cultural power here is formidable. From ice-drenched necklines to rocks sparkling below knuckles to diamonds embedded in teeth, the style helped define the aesthetic known as "ghetto fabulous" that ruled much of the iconography of videos, CD covers, publicity photos, and the wardrobes of the rapper lords and their entourages on their nights out. The essence of the hip-hop narrative has always been about the struggle of the individual against his or her environment and diamonds were seen as the crowning mark of personal triumph over adversity, the exterior mark of gangsta knighthood and sexual prowess. It was a sartorial style reminiscent of white Chicago crime lords of the Prohibition era—one that defined itself though visual excess, conspicuous decadence, and a certain dose of sly self-parody. One wealthy friend of Sean Gemini had a series of diamonds embedded in the rims of his SUV. He can now only park it in extremely secure locations.

This style grew out of the aggressive gold necklaces of the late 1980s worn by musicians like Big Daddy Kane, Slick Rick, and Kurtis Blow. The signature item, a chain made of hollow gold, was known as a "G-rope" because it was supposed to cost $1,000. Advertisements for the record label No Limit helped touch off the diamond ethic in 1992; they featured the CEO Percy "Master P" Miller sporting the logo of the label, a gold tank encrusted with diamonds.

The personal story of Master P spoke to the up-from-the-projects spirit of diamonds: he grew up amid crime, prostitution, and desperate poverty in New Orleans before getting into music and signing up winning acts like Snoop Dogg and Mystikal, as well as starting profitable auxiliary ventures in clothing, phone sex lines, gas stations, sports management, and shoes. Miller not only promoted the favorable image of thug-cum-businessman, he also helped usher in the era of "ghetto fabulous" in which the primary obsession of rap music turned from anger over social injustices (such as the brutality of police officers) to the fetishization of luxury items (such as diamonds). "They took all that political content of the late eighties, all the Public Enemy* stuff, and they wiped it all away," one music magazine writer told me. "They replaced it with nihilism and excess." Artists from all over the rap world began to imitate the style and diamonds became *the* indispensable thing to flash in nightclubs, as well as something to celebrate in verse. Rap was still focused on issues of power, but it became less about the power you did not have, and more about the power you could wear on your fingers.

"Every hip-hop artist has got to sing about it at some point," Sean Gemini told me. "It's *necessary*. You want to talk about what's relevant right now. You don't want to talk about saving the seals. It's about 'look at me, look at my chain.' I do not write fiction."

---

*A group most famous for the song "Fight the Power."

One of his earlier songs is called "Give It Up." The title refers to a command muggers give their victims.

> If you understand me
> You understand my 'hood
> I'm about money, bitches and cars
> I'm a superstar
> See the diamonds on my wrist
> They will blind your sight
> I'll put it down anytime

"It's about ghetto fabulous," he told me. "It's a Mercedes-Benz parked outside a bad building."

This was one of the original things about the bling style—its unabashed celebration of opulence in the midst of urban decay. Expensive goods such as cognac, private jets, and Rolex watches were portrayed alongside crack salesmen, carjackings, dilapidated tenements, and graffiti-covered walls with no seams between the two. It was two ends of an economic spectrum united by a common social fabric.

According to Bakari Kitwana, the former editor in chief of the music magazine *The Source*, this style emerged partly because of the resettlement patterns of middle-class blacks in the late twentieth century. As families got wealthier, they tended to stay put instead of moving out. "They didn't usually move out to the suburbs, so you have more of a proximity [of rich and poor]," Kitwana told me, citing the words of sociologists. This physical closeness, in turn, lends itself to a cultural continuum between the hard-luck and the well-to-do that is generally not seen among white families, for whom moving out of urban cores became a defining experience after World War II. For many successful young black people, the ghetto was the *only* place to be fabulous. Hence the Benz on the bad block, the snow-white sneakers that cost $200, the diamonds that could be ripped from the neck at any moment.

Bling style reached an apex of self-consciousness—some would say absurdity—in 1999 with the release of a smash song called "Bling Bling" by a New Orleans ensemble called B.G. The lyrics were saturated in the customary self-praise of hip-hop and it was difficult for some listeners to tell whether the song was satirizing diamonds or reveling in them (or perhaps some of both). "I be that nigga with the ice on me," went the most quoted couplet. "If it cost less than twenty, it don't look right on me." The song propelled the phrase "bling bling" into the mainstream and it became nearly impossible to use it on the street without a certain degree of irony. Three years later, the North American staff of the *Oxford English Dictionary* announced they would be including the term in new editions—effectively killing it for good.

The look may now be on the wane, according to Sean Gemini. He wasn't wearing any of his diamonds when we met at his Crown Heights studio, and he says many of his musician friends prefer to keep the jewelry under wraps when they're not performing. It can be dangerous to show it off in social circumstances. Many of his rapper friends have spent huge amounts of money to ice themselves out, only to be forced to sell it all for a cash loss when harder times set in. This is a familiar arc in the hip-hop world, one reminiscent of the "miner's disease" of the Brazilian highlands, the smugglers' markets of Central Africa, the Vancouver Stock Exchange in Canada, and other places where fantastic caroms between famine and feast are a routine circumstance, a ride fueled by the lusting for a clear white rock. Hip-hop has its own particular spin on diamonds: men are less shy about wearing them and the style tends to be super-charged. But the urge to possess them comes from exactly the same places in the heart as anywhere in the world. There is the same weakness for charms, the same yearning to be the room's alpha, and the same personal appropriation of a larger mythology. "It's a piece of something you can hold on to" Sean Gemini told me. "You can physically pick it up, touch it, hold it, bargain with it. You can't do that with a stock."

The rapper Kanye West added a twist in 2005 with his song "Diamonds (from Sierra Leone)," the first major release to point out the connection between jewelry and the civil wars of Africa. He specifically highlighted the disgusting conflict in Sierra Leone in which rebel troops hacked off the arms of civilians with machetes purchased with diamond profits. But many listeners read the song not so much as a condemnation of diamonds as a subtle endorsement—particularly given the singer's relationship with the New York firm of Jacob & Co., the famous ice-upper of Michael Jordan, Mariah Carey, Sean "Puffy" Combs, Faith Evans, The Notorious B.I.G., and Beyonce Knowles. In partnership with Jacob, West has developed his own line of gaudy pendants shaped like the head of Jesus Christ and festooned with diamonds. They retail for approximately $17,000.

I asked Sean Gemini about this apparent double vision and he said, once again, that he can see both sides of the question. It must be the Gemini part of his personality, he told me with a laugh. There is good to diamonds and there is great evil, and the only thing that matters is the angle from which you view them. Yes, he knows people get killed for diamonds overseas. Yes, he knows they present a twisted image of success to young boys and girls who deserve better role models. But it won't ever change the popularity of diamonds in American culture, nor the hunger to possess them.

"You can't go stop the killing in Africa, you have to accept what it is and just try to make life better over here," he told me. "A lot of people don't even want to talk about that stuff. They don't want to get all political. It's all about the here and now and being young and having fun. A lot of people say, 'I just don't give a fuck. *I* didn't do anything wrong to get this pendant, *I* didn't kill anybody.' That's the whole American mentality."

This must be admitted: they *are* chemically unique. They conduct heat more efficiently than any other known natural material. That's why they are always cold to the touch—just one of the reasons diamonds are known by the slang term "ice."

Their hardness is legendary. They are used to slice away skullcaps for brain surgery, punch through granite bedrock for oil drills, and cut steel plates for aircraft carriers. Their cube-shaped lock of carbon atoms has a toughness seen nowhere else in nature. It is a well-known fact that the Mohs Scale, which ranks the hardness of various rocks, put diamond at a 10 on a scale of 1 to 10, meaning that a more indestructible mineral has not been found. But even this offers an incomplete view, because the Mohs Scale rises exponentially in hardness when it passes the ranking of 8. A diamond is actually *four* times as hard as the next hardest rock at number 9.

The density of a diamond puts the brakes on the speed of light like no other mineral. The ordinary speed of light is around 186,000 miles a second. Put it through the turgid interior of a diamond, however, and it slows to around 77,000 miles a second. This has the effect of smashing the color spectrum apart into brilliant ribbons. A diamond thus becomes a fantastic chamber in which to bounce light around a series of angles, and fire off shards of violet, yellow, and red. Polish it the right way and the effect is even more striking. The Belgian cutter and mathematician Marcel

Tolkowsky revolutionized the art in 1914 when he published an academic paper theorizing that the most economical use of light for a diamond was to polish it into a kind of cylindrical pyramid, with facets aimed at precise angles to one another. This was the modern "ideal cut," which is today the classic shape of a diamond and the most popular shape for engagement ring consumers.*

Diamonds flash gorgeously under light, but that does not fully explain their prominence in Western popular culture. At the heart of the diamond lives an enduring riddle: What makes us want to take this piece of regurgitated carbon and attach it to ourselves?

The conventional explanation is Darwinian: Diamonds are merely a means of broadcasting one's social status and, therefore, one's genetic desirability as a mate. In a quirky book-length essay published in 1966 called *The Importance of Wearing Clothes,* Lawrence Langner argued that the wearing of gemstones played an important role in sexual selection and symbolized a critical shift in evolutionary development. At some point in the long journey from the rain forest, a man's mental abilities and his social status in the tribe became more important qualities than brute strength. Hanging glittering stones from the body was one way to advertise these powers—to flash the peacock feathers—and attract worthy mates. That argument seems straightforward, but Langner pushes his theory to suggest something darker.

"The desire to achieve superiority and to win the admiration of our fellow men and women is one of our deepest spiritual needs," he wrote. "Primitive man also possessed in his ornaments the equivalent of today's jewelry, but unlike the civilized man of today, he did not give them to his women until he had all he wanted to wear himself. He wore them for the same reason that we do—to show superior rank and authority . . . to provide aesthetic pleasure, and to compensate for the feeling of inferiority in himself and in his women."

The flash of a diamond, in other words, covers up our inadequacies and lets us unite ourselves with a piece of natural perfection. It is a drive that goes beyond ego. This suicidal desire to cloak the shabby self with beauty

---

*Central to Tolkowsky's idea is that the flat top—the "table"—should be at an angle to the slanted lower part—the "pavilion"—at a ratio between 58 and 62 percent. This is known as the "depth," and is the most important statistic used to determine the value of a polished diamond. Most jewelers won't disclose it unless you ask.

is a form of the urge to worship, to be dissolved into something vast and complete.

I have always been fascinated with tourists who casually ask to have their pictures taken in the foreground of the Grand Canyon or the Dover Cliffs or Mount Fuji or some other striking piece of earth whose depth and complexity they can never hope to fully appreciate. They stay only for a second, never long enough to know it, to run their hands over its stone faces, sleep in its crevasses, watch the sun make shadows on its boulders. But they still want to *own* it, to have their own image laid on top of it, if only for second. In the view of geological time, people are as superficial as raindrops on the rocks; they disappear as fast as they arrive. Yet we yearn for that brief moment of identification with something larger than ourselves. *I was here,* say those vacation photos. *I was a participant in this.* This is our natural response to the sublime—almost sexual in its urge to coexist with loveliness as a single unit. We want to pull that beauty over us, merge with it, make it a part of ourselves, bring it inside like a communion wafer. We want to cling to it because we believe it will fill up the emptiness inside.

It was the maverick American economist Thorstein Veblen who noted that the modern idea of "success" tended to lie in attaining a state of opulence, and not in making the collective lot of mankind any better. Society is oriented toward the public enjoyment of frivolous goods, he said, and the more ridiculous the better. The most vivid example of this tendency is the Potlatch ceremony of the Kwakiutl Indians of the Pacific Northwest, where local chiefs demonstrated their power by tossing valuable goods onto a bonfire. The entire point was to shame the neighbors.

Veblen coined the term "conspicuous consumption" to define the need to conceal insecurities—about looks, about weakness, about death—by living as extravagantly as possible. Clothing fashions revolve so quickly in America and the rest of the affluent world because of a desire to maintain the appearance of being too rich to work. To wear last year's shoes is to unwittingly broadcast one's status as an outsider, which, according to Veblen, is viewed as a strange kind of moral failing. The worst possible sin against the herd is the failure to spend money. And so the display of the right kind of gewgaws on one's person registers high on the index of status because it suggests pleasure without effort. It is a false way to cover the pining inside, but it does bring a version of satisfaction in the moment. Beneath the colorless surface is a precipice of want. "In order to be reputable," wrote Veblen, "it must be wasteful."

So it is with a diamond—a perfect package of emptiness, full of nothing but slow light.

But this does not explain everything.

I remember the weekend I first knew I was hopelessly in love with Anne. It was Memorial Day, 2000, and we went camping in the Sierra Nevadas. On the drive up, we stopped in the town of Placerville to buy a bottle of wine and fill up the tank. That particular gas station happened to be running a promotion and they gave me a cheap sports watch as a gift. I handed it to Anne as I started the engine.

She fiddled with it, trying to figure out how to program it.

"This could be our little alarm clock," she said. She meant that it was going to be one of our household items in the vinyl tent we would be setting up on the mountainside that night.

We had forgotten cups, so we drank the wine straight from the bottle and held one another in front of the campfire and promised that we would not leave the other. I had never said such a thing to a woman before. It was not quite a proposal of marriage—that would come later—but it was a giant step in that direction. I remember kissing her and caressing her face in my hands and feeling a wild bliss burning inside.

The watch didn't have an instruction booklet and had defied our attempts to program it. I stashed it in the glove compartment after our trip to the mountains. It seemed worthy of saving. Something about the way she had called it "our little alarm clock" touched me. It told the wrong time, but it made one faint electronic beep at the turn of every hour. I could hear it only when the radio wasn't on.

After our engagement fell apart, I let the watch stay inside the glove box. By imperceptible degrees, the beep started to drift further and further from the top of the hour. It would make its tiny chirp, I would glance at the gray wall of the dashboard, and then return my eyes to the road. *Anne's watch*, I would think, *our alarm clock*, and my mind would drift elsewhere.

In the summer of 2003, I was idling at a red light in the north part of Phoenix when I suddenly realized that I wasn't hearing the watch anymore. I pulled it out and saw the numbers had disappeared from the face. The battery had given out. That watch had been buried in my glove box for two years before it died.

Psychologists have known for generations that human beings have the tendency to project emotions onto inanimate objects, like that watch. In 1929, the Swiss child psychologist Jean Piaget noted a tendency toward "animism" in children under the age of seven—that is, they assume flowers, trees, silverware, etc. have spirits and personalities. A particular girl cannot sleep, for example, unless she sees the Mickey Mouse nightlight smiling back at her. The British pediatrician D. W. Winnicott put a new spin on the phenomenon in 1951 when he coined the phrase "transitional object" to describe the teddy bear, soft toy, or a sucked thumb that becomes a substitute for the mother's body. The object tends to become the first thing the infant recognizes as different from itself or its mother—the *not-me*, as Winnicott called it. The *not-me* helps ease the pain of separation from the mother's body and, with it, the mother's constant love. The teddy bear or Mickey Mouse nightlight cannot give love itself, but it becomes the needful bridge between *love* and *not-love*.

This bridge typically disappears once we reach the age of six. For some, however, the ghost of it can linger on well into adulthood. One minor example is an occasional pang of sympathy for objects (stuffed animals, for instance). This bond between people and objects is a more advanced form of animism, called "participation mystique" by Carl Jung. These beliefs often turn up in sophisticated religious systems: the nature worship of the Bantu tribes in Africa, for instance, or the Shinto faith of Japan, where trees, rocks, streams, and other features of the landscape are believed to be the play-masks of the *kami*, the spirits that roam the earth. The Roman Catholic Church, of course, believes the body and blood of Jesus are present in the wine and the wafer of communion.

The displacement of emotion into objects—like that gas station watch—is just one shading of that uniquely human habit of looking for meaning in the things and events around us. This is a cerebral processor we cannot switch off. It comes as naturally to us as breathing.

One of the foremost contributions to the field of psychiatry in the twentieth century was made by a Viennese doctor named Viktor Frankl, a survivor of four different Nazi concentration camps. His wife, as well as his father, mother, and brother, all died; only he and a sister survived. In his masterwork *Man's Search for Meaning*, Frankl described his months as inmate #119,104, surrounded by starvation and random murder. He noticed something remarkable among his fellow inmates. Those who could see no point in their suffering were the ones who tended to die of exhaustion or starvation. But those who tried to find some purpose in their suffering were the ones who, in the midst of their wretchedness, managed to be fully alive. While staggering to work at camp in the freezing cold, Frankl began to have an imagined conversation with his wife. He was unsure if she was even alive. But he still told her how much he loved her, and how much joy she had brought to him in the short time they had been together.

"Then I grasped the meaning of the greatest secret that human poetry and human thought and belief have to impart." He wrote later. "The salvation of man is through love, and in love."

Frankl concluded that the chief function of the mind was not wrestling with sexual imprints left over from childhood, as Sigmund Freud had said. The true preoccupation of the mind, rather, is the urge to derive some kind of *purpose* from the confusing mass of stimuli constantly thrown at us by the world. Frankl himself had decided at Auschwitz that the overarching meaning of life was to love all humankind. Others may decide on a different script. But the journey toward that conclusion is where the power lies. We spin constant webs of meaning around the things that swim into our vision. Raw data flows into our minds like cotton and gets loomed into tapestries. Far from being an illness, this is instead the apex of mental health. We ceaselessly file people, events, memories—and objects—into categories that fit an internal narrative, even if the ultimate significance of it all is so obscure that we can barely articulate it.

In the face of a baffling universe, and with the foreknowledge of certain death, is it any wonder that the mind gravitates toward something claiming to be eternal that we can grasp in our hands? When it came to professions of love, man's quest for meaning had lit upon a rock. De Beers had supplied a mythology to lead us there. We crave the thing that is said to be the hardest to find, that raises us over everyone else in a twinkling, as if to emphasize the emotional poverty of ordinary life. A diamond is the thing set apart, a heart outside of the heart, the one shining irreducible moment in clear carbon that is supposed to make us forget our failings and mortality. From the river mines and battlefields of Central Africa to the suffocating polishing factories of India and the Arctic camps and Siberian labs where men and women risked their lives in pursuit of the star that stands for love, they all bent to serve the myth around which we wound our hungry dreams.

The jewelry store was on a two-lane highway, across the street from a car dealership and a Starbucks. Beyond the retail strip were sycamore trees and tidy suburban houses made from native timber and gray Pennsylvania schist. There was a Quaker college just down the road that had a lake with duck feathers on the edge. I was a continent away, more or less, from San Francisco where I had bought Anne's ring more than four years ago.

The jeweler was a gregarious man and he chatted with me as he worked on the gold prongs that held the diamond in place. Sweat glistened on his cheeks, though the store was air-conditioned.

"You're lucky," he said. "The other day, this guy came in with a ring from a busted marriage. It was radiant-cut, pretty big, but it was all twisted in the middle. I couldn't give him anything for it. Now this stone, this is marketable. I can get rid of it."

"What's going to happen to it?" I asked.

"I'll put it into a new setting, try to sell it in the store. It could move in two weeks. It could move in a year, I don't know. If it doesn't move, I'll take it up to New York."

The jeweler freed the gem from its setting and set it on a piece of tissue paper colored baby-blue. With the gold now stripped away, light could stream through the entire pavilion and Tolkowsky's light-bouncing trick could be seen at full effect. I thought it had never sparkled so brilliantly— not since the day I had acquired it when I was brimming with love.

I looked at it for what I knew would be the last time. Soon, it would be on the finger of a stranger who would be ignorant of its history, the same way I had known nothing about it at all when I had made it the embodiment of my feelings for Anne. Its memory would be erased the second I walked out of the door.

The jeweler seemed to know what I was thinking. He was one of the few people in this part of the city who bought secondhand rings and he conducted transactions like this all the time.

"It's not going anywhere," he told me. "A million years from now, your family might be extinct. Humanity might be extinct. But this diamond will still be here. It won't have changed a bit. Time doesn't wear them down."

He repeated: "You're lucky. This is a very tradable stone. It's got everything you could want."

I watched him seal it in a plastic envelope and file it away with several other diamonds of similar size. He gave me a check and we shook hands good-bye. I left with the empty box in my pocket.

NOTES ON SOURCES

This is a work of nonfiction. The events and the people described here are real; no pseudonyms have been used. Many interviews overseas were conducted with the aid of a translator, particularly in Africa. In a handful of instances, the contents of a lengthy conversation were compressed into a single running paragraph, with my triangulated questions eliminated for the sake of narrative simplicity. Numerous government documents, corporate reports, books, magazine articles, newspaper stories, and academic journal articles provided important background and context. Those not directly cited in the text are listed below.

One: Dying Stars

An overview of alluvial mining techniques is contained in "Diamonds in the Central African Republic," an unpublished manual written by Joseph N'gozo. Smuggling methods are outlined in a declassified diplomatic cable sent from the U.S. Embassy in Bangui to the U.S. State Department, on October 24, 2002, as well as in an advocacy report entitled *Hard Currency: The Criminalized Diamond Economy of the Democratic Republic of the Congo and Its Neighbours* (Ottawa: Partnership Africa Canada, 2002). One of that study's authors, Christian Deitrich, followed up with a January 10, 2003, report entitled *Diamonds in the Central African Republic: Trading, Valuing and Laundering*. Deitrich also generously volunteered additional insights with me in a phone conversation. The reign of Bokassa is examined in Alex Shoumatoff's essay "The Emperor Who Ate His People," reprinted in his book *Africa Madness* (New York: Alfred A. Knopf, 1988). General information on late colonial Africa comes from *Inside Africa*, by John Gunther (New York: Harper & Brothers, 1953), one of the classics of his *Inside* series, and one that remains remarkably timeless after six decades. Further background on the continent, and a vivid firsthand account of Bokassa's coronation, is taken from *The Africans: A Noted Foreign Correspondent's Encounters with Black Africa Today*, by David Lamb (New York: Random House, 1982).

Two: Midnight Sun

Vilhjalmur Stefansson's adventures and ideas are recounted in *Canada's Colonies*, by Kenneth Coates (Toronto: James Lorimer & Co., 1985), and *Stefansson and the Canadian Arctic*, by Richard J. Diubaldo (Ottawa: McGill-Queens University Press, 1999). Early maritime explorations of Canada—and the subsequent attempts to find John Franklin—are covered in *The Search for the Northwest Passage*, by Ann Savours (New York: St. Martin's Press, 1999); *The Search for the Northwest Passage*, by Warren Brown (New York: Chelsea House Publishers, 1991); *Ice Blink*, by Scott Cookman (New York: John Wiley & Sons, 2000); and *Search for Franklin*, by Leslie H. Neatby (New York: Walker & Co., 1970). Richardson's discovery of Victoria Island is told in *Banks, Victoria and Stefansson Islands, Arctic Archipelago*, by R. Thorsteinsson and E. T. Tozer (Ottawa: Geological Survey of Canada, 1962). Background on Chuck Fipke, as well as the glacier puzzle of Wisconsin and Jacques Cartier's lasting gift to French idiom, is drawn from Kevin Krajick's excellent *Barren Lands: An Epic Search for Diamonds in the North American Arctic* (New York: Times Books, 2001). This book will surely be recognized years hence as the most thoroughly researched account of this aspect of Canadian mining history. This chapter also drew on newspaper accounts published in *The Globe and Mail*, *The Wall Street Journal*, and the *yellowknifer*, and magazine articles in *Up Here*, *The Walrus*, and *Canadian Diamonds*.

Three: Desired Results

Insights on the "bright life" and postwar Japanese consumer thinking are drawn from *Assembled in Japan: Electrical Goods and the Making of the Japa-*

nese Consumer, by Simon Partner (Berkeley: University of California Press, 1999). Partner, a professor of history at Duke University, was also generous with his time over the phone with me. I have quoted from corporate memos from N. W. Ayer & Son on file at the Smithsonian Institution, including "De Beers Diamond Engagement Ring" (author unknown, 1991), "Consumer Ayerplan" (ibid.), and a letter dated October 30, 1987, from Frances Gerety to F. Bradley Lynch detailing the creation of the world's most famous ad slogan. The initial report to De Beers from Lauck is excerpted in a March 23, 1945, affidavit from Ayer vice president Warner S. Shelly on file at the National Archives. Other key Ayer documents were first disclosed by Edward Jay Epstein in the seminal article "Have You Ever Tried to Sell a Diamond?" in *The Atlantic* (February 1982). Epstein also gives a brief account of the first De Beers campaign in Japan in his book *The Rise and Fall of Diamonds: The Shattering of a Brilliant Illusion* (New York: Simon & Schuster, 1982). Early dealings between Ayer and Harry Oppenheimer are also recounted in *The Last Empire,* by Stefan Kanfer (New York: Farrar, Straus & Giroux, 1993), and the end of the relationship is covered in *The Encyclopedia of Advertising,* edited by John Mcdonough (New York: Fitzroy Dearborn Publishers, 2002).

Statistics on recent diamond sales came from several untitled documents on file at Tokyo's Japan Jewellery Association. Copies of Japanese and American magazine advertisements, the activities of Ayer's publicists in Hollywood, and details on other marketing efforts were partially drawn from multiple papers and letters from the J. Walter Thompson Collection at the John W. Hartman Center for Sales, Advertising & Marketing History at Duke University, including most notably "Has Anyone Seen Merle Oberon's Matching Bracelet?" (author and date unknown), "Diamond News Spring Edition" (author unknown, February 1996), and "De Beers Activity in Japan" (author unknown, 1996). A U.S. Justice Department memo from Raymond D. Hunter entitled "Diamond Case," dated February 21, 1945, was also enlightening. Akiro Kurosawa's account of the emperor's radio address was taken from his *Something Like an Autobiography* (New York: Vintage, 1983). I learned of it from Patrick Tyler's *Japan: A Reinterpretation* (New York: Vintage, 1998), which was valuable for much more than the quote.

Four: The Strong Man

The unhappy history of diamonds in the Jequitinhonha region is partially drawn from *The Golden Age of Brazil: Growing Pains of a Colonial Society 1695–1750*, by C. R. Boxer (Berkeley: University of California Press, 1962); *"Licentious Liberty" in a Brazilian Gold Mining Region*, by Kathleen Higgins (University Park, PA: Pennsylvania State University Press, 1999); *Travels in the Interior of Brazil, Particularly in Gold and Diamond Districts of That Country, by the Authority of the Prince Regent of Portugal, Including a Voyage to the Rio De La Plata and a Historical Sketch of the Revolution of Buenos Ayres*, by John Mawe (London: Longman, Hurst, Rees, Orme & Brown, 1812); *The Highlands of the Brazil*, by Sir Richard Burton (London: Tinsley Brothers, 1869); and "In the Diamond Fields of Brazil," by Harry Franck in *Century* magazine (September 1921). Mining law and tax dodging are discussed in the advocacy paper "The Failure of Good Intentions" (Ottawa: Partnership Africa Canada, 2005). This chapter also drew on corporate and government reports, including *Mineral Summary 2004* from the Ministry of Mines and Energy, National Department of Mineral Production, Brasilia; *COMIG 10 Years: The Mining of the 21st Century*, from the Minas Gerais Mining Company, Belo Horizonte; and *2004 Annual Report* from Brazilian Diamonds, Ltd., Vancouver, B.C. Excellent portraits of the nation can be found in *The Brazilians*, by Joseph Page (New York: Addison Wesley, 1996), and *Brazil: The Once and Future Country*, by Marshall Eakin (New York: Palgrave Macmillan, 1998).

Five: The Cartel

Details from the rush on the Vaal River and on the farm of the unfortunate De Beer brothers were drawn from *South Africa's City of Diamonds: Mine Workers and Monopoly Capitalism in Kimberley, 1867–1895*, by William H. Worger (Craighall, South Africa: A. D. Donker, 1987); *Knights of the Shovel*, edited by George Beet (Limited edition published by Friends of the Library, Kimberley Africana Library, 1996); and *Graves and Guineas*, by J. T. McNish (Cape Town: C. Struik, 1969). The megalomania of Cecil Rhodes is put under the microscope in *Rhodes*, by Antony Thomas (New York: Thomas Dunne, 1996). The later history of the cartel is limned in the richly detailed dual biography *Oppenheimer and Son*, by Anthony

Hocking (Johannesburg: McGraw-Hill Book Co., 1973). The single best book ever written about De Beers, however, is *The Last Empire*, by Stefan Kanfer (see chapter Three), which helped inform the early parts of this chapter. Kanfer also shared several current observations with me over the phone and pointed me to De Beers–related material in the Sterling Library at Yale University. Other good overviews can be found in "De Beers and the Diamond Debacle," by Peter W. Bernstein, *Fortune*, September 6, 1982; and "Million-Carat Colossus," by Sally Angwin and Selhurst Trewier, *Town* (London, November 1963).

Three books with useful sections on the De Beers sightholder system are *Diamond Stories: Enduring Change on 47th Street*, by Renee Rose Sheild (Ithaca, NY: Cornell University Press, 2002); *Diamond: The Spectacular Story of Earth's Rarest Treasure and Man's Greatest Greed*, by Emily Hahn (New York: Doubleday & Co., 1956); and *The Diamond People*, by Murray Schumach (New York: W. W. Norton & Co., 1981). Current sightholder criteria can be found in "Sales and Marketing at the DTC," by K. Goodram, published in *Diamonds—Source to Use* (Johannesburg: South African Institute of Mining and Metallurgy, 2003).

The strange story of the Arkansas pipe is skillfully examined in the doctoral thesis of John C. Henderson entitled *The Crater of Diamonds: A History of the Pike County, Arkansas Diamond Field* (Denton, TX: University of North Texas, 2002). There are a few colorful anecdotes in Howard Millar's memoirs, *It Was Finders Keepers at America's Only Diamond Mine* (New York: Carlton Press, 1976). An examination of the disputed shape of the ore body is contained in "Summary of the 1990s Exploration and Testing of the Prairie Creek Diamond-Bearing Lamproite Complex, Pike County, Arkansas, and a Field Guide," by J. Michael Howard, published in *Contributions to the Geology of Arkansas* (Little Rock: Arkansas State Geology Commission, 1999). This section also drew upon several unsealed memos from lawyers at the U.S. Justice Department, most notably a study from Herbert Berman for Edward S. Stimston entitled "Legal Problems Involved in a Suit Against the Diamond Cartel," dated January 6, 1944. Janine Roberts, the author of *Glitter & Greed* (New York: The Disinformation Company, 2003), found some De Beers–related documents in the National Archives that I missed, as well as a good quote from Ernest Oppenheimer on the philosophy of scarcity. Kevin Krajick's *Barren Lands* (see Chapter Two above) also has an excellent section on early century happenings at Murfreesboro. Some of the activities of the IDSO are recounted in Ian Fleming's only nonfiction book, *The Diamond Smugglers* (London: Jonathan Cape, 1957). The James Bond quote comes from the novel *Diamonds Are Forever* (London: Jonathan Cape, 1956), whose plotline is notably different than the 1971 United Artists movie of the same name.

Six: The New Era

An elegant portrait of the Aboriginal Dreamtime traditions is *The Songlines*, by Bruce Chatwin (New York: Viking, 1987). Background on Argyle's geology comes from "Discovery and Mining of the Argyle Diamond Deposit, Australia," by Jim Shigley, John Chapman, and Robyn K. Ellison, in *Gems & Gemology* (Spring 2001), and *Sustainability Report 2003*, published by Argyle Diamonds Australia, West Perth, W.A. The pricing dispute is summarized in "Argyle's Bitter Diamond War," by Tim Treadgold, in the Australian *Business Review Weekly*, November 4, 1996. Cogent analysis of recent De Beers decisions is contained in a case study entitled "Forever: De Beers and U.S. Antitrust Law," published April 20, 2000, by the Harvard Business School. The Supplier of Choice business model is examined in "De Beers New Direction," by Rob Bates, in *JCK-Jewelers Circular Keystone*, June 1, 2003, and in "Conjecturing About 'Incredibly Hidden' Strategies Behind the Dropping of So Many U.S. Sightholders," by Chaim Even-Zohar, in the newsletter *Diamond Intelligence Briefs*, June 12, 2003.

Seven: Blood Diamonds

Accounts of Savimbi's death by gunshot are drawn from initial reports from the British Broadcasting Company and from "Chevron Oil and the Savimbi Problem," by James P. Lucier, *Insight on the News*, April 29, 2002. Clues to his personality are contained in "Jonas Savimbi: Washington's Freedom Fighter, Africa's Terrorist," by Shana Wills, *Foreign Policy in Focus*, February 27, 2002. The smuggling through Antwerp is detailed in *Final Report of the Monitoring Mechanism on Sanctions Against UNITA (Angola)*, by the staff of the United Nations, New York, released on December 21, 2000, as well as in an unpublished investigation in 2001 from Belgium's Intelligence and Security Services titled "The Illegal Trade in Diamonds from Angola: The Part Played by Belgium" (author unknown). Further details were drawn from the advocacy report *A Rough Trade: The Role of Companies and Governments in the Angolan Conflict* (London: Global Witness, 1998). The vivid description of an arms airlift comes from *Diamond: A Journey to the Heart of an Obsession,* by Matthew Hart (New York: Walker & Co., 2001).

The restive situation in the northeast is examined in the unpublished November 2003 document "Report on Fact-Finding Trip to Lunda Norte and Lunda Sul," by Rafael Marques of the Open Society Initiative for Southern Africa, as well as *War, Peace and Diamonds in Angola,* by Justin Pearce, published by the Institute for Security Studies, Johannesburg, South Africa, June 25, 2004. Background on the nation's diamond business and complex ownership structures can be found in *Diamond Industry Annual Review—Republic of Angola,* edited by Christine Gordon and published by Partnership Africa Canada, Ottawa, July 2004. The boomtown culture of Cafunfo is given a sociological treatment in "Garimpeiro Worlds: Digging, Dying and Hunting for Diamonds in Angola," by Filip De Boeck in the *Review of African Political Economy,* 2001. General background was drawn from *Country Profile 2004, Angola,* published by The Economist Intelligence Unit, London, and the unforgettable portrait "Oil and Blood," by Jon Lee Anderson, in *The New Yorker,* August 14, 2000. The section on the Ivory Coast also drew on fine overseas reporting in *The Washington Post.*

Eight: The Stone Mills

Though it does not cover diamond polishing, *Born to Work,* by Neera Burra (New Delhi: Oxford University Press, 1995), contains a cultural overview of child labor in India and an examination of its role in several economic sectors. William Langewiesche's article "The Shipbreakers" in *The Atlantic* (March 2000) has several insights on the regulatory climate in the state of Gujarat. Some ancient history was taken from *Great Diamonds of India,* by Monisha Bharadwaj (Bombay: India Book House Pvt, 2002). Health problems associated with diamond polishing are examined in the following medical journal articles: "Occupational Asthma with Paroxysmal Atrial Fibrillation in a Diamond Polisher," by E. Wilk-Rivard J. Szeinuk, in *Environmental Health Perspectives* (December 2001); "Cobalt Lung in Diamond Polishers," by M. Demedts, et al., in *American Review of Respiratory Diseases* (July 1984); and "Pulmonary Function Studies in 15 to 18 Years Age Workers Exposed to Dust in Industry," by N. M. Rao, et al., in *Indian Journal of Physiology and Pharmacology* (January 1992). The rise of the polishing industry is recounted briefly in the article "Uncommon Brilliance," by Aravind Adiga, in *Time Asia*, April 12, 2004.

I also used several stories from the archives of *The Times of India* to recount the recent history of Surat, most notably "Multinationals Urged to Stop Using Child Labor," by Nitin Jugran Bahuguna, October 29, 1997; "Health and Hygiene Transform the City of Dirt and Diamonds," by Shabnam Minwalla and Rafat Nayeem Quadri, November 9, 1996; "Plague Offers Surat Chance for a Facelift" (author unknown), September 26, 1995; and "Back on the Road to Hell," by Shabnam Minwalla, September 10, 1995. Background on the fascinating nation of India was drawn from *In Light of India*, by Octavio Paz (New York: Harcourt, 1997), and *Portrait of India*, by Ved Mehta (New York: Farrar, Straus & Giroux, 1970).

Nine: Alchemy

A technical explanation of the BARS process can be found in a translated version of "Growth Conditions and Real Structures of Synthetic Diamond Crystals," *Russian Geology and Geophysics*, vol. 38, no. 5 (1997). The art of synthetic detection is recounted in the excellent primer *Laboratory Created Diamonds*, by Sharrie Woodring and Branko Deljanin, published by the European Gemological Laboratory USA, 2004. The most informative magazine piece yet written about the Gemesis Corporation is "The New Diamond Age," by Joshua Davis, in *Wired* (October 2003). Further background comes from the trade journal articles "A Diamond Is a Diamond?" in *Rapaport Diamond Report*, October 3, 2003; "Gemesis Laboratory-Created Diamonds," by Jim Shigley, Reza Abbaschian, and Carter Clarke, in *Gems & Gemology* (Winter 2002); and "Tuesday's Diamond in Wednesday's Ring," in *IDEX* magazine (August 2004). A detailed chronology of gem-making efforts from 1880 onward is found in *The Diamond Makers*, by Robert Hazen (Cambridge: Cambridge University Press, 1999). The fascinating history of Akademgorodok is related in Paul Josephson's *New Atlantis Revisited* (Princeton: Princeton University Press). The European reluctance to embrace cultured pearls is briefly discussed in the hagiography *The Pearl King: The Story of the Fabulous Mikimoto*, by Robert Eunson (New York: Greenberg, 1955).

Ten: The Big Nothing

Retailing data was drawn from several industry reports, including: *The Cost of Doing Business Survey*, published by the Jewelers of America in May 2004; *Top 50*, published by *National Jeweler* on May 16, 2004; and *Luxury Goods: The Global Jewelry and Watch Market*, published by Bear Stearns & Co. in September 2004. Also helpful were the articles "Diamond Industry 2004," in *Rapaport Diamond Report*, November 5, 2004, and "Romance Killer," by Victoria Murphy, *Forbes*, November 29, 2004. De Beers' newest ad blitz is discussed in "The Right-Hand Diamond Ring," by Rob Walker, *The New York Times Magazine*, January 4, 2004.

Martin Rapaport's pugnacious history with the old guard was covered in "A Diamond Maverick's War with the Club on 47th Street," by Sandra Salmans, *The New York Times*, November 13, 1984; "Secretive Club Polishes Its Image Amid Fight Over Pricing Disclosure," by Kathleen Day, *Los Angeles Times*, August 18, 1985; "Mike Rapaport: Prophet or Pariah?" by Joe Thompson, *JCK—Jewelers' Circular Keystone* (March 1982); and "Sparkle Street, USA," by Margaret Hornblower, *The Washington Post*, March 10, 1985. Reflections on the history of Forty-seventh Street are in Murray Schumach's well-reported book *The Diamond People* (see chapter Five above).

The chemical aspects of a diamond are given expansive treatment in *The Nature of Diamonds*, edited by George E. Harlow (New York: Cambridge University Press, 1998). Some biography of a key hip-hop magnate was taken from "Assessment: Master P," by David Plotz in the Internet magazine *Slate*, July 4, 1998. Thoughts on the psychology behind the lust for diamonds can be found in *The Importance of Wearing Clothes*, by Lawrence Langner (New York: Hastings House, 1959); *Through Paediatrics to Psycho-Analysis*, by D. W. Winnicott (New York: Basic Books, 1958); *The Gift: Forms and Functions of Exchange in Archaic Societies*, by Marcel Mauss (New York: W. W. Norton & Co., 1967); *The Theory of the Leisure Class*, by Thorstein Veblen (New York: Macmillian, 1899); and the magnificent Victorian novel *The Moonstone*, by Wilkie Collins (Hertfordshire: Cumberland House, 1993). Viktor Frankl's *Man's Search for Meaning* (Boston: Beacon Press, 1959) contains not a word about diamonds, but offers much, much more.

ACKNOWLEDGMENTS

In the United Kingdom, I am grateful to Alex Vines of the Royal Institute of International Affairs at Chatham House for sharing contacts and information, as well as to Gillian Nevins of Amnesty International in London. Alex Yearsley of Global Witness, Ltd., supplied me with several key documents and insights related to gem smuggling. Richard Wake-Walker at WWW International Diamond Consultants was generous with his time and expertise. Thanks as well to Harry Levy of Levy Gems, Ltd., and Andy Bone and Susan Spencer at the Diamond Trading Company.

In the Central African Republic, I am grateful to Phillipe Makendebou, David Greer, Joseph Benamse, Andrea Turkalo, Louis Sarno, Assan Abdoulaye, Kevin Kounganda, Honore Mbolihoudie, and to the people of Kate Bombale. Justin Oppman was helpful with tips for navigating African roads and bureaucracy.

In Canada, I owe immense thanks to Diamonds North Resources, Ltd. and Teck Cominco for allowing me virtually unlimited access to their Arctic explorations in the summer of 2004. Mark Kolebaba and Nancy Curry were of particular help. Michael Podolak of Great Slave Helicopters gave me a ride I will never forget. Denise Burlingame of BHP Billiton took me around the Ekati mine and Doug Ashbury of Diavik Diamond Mines ensured that I saw the dike around pipe A-154. Thanks also to Andrew Raven, Chris Woodall, and Aaron Whitefield of the *yellowknifer* newspaper; Jake Kennedy of *Canadian Diamonds* magazine; Mike Vaydik of the NWT & Nunavut Chamber of Mines; Terrance Pamplin and Ryan Silke of the Prince of Wales Northern Heritage Center; and Willy Laserich of Adlair Aviation.

In Japan, I am grateful to Hishasi Ashino of the Japan Jewellery Association for sharing some internal documents and translating them for me. Catherine Porter provided hours of necessary laughter in Tokyo. Rakesh Shah and his family were generous with their friendship and expertise. Dennis Weatherstone got me in a few doors that would have otherwise been closed. Beijing native Yuan-Yuan Lee translated Japanese for me in his adopted home country, with additional help from Kumiko Igarashi and Akiko Sato.

In Brazil, I am indebted to translators Francisco Santoro, Shelia Borges, Bryan Rott, Gislene de Jesus Costa, Rodolfo Lautner, and Neuza Batista da Silva. Geologist Cristina Pletschette helped me with statistical data. Alberto Pinho of the Cooperative Regional dos Garimpeiros de Diamantina walked me through the thicket of Brazilian mining law. Julian Humphryes and Doug Thayer provided insight on mining techniques. Tião Fernandes was the first one to tell me about Strong Man and helped me locate him. Thanks also to Aurelio Caixeta de Melo Ferreira for the hospitality in Patos de Minas and to Roanne Nubia and Fabiana Araujo for the friendship in Coromandel.

In South Africa, Karen Williams of the Institute for War and Peace Reporting served up exuberant rounds of cocktails and conjecture in Johannesburg. Thanks, too, to Kara Greenblott for her hospitality. Tom Tweedy of De Beers dispensed a bit of information. Justin Pearce provided several nuanced insights on African politics and made me think harder about my conclusions. Kokkie Duminy of South Africa's Kimberley Public Library helped me navigate that institution's peerless Africana Collection. Thanks, too, to Barbara Els at the Transnet Heritage Library in Johannesburg.

In Australia, Anitra Ducat and Kerri Redfern of Rio Tinto, Ltd., showed me just about everything I wanted to see at the Argyle mine. Russell Moar, Rick Stroud, Scott Ramsey, Alan Tietzel, Ray Piotrowski, and Kevin McLeish patiently answered my questions at the mine site. David Rose volunteered some expertise on block caving. Thanks, too, to Gareth Parker of the *West Australian* newspaper in Perth and James Morrow of *Investigate* magazine in Sydney.

In Angola, I am grateful to Anselmo Ribeiro, who translated several interviews from Portuguese and displayed a noteworthy combination of courage and tact. Additional translation was provided by David Flechner, who helped me laugh through several bizarre situations. Thanks also to Susan Grant of Save the Children UK, Zoe Eisenstein of Reuters, Sebastião Panzo of Endiama, João Pinto of Radio Ecclesia, and also to Tako Koning, Daphne Eviatar, Robert Miller, and Antonia Leao Monteiro.

In India, I am grateful to editor Bharat Desai and reporter Swati Bharadwaj Chand in the Ahmadabad bureau of *The Times of India*. Oswald Crasto helped get me inside several offices in Prasad Chambers. Dilip Mehta of Rosy Blue, Inc., facilitated key interviews in Bombay, as did U.S. Ambassador David Mulford and former UN Deputy Secretary-General Prakesh Shah. Sunil Desai was helpful with much more than translating Gujarati for me in Surat.

In Russia, I am very thankful to Yuri Palyanov and his team of scientists, and also to Valentin Afanasjev, Nikolai Sobolev, Victor Vins, and to Sergey, Antonio, and Julechka for their friendship in Novosibirsk. Jeffrey and Tatyana Tayler showed me a vodka-soaked good time in Moscow. Natalia Yakimets translated interviews from Russian.

In the United States, I am thankful to Sharrie Woodring of the European Gemological Laboratory for sharing expertise on methods of synthetic growth. Britta Schlager of the Gemesis Corporation let me borrow an expensive stone. Steven Anker of Anker Diamond Cutting, Inc., disclosed some of the peculiarities of the trade. James Butler and Boris Feigelson of the U.S. Naval Research Laboratory walked me through the irradiation process in language I could understand. Gary Roskin of *Jewelers' Circular Keystone* and Victoria Gomelsky of *Couture International Jeweler* did truth-squad duty, as did Robert Hammerman. The hip-hop section could not have been written without the expertise of Elizabeth Mendez Berry. I am grateful, too, in no particular order, to Joseph Rott, Bernie Silverberg, Michael Coan, John Anthony, James Auburn, Toni Greene, Susan Moynihan, Michael Romanelli, John Kaiser, and Laura Babcock.

Thanks to the archivists at the Smithsonian National Museum of American History in Washington, D.C., and especially to Faith Davis Ruffins, who helped track down old files from the N. W. Ayer agency. Lynn Eaton offered tireless good cheer and valuable assistance with the J. Walter Thompson Collection at the John W. Hartman Center for Sales, Advertising & Marketing History at Duke University in Durham, N.C. Diane Kaplan was helpful with Cecil Rhodes's correspondence at the Sterling Library at Yale University in New Haven. Fred Romanski and

John Taylor helped me find what I was looking for in the National Archives in College Park, Maryland. Marsha Appel opened up the private holdings of the American Association of Advertising Agencies in New York. Thanks, also, to the staff at the Reading Room of the New York Public Library.

My editor at St. Martin's Press, Michael Flamini, and his assistant, Katherine Tiernan, saw this manuscript through to publication and brought substantial improvements to the text. Friends and colleagues Susannah Donahue, Sarah Rutledge, Barbara Kiviat, Kim Sevcik, Deborah Siegel, Stacy Elise Sullivan, and Lawrence Viele read selected portions and offered valuable suggestions, as well as encouragement. No writer could have asked for a better cheerleader, adviser, and friend than Ellen Ruark. Thanks to Gabrielle Giffords for believing. Fellow mining enthusiast Marc Herman was a constant example of what it means to chase a story back to its source; his groundbreaking book about gold, *Searching for El Dorado,* also served as a narrative model. My family in Arizona was a rock of support, and they have my eternal gratitude for so much more than can be said here. This book would not exist were it not for the insight and talent of my agent, Brettne Bloom, who first conceived the idea of a comprehensive look at the diamond industry and whose enthusiasm for this project has never wavered. Final thanks go to Kevin Gass, a true friend and brother-in-arms, who first journeyed with me into Africa and always had my back—there and here.

—*New York City, January 2004–May 2005*

INDEX